SOUL VIBRATIONS

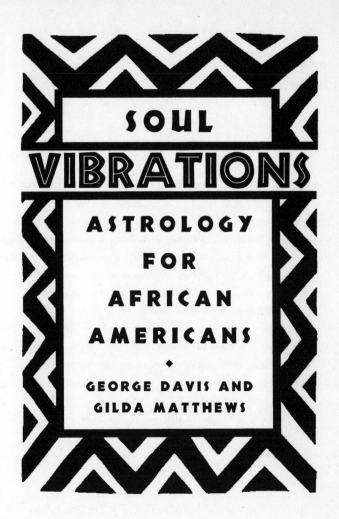

SOUL

VIBRATIONS

ASTROLOGY
FOR
AFRICAN
AMERICANS

•

GEORGE DAVIS AND
GILDA MATTHEWS

QUILL
WILLIAM MORROW
NEW YORK

It is the policy of William Morrow and Company, Inc., and its imprints
and affiliates, recognizing the importance of preserving what has been written, to print
the books we publish on acid-free paper, and we exert our best efforts to that end.

Library of Congress Cataloging-in-Publication Data
Davis, George.
Soul vibrations: astrology for African Americans/George Davis and Gilda Matthews.
p. cm.
ISBN 0–688–14601–5
1. Afro-American astrology. I. Title. II. Matthews, Gilda.
BF1714.A37M37   1996   133.5'089'96073—dc20
95–35908 CIP

Printed in the United States of America
First Edition
3 4 5 6 7 8 9 10
BOOK DESIGN BY LEAH LOCOCO

This book is dedicated to the memory of Rev. Clarence Davis, a Methodist minister, who stayed true to his religious calling, but was forever toying with astrology as a means of keeping himself open to, and accepting of, the great variety of human behavior. His life was a constant expression of his love for humanity.

ACKNOWLEDGMENTS

The creators of this book acknowledge their debt to the many astrologers whose insights deepened their understanding of the subject, and to the many cultural historians whose insights were even more vital to the creation of the book.

In addition, thanks is extended to the many people who helped in ways too numerous to mention to make this entire project a success.

CONTENTS

INTRODUCTION   XI

THE HISTORY OF ASTROLOGY   1

ASTROLOGY, SCIENCE, AND MODERN LIFE   5

THE SIGNS OF THE ZODIAC

     ARIES   11

     TAURUS   33

     GEMINI   53

     CANCER   73

     LEO   93

     VIRGO   115

     LIBRA   135

     SCORPIO   157

     SAGITTARIUS   177

     CAPRICORN   197

     AQUARIUS   219

     PISCES   239

INTRODUCTION

Whether for fun or as a pathway to the mysteries of the soul, African Americans have shown an enduring interest in the ancient art of astrology. Yet this is the first astrology book that combines the intrigue and entertainment of sun-sign astrology with African-American history and culture.

In one way this is a book for those who think of astrology as no more than a parlor game or a topic of small talk: What sign is Janet Jackson? Magic Johnson? Maya Angelou? Do Leos get along well with Virgos? Like daily newspaper horoscopes or fortune cookies, it provides good, old-fashioned entertainment.

However, this is also a book for those who think of astrology as a divine science to be enlisted as an aid in the quests for love, self-awareness, fortune, and happiness. Astrology is often invoked to communicate information about the personalities of friends, relatives, and lovers. Many of us with surprising accuracy can guess an individual's sun sign by observing his or her behavior. Astrology has taught us how to "read" the distinct vibrations of each of the twelve sun signs.

Since ancient times astrology has endured as one of humankind's most accessible ways of talking about behavior and cosmic events. I have long used astrology in my work in psychospiritual counseling as a springboard for getting people to open up about themselves and for initiating positive dialogue about relationships and spirituality. When my colleagues and I brought astrological portraits of African Americans into an inner-city school system, we were astounded at the strong and long-lasting positive impact on a youngster who finds, for example, that General Colin Powell is an Aries like himself; or in another instance, that

Madame C. J. Walker, who was one of history's most successful black tycoons, "was born on the same day as me."

This is just one of the affirmations we had that astrology is a powerful way to present the beauty and variety of the African-American experience. Astrology is one of many ways of organizing our perceptions about that experience. It affords the possibility of a nobler, more exalted, and therefore truer (in a spiritual sense) way than does conventional history texts or limited, fact-based journalism. And we also discovered that while astrology accentuates each person's individuality, its most profound and peace-giving function comes from its capacity to symbolize the complex relationship between the individual and the sun, moon, stars, and the infinite universe.

In this fun-filled guide to the zodiac for African Americans you will find detailed traits of each sign and insights into love and compatibility. Using examples from African-American folklore, history, contemporary life, and a cavalcade of eminent characters—from Nat Turner to Tina Turner—*Soul Vibrations* reveals, for the first time, the age-old relationship between the stars, the African-American experience, and you.

THE HISTORY OF ASTROLOGY

SOUL *VIBRATIONS* IS THE FIRST ASTROLOGICAL look at the black American experience, but the courtship between black people and this ancient art has lasted longer and more ardently than with any other ethnic group.

One of the oldest existing horoscopes was drawn in ancient Egypt more than 2,300 years before Christ by Imhotep, a black man. (Imhotep, incidentally, could be considered the grandfather of modern medicine since it was he who pioneered many of the procedures that Hippocrates later documented.) The Imhotep horoscope was drawn for the great Step Pyramid at Saqqâra, whose design was based on astrology. Like most pyramids, it had a dual purpose: It was used as both a burial place for the pharaohs and an astrological calculator. The sloping corridors leading into the interior were used as precise sighting tubes through which astrologers could view the stars.

But the history of astrology can be dated even farther back. From the earliest times man has wondered about his place in the universe. The ancient Chaldeans, black people who settled in the region of the Fertile Crescent, near the Persian Gulf, were the first real astrologers. For centuries they patiently observed and noted the relationship between events on earth and the procession of celestial bodies across the Mesopotamian skies. They built towers called ziggurats and painted them in seven colors to represent the seven known "stars" of the solar system.

The Tower of Babel, mentioned in the Bible, was the most famous of these ziggurats. Priests, or astronomer-astrologers, ascended the ziggurats to get unobstructed views of the sky as well as to find solitude and undisturbed periods of meditation.

This region of the world is commonly known as the Cradle of Civilization. All the major religions of the Western world—Christianity, Judaism, Islam—originated there and are based largely on the same body of "ancient doctrine" amassed by the priest-astronomers. Each religion adapted this doctrine to fit its own needs, and each denounced all other interpretations. The fact that they came from the same source accounts for the similarities between the Torah, the Bible, and the Koran.

The ancient doctrine was successfully modified for various reasons by various people. Few Christians know or would acknowledge that the Three Wise Men who attended the birth of Christ were, in the original text, three Chaldean astrologers.

Few Jews know or would acknowledge that the twelve tribes of Israel are spiritually based on the lore surrounding the twelve signs of the zodiac, as indeed are the twelve disciples of Christ.

Astrology differed from other interpretations of the ancient doctrine in that it attempted to link knowledge of the human spirit with astronomy and therefore with the science of mathematics. The Babylonians who conquered and settled Chaldea began this process by systematically noting the relationship between behavior and the movement of the most obvious extraterrestrial objects—the sun, moon, and the then visible planets, which they called wanderers. The constellations, or groupings of stars, that formed a backdrop for the "wanderers" were given animal names, making the path they traveled a kind of heavenly zoo, which is how the term *zodiac* originated.

Particular animals were chosen to characterize most constellations because those animals were thought to possess traits similar to most of the people born during the time the sun traversed those particular sections of the zodiac. For example, when people born during a certain period were observed to be stubborn and steadfast, the constellation behind the sun at that time was named Taurus (the Bull). Similarly, when people born during another period were observed to be proud and regal, the constellation was called Leo (the Lion).

The Greeks and Romans added mathematical refinements and a more complex mythology. But after the fall of Rome astrological interest almost disappeared from Europe. It was revived again during the Middle Ages, even though the Catholic Church continued to attempt to exterminate all manifestations of the ancient doctrine not sanctioned by papal authority. Astrologers and astrological texts were burned. The Arabs became the primary trustees of the banished form of the ancient doctrine. There were, however, some older versions of these doctrines that had been taken to the Far East, where they had found favorable reception. These versions did not surface in the West until the Renaissance, when they became popular among the wealthier classes. Since then astrology's popularity has continuously waxed and waned in European and American society.

Among African Americans, however, interest in astrology has for the most part remained at a high level, as black Americans have shown an enduring curiosity about the ancient art. Despite this interest, until now no book has used astrology as a prism through which to take a valuable, largely positive view of African-American life.

ASTROLOGY, SCIENCE, AND MODERN LIFE

THE MOST THOUGHTFUL ASTROLOGERS HAVE never claimed that the placements of the sun, moon, and planets at the time of birth *cause* the twelve different personality types.

Instead, for a long time astrologers have been saying what quantum physicists are only now discovering. We are all part of a single, infinite, unbroken stuff. This supports the astrological contention that the placement of celestial bodies does not cause certain personality types. The relationship between placement and personality is based on the principle of synchronicity, an illusion of simultaneous occurrence, which produces the illusion of cause and effect in the time-space continuum.

But even before quantum physics, scientists affirmed that sun and moon cycles do produce profound effects on the earth's atmosphere and climate. It has also been accepted that the electromagnetic fields of all the planets affect all other electromagnetic fields, including those within the atoms that make up the human body. Furthermore, traditional Newtonian physics established that the gravitational pulls of all the major celestial bodies in our solar system affect all fluids on earth. And since the human body is composed largely of fluid, the positions of celestial bodies would logically have some effect on us.

From ancient times, long before the invention of the telescope, astrologers insisted that planetary aspects (the angular relationship between two planets) produced noticeable effects on human beings as well as on worldly events.

John H. Nelson, an engineer employed by RCA, discovered that radio waves suffer the greatest disturbance when two planets are in a 180-degree or 90-degree relationship with the sun. These waves are relatively disturbance-free, however, when planets are aligned in 120-degree or 60-degree aspects with the sun.

There are many ways that astrological beliefs are supported by traditional physics and have been accepted by logic-bound modern people.

The National Aeronautics and Space Administration (NASA) uses astrology not only to choose astronauts but also to predict the weather during spaceflight.

Far more often than the average citizen thinks, the rich and famous as well as the infamous frequently use astrology in many ways. The Morgans and the Vanderbilts are among the wealthy American families who regularly employed astrological advisers in decision making; Adolf Hitler used an astrologer in devising his nearly successful conquest of Europe. More recently Nancy and Ronald Reagan were shown to be believers.

Some doctors use it in fertility studies, and many prominent attorneys use it as an aid in selecting jurors in important cases.

An extraordinary number of luminaries in the entertainment industry believe in it so much that they do not publish their birth dates for fear of someone's using astrological knowledge of their character against them.

THE SIGNS OF THE ZODIAC

THE TWELVE SIGNS OF THE ZODIAC HAVE TRADI-
tionally been organized in several different ways, and each way
reveals something meaningful about how they are both alike and
different from one another. For instance, they may be grouped according
to the four zodiacal elements—fire, earth, air, and water. Each of these
elements (sometimes called triplicities) comprises three signs.

Aries, Leo, and Sagittarius are the fire signs; they represent dyna-
mism, self-expression, and enthusiasm. The earth signs are Taurus,
Virgo, and Capricorn; they represent stability, practicality, and materialism. Gemini, Libra, and Aquarius are the air signs; they represent
communication, the various stages of personal relationships, and intellectualism. The water signs are Cancer, Scorpio, and Pisces; they represent the emotions, intuition, and receptivity.

The signs of the zodiac are also classified according to the three
zodiacal "qualities": cardinal, fixed, and mutable. Each of these qualities
(sometimes called quadruplicities) comprises four signs.

The cardinal signs are Aries, Cancer, Libra, and Capricorn; these
signs place high value on initiative, enterprise, and achievement. The
fixed signs are Taurus, Leo, Scorpio, and Aquarius; they are noted for
determination, order, and rigidity. The mutable signs are Gemini, Virgo,
Sagittarius, and Pisces; these signs are noted for adjustability, versatility,
and mediation.

CARDINAL SIGNS	FIXED SIGNS	MUTABLE SIGNS
Fire: Aries	**Fire:** Leo	**Fire:** Sagittarius
Water: Cancer	**Water:** Scorpio	**Water:** Pisces
Air: Libra	**Air:** Aquarius	**Air:** Gemini
Earth: Capricorn	**Earth:** Taurus	**Earth:** Virgo

Although the zodiacal signs, or vibrations, have their own specific traits, each also mirrors some of the characteristics of the element and quality under which it is classified.

In addition, each sign is said to be ruled by a particular planet; thus the sign has the same associated traits as the planet which rules it. In fact, the positions and movements of the ten planets (including, of course, the Sun) as seen from the perspective of the earth are what all astrological interpretations are based upon. The chart below lists the ruling planet of each sign and its area of influence.

PLANETARY RULER	ZODIACAL SIGN	ASSOCIATED TRAITS
SUN	Leo	Willpower, self-expression, vitality
MOON	Cancer	Emotion, intuition, empathy, patience
MERCURY	Gemini and Virgo	Communication, objectivity, mental dexterity
VENUS	Taurus and Libra	Personal relationships, harmony, love, tactfulness
MARS	Aries and Scorpio	Passion, physical energy, aggressiveness, initiation
JUPITER	Sagittarius and Pisces	Expansion, wisdom, good fortune
SATURN	Capricorn and Aquarius	Limitation, restraint, consolidation
URANUS	Aquarius	Higher values, optimism, sudden transformation
NEPTUNE	Pisces	Spirituality, creativity, seclusion
PLUTO	Scorpio	Death and regeneration, extrasensory perception

Although the astrological Sun determines the essence or the intention and direction of an individual's personality, the placement of the planets at the time of birth will tell us how that essence has been modified by celestial influence.

For example, two people have a Leo sun sign, but the one with Mars in Pisces at the time of birth will be different from the one with Mars in Aries. Two people might have a Cancer sun sign and both have Mars in Pisces, but the one with Venus in Gemini will be different from the one with Venus in Leo at the time of birth. The combinations and angles (or aspects) are infinite.

Another crucial astrological factor is the Ascendant, or rising sign, which is the sign of the zodiac that appears on the eastern horizon at the exact time and place of a person's birth. According to astrology only the signs of the Sun and Moon are as important as the sign on the Ascendant in delineating a picture of an individual. *Soul Vibrations,* however, is a book about sun signs only, so the book does not discuss the actual infinite variety of human manifestations. Enjoy!

MARCH 21ST TO APRIL 20TH

ARIES

THE RAM

THE SIGN OF THE PIONEER

◆

IMPULSIVE, ASSERTIVE,

ENERGETIC

◆

Ruled by Mars

COLOR: Bright Red

METAL: Iron

GEMS: Diamond and Amethyst

LUCKY NUMBERS: 7 and 6

FORTUNATE DAY: Tuesday

THE ARIES VIBRATION

ARIENS ARE USUALLY VERY BOLD AND DIRECT. Even in the field of poetry, where subtle or clever wording is often the goal, Maya Angelou has made her mark with bold, blunt expressions of simple, straightforward emotions. None of that subtle tiptoe-through-the-tulips poetry for her. Her poems are usually calls to action. "Courage is the most important virtue, because without courage you can't have the other virtues," she said. This might not be true for other signs, but it is certainly true for Ariens.

Gil Scott Heron, the Arien musician and poet, is even more outspoken and direct in his musical monologues. His mid-1970s hit "The Revolution Will Not Be Televised" was one of the boldest, most direct political statements made in a popular song prior to the Gangsta Rap of the 1990s.

And Martin Luther King, Jr.'s daughter Bernice King—an Arien lawyer, Baptist minister, and civil rights activist—is known for saying exactly what is on her mind, whether she is speaking to national leaders or young African Americans. "We have brothers and sisters with forty- and fifty-dollar hairstyles and a nickel's worth of brains," she said at a speaking engagement attended by brothers and sisters with forty- and fifty-dollar hairstyles. Nothing subtle there.

Ariens are most successful when they come on very strong. They prove themselves by their action and not by their planning and debating back and forth. Because they are children of the first astrological sign, Ariens are much like the new kids on the block. They are eager to show what they can do. Ariens are usually very impatient. "Let's go. Let's do it," they say.

You might have to say, "Wait a minute," if you are dealing with one of them. "Slow down. Let's think about this."

In action they can be confident, witty, dynamic, and charming. Associates of General Colin Powell, the former chairman of the Joint

Chiefs of Staff and "Desert Storm" leader, described him as "a facilitator rather than a thinker."

Ariens would rather do it than think about doing it, or even think about how to do it. Most of them would rather get started and discover *how* to do it on the way. Even an educator like Booker T. Washington was more of a doer, builder, and pioneer than an intellectual. His native optimism was the key to his incredible rise from slavery and menial labor to becoming the founder of Tuskegee Institute and the most powerful black man in America during the early 1900s. *Up from Slavery,* the autobiography that chronicles his life, reads like an adventure story, with one bold action following another.

Ariens are driven by a spiritual life force that compels them to act. Ready or not, they are going to push ahead and get the show on the road.

When they are not operating at their best, they can be overly aggressive, impatient, headstrong, and careless. They can be self-centered and quick-tempered.

Nonetheless Ariens are very optimistic people, eager to look on the bright side of life. For example Clara "Mother" Hale's middle name could have been "Optimism." She was practically destitute and barely educated when her husband died in 1942, but without the assistance of outside agencies, she still managed to found Hale House, a foster home for the children of heroin addicts in Harlem. Her untiring efforts saved the lives of scores of children; and she remained in touch with the hopeful side of life even after she herself was well past seventy years old.

Ariens are at their best when they rely on their ability to see the brighter side of life instead of trying to understand its deeper motives and undercurrents, as a Scorpio might.

High energy and intensity is an attribute of all fire signs, but as the first and most aggressive of those vibrations, Ariens burn hotter than even Leos and Sagittarians. Such successful performers as the legendary blues vocalist Bessie Smith, jazz vocalist Sarah Vaughn, and superstar soul singers Diana Ross, Marvin Gaye, Al Green, and Teddy Pendergrass, are appreciated more for their sheer energy than for pure musical talent, as a Piscean or Tauran would be. Ariens can trust their powerful energy more than almost any other characteristic of their personalities.

They are usually very sociable people, with generous spirits. Giving of themselves will bring more good things to them than they will ever have by holding on to the things they get along the way.

This is usually not difficult since, as the youngest sign in the astrological cycle, they are not at all fearful. Like many young people, they are rather idealistic and naive about human life and its requirements. They are confident because their experience has not taught them much about danger. For most Ariens the world is an uncomplicated affair; they do not see many of its mysteries and puzzles. They accept people and what people say at face value and are often disappointed or tricked by others who use flattery to manipulate.

Theirs is a light and friendly vibration, but they are also very aggressive. And sometimes that aggression, combined with their optimism and confidence, can lead to egotistical and selfish behavior.

Aries is like a youth seeking to reassure himself in the face of inexperience. The ego must be defended at all costs. I AM are the key words of the sign: "I am first," "I am here," "I am sure," or simply "I am" is music to the young Arien soul. In friendship or love the ego must be massaged. In competition it must win. In arguments it accepts nothing short of the other person's surrender.

Insistent Ariens need to get their point across immediately. After the argument they can be sweet, forgiving, and generous; after all, they know that they could have been wrong all along.

In many ways the Aries vibration reflects the emphasis on attitude and in-your-face confrontation that currently flourishes in the sports and entertainment worlds as well as in everyday life on the street in the 'hood, where macho posturing and swagger reign. On stage, Aries comedians Eddie Murphy and Martin Lawrence project a brash, cocksure attitude that is typical of their Aries sun signs.

The astrological symbol for Aries is the Ram, the driving, musky little animal who gets ahead by running headlong into things and butting them out of the way.

People born under the sign usually think that the easiest route between two points is always a straight line, even if there is a brick wall separating the two points. Ariens need to learn how to walk around some of these walls rather than run through them. It's all a matter of discipline.

Booker T. Washington commented that he felt his success was based on the discipline that he received at the hands of his early schoolmasters. He thanked them for being so strict. At Tuskegee, the college he eventually founded and ran, he instituted a system of education with discipline as the primary ingredient.

Colin Powell said that he learned very early that his energy would be better focused by military life, which continued the discipline of his strict, Jamaican-born parents.

Aries is also the sign of the warrior. It is ruled by the planet Mars, and in Roman mythology Mars is the god of war. As a result Ariens love confrontation—no sign is more combative or more at ease with strife and conflict.

Colin Powell, who earned both a Purple Heart and the Bronze Star during two tours in the Vietnam War, is of course not only one of the most celebrated Ariens but also one of the most famous modern warriors. Former Secretary of Defense Caspar W. Weinberger described Powell as "a superb soldier whose greatest ambition has been to command troops in the field."

One of the most self-centered, defiantly optimistic warriors in American history was Arien Jack Johnson—the first black man to win the heavyweight championship of the world. Johnson not only battled ring opponents and inspired a frantic search for the "Great White

Hope" but, because of his extravagant lifestyle and open defiance of racist laws outside the ring, also had to contend with public opinion, both black and white, and eventually the United States and British governments.

Within most Ariens there are a thousand competing ambitions, and many natives believe they have enough energy to fulfill all of them. Eddie Murphy, for instance, had established himself as one of America's wittiest and most popular comedians before he turned to acting and became Hollywood's biggest box office draw. Soon after establishing himself in films he launched a career as a singer.

Still, many Ariens overestimate their strength and make foolhardy attempts to do more than they can. As a result they can leave many things half done. I know a young Aries woman who has nearly a dozen books lying around facedown in her apartment. She had the ambition to start all of them but didn't have enough patience to finish any.

Ariens also love to bluff and tend to oversell themselves, sometimes promising more than they can deliver. An example is a young woman acquaintance at a New York college who vowed she would destroy all racism, change the syllabus, and replace all the textbooks in her lily-white history department in a single semester.

Discipline, however, can turn an Aries's competing ambitions and overzealousness into a wide variety of accomplishments. Paul Robeson, who was born with his Sun in Aries, is an excellent example. He attributed much of his success to his father, who provided "a source of tremendous discipline which lasted through the years." Of his childhood he wrote, "I knew what I must do—when to come home from play, my duties in the household, my time for study—and I readily yielded to his quiet discipline."

When he graduated from Rutgers University in 1919, he was number one in his class with a 97-plus average. He was also elected to Phi Beta Kappa and earned varsity letters in four sports, including All-American honors in football. By 1924 he had finished law school at Columbia University and was about to embark on a film career that might have established him as the first black movie star. Critics rate him one of the great Shakespearean actors of all times.

In order to bring Negro spirituals to the concert halls of the world, he taught himself to sing in nine languages. He remains one of the greatest baritones that the century has produced and one of the century's most courageous fighters for the rights of oppressed people.

Discipline allowed him to pursue and realize more of his wide-ranging ambitions than any man coming of age in the twentieth century.

Among female Ariens the title of "Most Versatile" might go to Maya Angelou. She has been a Creole cook, San Francisco's first black woman streetcar conductor, an actress, and singer on the international stage.

She was a fighter for civil rights with Dr. Martin Luther King, Jr., a journalist in Ghana, a college teacher, the author of *I Know Why the Caged Bird Sings,* and several other best-selling autobiographical works, and the creator of ten one-hour programs for National Educational Television.

In 1992 she was selected to write a poem to be read to the nation on the occasion of President Bill Clinton's inauguration. The poem was a call for courage and forceful action.

Ariens are rebellious and eager to establish a sense of self, a separate identity, through their own actions. In the sign of Aries, humankind seeks to challenge the universe and believes that it can be controlled. As the first sign of the zodiac Aries imparts to those born under it all the qualities needed to start the new cycles of life that begin after the twelfth incarnation, Pisces.

The ever-present cycle of life moves from youth to maturity, from innocence to wisdom, from pioneer to poet. Pisces is the poet. Aries is the pioneer—rugged, uncomplicated, and courageous, with a great spirit of initiative and enterprise and a love of conquest and competition.

In fact the Aries vibration often needs an opponent in order to fully express itself. If an obstacle is not readily available or easily found, the Arien will often create one. Defiance is one of their most prominent characteristics.

Stirring up opposition helped Jack Johnson maintain his edge in the ring, and Booker T. Washington created enemies in order to kindle his goal of educated young African Americans during Reconstruction.

When enemies are real and injustice is obvious, Ariens can be the fiercest fighters in the world.

Although the exact date of Harriet Tubman's birth is not known, historians have established that she was born in springtime, and astrologers claim that because of the nature of her rebelliousness and fiery temperament she must have been an Arien.

As a child she defied slave custom and renamed herself against her master's will. Although a small woman, she was one of the two most famous conductors of the Underground Railroad. She made nineteen trips into the slaveholding South and rescued more than three hundred African Americans from slavery.

She was not intimidated by the Fugitive Slave Act or the forty-thousand-dollar reward offered for her arrest. In the North she was severely beaten for leading a group that rescued an arrested slave from police in Troy, New York.

She went South and rescued her aged parents and bought land upon which to settle them. With the outbreak of the Civil War she fought for her right to join the war effort and eventually worked for the Union Army as a cook, nurse, scout, and spy. After the war she worked to establish a school in North Carolina for freed slaves. In the twilight of her years she was active in the temperance and women's rights movement.

Another person of action whose birthdate is not known but who is usually accepted as an Arien is Frederick Douglass, who was born in the spring of 1817, in Tuckahoe, Maryland. Among Douglass's first acts of defiance was learning to read at a time when it was forbidden for slaves.

As a teenager he fought and defeated the most feared slave breaker on the Eastern Shore of Maryland. Douglass fought within the American system for the abolition of slavery. His writing was characterized by fiery, spontaneous outbursts against injustice.

Unlike outraged Taureans David Walker or Malcolm X, or fiery revolutionary Aquarians Huey Newton or Bob Marley, who struck out at the system itself, Douglass worked within the system to fight injustice.

Like many Ariens, he maintained a strong, active life even in his later years, when he was a crusader for women's rights and the rights of freedmen. He also held a variety of jobs for the federal government, including recorder of deeds for the District of Columbia, and minister to Haiti.

Vettius Valens, an astrologer who lived in the second century A.D., wrote that Ariens are "notable, famous, commanding, just, a hater of trickery, freedom-loving, domineering, bold in their opinions, boastful, high-minded, unreliable, capricious, quick-changing, and resourceful."

The truth is that Ariens are drawn to lofty ideals and grand schemes as well as to innovation. Ariens like to concentrate on the big picture and let others worry about the small details. In their personal lives they have the ability to defeat giants, only to be nibbled to death by ants.

Jack Johnson's life was eventually consumed by this fate as the authorities closed in on him. But he never retreated from his proud Arien stance. Even when he was on top, there was none of Joe Louis's Taurean modesty, none of Muhammad Ali's Capricornian cleverness and calculation. There was only the clean, unadorned arrogance of a candid, uncomplicated personality. "Now I am champion," he asserted, and flashed his famous golden smile.

RELATIONSHIPS

Ariens are extroverts. They make friends easily and tend to trust others very quickly—sometimes too quickly. It takes only a very short time for them to establish close relationships with new friends. They are witty conversationalists who love to chat with people who agree with them. Their social life is very important to them.

But despite their outgoing natures and easy friendliness most Ariens are not as socially successful as they might be. They're ever ready to strike up new acquaintances, but they often neglect their good friends in order to do so. Relying on an instant evaluation of others, as they often do, they have a tendency to trust many undeserving types. "Hey, this is a great guy. He and I get along perfectly. This is the partnership I've been waiting for," they seem to think, instead of holding back and determining what their new acquaintance is really like. They are eager to share their youthful energy, optimism, goodwill, and generosity. They'll give the moon to a total stranger if they are sufficiently impressed.

In social situations they often live too much in the present and the future. They often forget about that old friend who has done more to deserve the gift of the moon. Extreme loyalty doesn't come naturally to them. In rare cases they are loyal only to the person who can help them further their scheme of the moment. They believe in their ability to patch up things with old friends later. Once this is accepted by others, they can be very dependable friends, and all of their sympathy, zeal, idealism, concern for the underdog, and warmth will usually be available when called upon.

LUCK, MONEY, AND WORK

It isn't easy to decide if Aries is a good-luck or a hard-luck sign. Ariens attract money, but they can waste it as fast as they acquire it. Aries is a sign of great opportunity. Ariens are achievers; they have a capacity to work diligently, and often rise to positions of power and influence. But good fortune also comes to them out of the blue. Although not as lucky as Sagittarians, they are fortunate enough. Still, there is in the sign a tendency to spend foolishly or, when things are going well, to be too generous and careless. Ariens are not usually thrifty.

They have too much confidence in themselves to waste a lot of effort squirreling money away for a rainy day. They are daring and like to gamble. They believe fate will be kind and they get deep satisfaction out of beating the odds. Their nerves are perfect for quick games of chance, whether it be business, blackjack, or love.

They would rather let the wheel turn and take a chance than inch forward piling up a fortune penny by hard-earned penny. They tend to be impulsive and somewhat reckless, but the decisions they make on the spur of the moment are usually more reliable than those derived from endless reasoning and analyzing. The sign of the Ram is more inclined to intuition and action than intellectuality or scholarship.

Money means different things to different people. To Taurus it means security and comfort; to Cancer it means security and the opportunity to protect loved ones; to Sagittarius it means freedom; to Capricorn it means power and the ability to control people's efforts for a material purpose. To Aries, however, money is a symbol of triumph. Money, along with fame, are the rewards the world offers to those who succeed. Recognition is the prize. Wealth is a trophy, something to be shown. This is why Ariens are so easily impressed by expensive things.

Most Ariens don't take orders well because the loudest voice they hear is their own—which usually urges them to make their own decisions and act according to their own methods, impulses, and urgent sense of timing. They are individualistic. They like to be told what the job is and left alone to do it. This is why they're often so quarrelsome and unsuccessful when involved in close cooperative efforts. They are creative, but they often need someone of a more patient temperament to work out the details of a project. They like to do things quickly because when a task is not completed in a relatively short period of time, they tend to get bored or diverted to new challenges.

They often make good policemen, firemen, and soldiers, since in these positions promotions are often awarded to those who perform in a courageous or even reckless manner rather than to those who steadily follow exact orders.

A great number of Ariens can be found in the prestigious professions of law and medicine. Ariens usually prefer the hectic pace of large cities over the leisurely lifestyle common in rural areas. They are always better suited for active professions than for stationary jobs such as secretarial work, accounting, or bookkeeping.

MENTAL AND PHYSICAL HEALTH

Ariens are robust people. They're seldom sickly or delicate by nature. They're usually not self-pitying enough to become hypochondriacs and load themselves down with psychosomatic illnesses. Women of this sign are more often hardy than fragile. But Ariens aren't usually the kind of people who take good care of themselves. They tend to abuse or neglect their physical health. "I'm okay," an Arien often says when he or she is sick or overtired and should be in bed. Constant activity puts a strain on the body, as do worry, excitement, and anger.

Ariens have a lot of trouble with their nervous systems, stomachs, and digestive tracts—all a result of emotional strain and "nerves," as the old folks called it. Ariens should be on special guard against high blood pressure. Most of them are too highstrung to relax properly. Even when they're physically inactive and trying to relax, their minds and nervous systems are active. They should take relaxation lessons from good old Taurus, who knows better than anyone how to lie back and take it easy.

LOVE AND SEX

People born under this sign aren't sophisticated lovers, but what else could be expected of the youngest sign of the zodiac? Youth believes that passion, vigor, and directness are more important in a love affair than tact and timing. Ariens don't like to wait or use a coy approach. Often they refuse to take no for an answer. If they dig you, they'll let you know, then chase you down if necessary.

Some women complain that Arien men come on too strong; other women like them because of their aggressiveness. They're warm, demonstrative men with a flair for the dramatic. They like to sweep women off their feet. No male pursues more vigorously than the Arien on the hunt.

Ariens, particularly males, are famed for their pursuit of the opposite sex, and few other signs are likely to love as frequently or as foolishly as Ariens. Too often, natives of this sign do not form a realistic picture of the mate they swoon over. They love passionately and are very generous and open with their affections. But often they are in love with nothing more than a reflection of their own ideals, a projection of their own needs.

Arien men are often attracted to surface appearances. They can fall deeply in love with a woman simply because she is beautiful, because she looks like a trophy worthy of a victorious warrior. They tend to ignore inner qualities as well as those unique personality traits that give their mates true individuality and distinctiveness. They might fall in love with a woman they think is easy to dominate, or one they can use as a sexual convenience, or one with money or social standing, hoping that later they can make this person into the type of individual they want her to be. When they discover that most people are not so easily changed, they are disappointed and often feel betrayed. They are likely to have a past strewn with unwise romances.

Arien women seldom find fulfillment in just keeping house. They need a larger field for their expansive energies and ambitions. They make up more than their share of successful career women. They are ardent, active lovers, and many of them are more strong-willed and aggressive than most men. They don't mind taking the lead in sexual affairs if the man seems hesitant. A typical Arien woman wouldn't be reluctant to call up a man she liked and ask him to take her out; and if he were a little too slow in asking her to bed, she wouldn't hesitate in asking him. For instance there's a young woman in Sacramento who has been married three times, and each time she did the proposing. When she fell out of love, *she* initiated the divorce proceedings. She often says that she was too much woman, both physically and mentally, for the men she married. This is a problem that many of her Arien sisters share. Dancer, producer, actress, writer, and civil rights worker Maya Angelou once told a reporter that her biggest problem in life has been finding a man strong enough for her.

LOVE AFFAIRS

(See the other chapters for love affairs between
Aries men and women of the other signs.)

ARIES WOMAN, ARIES MAN

This may not be a very stable relationship, but it is likely to be an exciting one. Two pioneers are bound to lead each other into some fresh experiences. You both like to be involved with a great variety of things. The love affair can be nothing other than explosive. It's bound to be very intense at first—full of idealism and expectation, passion and promise; but jealousy and arguments will be common also, since no two people are likely to enjoy arguments more than the two of you. A deep insecurity might cause each of you to try to bind the other closer than you let yourself be bound. This might cause the kind of tension that will ruin a love affair that started off in such heat. Ariens are idealists. They don't like to compromise, but you two will have to compromise a lot if you're to have anything more than a short, passionate affair.

ARIES WOMAN, TAURUS MAN

His pace is very different from yours. His is patient or leisurely while yours is impulsive. You're inclined to outbreaks of temper, and though he's rather peace-loving, he will get furious or at least stubborn when you try to push. This would be okay if you knew when to let up, but you may be too courageous for your own good. If you persist, you'll provoke a temper the likes of which you've never seen. He's so practical and realistic that he might seem boring to you. You're so impatient and impulsive that you might seem foolish to him. He tends to be financially conservative and materialistic. The fights over money could be enough to end this affair. The sexual bond is a connection of opposites. He is slow and sensual. He needs a lot of prolonged sexual satisfaction. You might need to slow your rhythm down and he might need to bring you more excitement and stimulation.

ARIES WOMAN, GEMINI MAN

One of the stronger men born under Gemini might be ideal for you. If he thinks fast enough, that could make up for what he lacks in willpower. He'll probably not be as forceful as you, but he may be much more clever. Like you, he's likely to be rather restless, so you should agree on a rather active social life. He's probably not jealous, but it's likely that you are. He's probably moody, and you're not the kind to let him alone when he's in one of his moods. Both of you argue a lot, but the arguments will mean more to you than they do to him. You might desire a lot more sexual attention than he gives, but when he puts his mind to it, he's likely to be more uninhibited, and though not overly affectionate or emotional, he can be very entertaining. Unfortunately he's not likely to be as deeply involved or as serious about many of the things you're serious about. You're both very easily bored, so you need a lot of friendship to substitute for intensity of affection.

ARIES WOMAN, CANCER MAN

You move a little too fast for a cautious, suspicious man like him. He might be attracted to the way you zoom around, but he's not likely to feel comfortable with you because he knows how little joy you get out of domestic life. He is emotionally protective. You can be emotionally impulsive. This makes him nervous. He throws you off of the frantic pace that you like by requiring more sensitivity to his touchy emotional nature than you usually like to give. His great imagination can be stimulating to you, but it might be too withdrawn from the real world of action that you enjoy. Much understanding is needed if you are to reap the rewards that your enterprising natures could produce, if you could ever get them together.

ARIES WOMAN, LEO MAN

Love almost never runs smoothly for a woman like you. Your smoothest combination would be with Mr. Sagittarius, but the most dynamic and dramatic might be with Mr. Leo. He's the man you could fall in love with suddenly, perhaps at first sight. The affair will be full of ecstasy. It's the kind of affair that causes the heart to flutter, the kind that makes you wonder, *Where has he been all my life?* You're very attracted to external appearances, and he cuts a finer caper than any man around. He's confident, friendly, ambitious, but not plodding and materialistic. The trouble is that he's egotistical, just like you. And he demands a lot of attention, just like you. There'll be plenty of competition to see who is the darling of this relationship. The title will swing back and forth through many arguments. Even the lovemaking will be a kind of competition for the title. It's a struggle that will never end, which is good since both of you hate boredom more than anything else.

ARIES WOMAN, VIRGO MAN

He might be a little too self-contained and undemonstrative to attract a vivacious girl like you. You're likely not to be perceptive enough about human nature to appreciate his virtues, and even if you got to know him well, you might find him a little too fussy for a girl who likes things to be done in a big, splashy way. He is probably very analytical and possesses a keen, critical intelligence. You might want him to be more enthusiastic, and he'll wonder why you get so excited and combative over the little critical jabs he throws out almost without thinking.

Staying together will require more mutual understanding than most two-somes. A lot of mutual understanding.

ARIES WOMAN, LIBRA MAN

Temper! Temper! Watch your temper. Libran men don't like discord. Even though they can hold their own, they usually prefer harmony, while excitement seems to stir you more. As the relationship gets started, this affair might be easier for Mr. Libra than it is for you, because you're likely to be more emotionally involved than he is. You might want to pin down, which will be uncomfortable for him. He might want to manipulate to gain control, which will be uncomfortable for you. You might do better to back off and be friends and lovers, but there's an all-or-nothing streak in you that might make this impossible. It's not hard for you to understand each other, and you both like the same kind of active, socially adventurous life. The sexual vibrations would be good if he were a little less flirty and fickle and you were a little less pushy and possessive. Still, if handled right, this one could work out.

ARIES WOMAN, SCORPIO MAN

You're both very proud and combative. He's proud, reserved, and usually secretive. He doesn't trust many people, and it's hard for him to love anyone he doesn't control in some way. You're proud but very friendly. You trust many people but are suspicious of those who are too secretive. He can be very sarcastic and critical; you are not inclined to sit still and be criticized. He won't change his mind easily, and after you've changed yours a few times to suit him, you'll expect him to give a little too. If he doesn't, you'll feel justified in making a verbal assault that can only cause more bickering and finally more silence. This is a shame since if the two of you were working together, there would be very little that you couldn't accomplish, and if everything else were going well, the sexual vibrations would improve as he opens up and learns to trust and you settle down some.

ARIES WOMAN, SAGITTARIUS MAN

Things might work well because he might come to understand you as well as you understand yourself. He knows your faults because they are very much like the ones he may have corrected in himself—impatience, impulsiveness, an excess of idealism or an excess of cynicism. He doesn't mind arguing with you about them because he is clever enough to win by letting you think you have won. You're more powerful and domineering than he, but you'll be surprised how often you end up doing things his way. His admiration for your finer qualities is genuine. He likes a woman who is friendly, confident, energetic, curious about life, ambitious, trusting, warm, and spontaneous. And you'll like him because he possesses all of these qualities, too, in more moderate quantities, which makes him a little the wiser of the two and you a little more aggressive. He may be a little footloose and flighty at first, and you a little too jealous for him. But if you loosen up a little and he tightens up a little, things will work out well. In love both of you possess a good combination of realism and idealism. You both think you're more romantic and sensual than you are. The truth is probably that you each experience moments of intense passion interspersed with your equally intense and more persistent desire to win the game of life—for ego's sake. If careers and egos take center stage, as with superstar singer Diana Ross and record mogul Barry Gordy, the relationship may end, but the friendship is likely to continue long afterward.

ARIES WOMAN, CAPRICORN MAN

It's hard for a love affair to survive direct clashes of personalities, and this one is likely to be full of them. Capricorn men like to manage things, and Aries women don't work well under nagging supervision. He has fits of gloom and pessimism that will be hard for you to endure sometimes. Unless he's much older than you are, or much wealthier, you're not likely to be inclined to accept his habit of dedicating almost his entire life to his career. You like more variety and you're likely to have a career of your own. For his part he might find you too impulsive and impatient. He'll try to control your diverse energy. With that kind of energy you might not feel inspired by his often uninspired but extremely strong sexual appetite.

ARIES WOMAN, AQUARIUS MAN

Because you're an idealist, there's no doubt that you could be very attracted to Mr. Aquarius. He wants to change the world, to make it a better place for all. He has great sympathy for the underdog and he finds it easy to get along with people from all walks of life and all levels of society. His stubborn streak barely shows. When you first meet him, you might think that if he were a little more of this and a little less of that, he'd be perfect for you. But to get him to change that little bit is like trying to move a mountain. He's not genuinely materialistic and never will be. He might like nice things, but he could as easily live like a bohemian. He'll insist on a lot of personal freedom, and no bargain will tempt him to give that up. He is strongly opinionated and usually refuses to compromise. And though he is kindly and sympathetic, he is not at all emotional. In fact he's about the most coolly detached of all men. In sexual matters his personality is tuned more for nonchalance or playfulness than for the extremes of passion, possessiveness, and jealousy that you seem to prefer.

ARIES WOMAN, PISCES MAN

No two people could be more unlike each other. There is bound to be an immediate recognition of this, so if you get together at all, you each must have decided to put up with the other because of what each has that the other lacks. You are aggressive, self-confident, impulsive, careless, idealistic, trusting, and egotistical. It's easy to see how you could be taken in by such an apparently lovable character as Mr. Pisces. He's a dreamer who tends to be indecisive, evasive, and unstable, but also sweet, musical, sensitive, sensual, and seething with concealed passion. He's very clever, especially in relationships with very aggressive people.

He attempts to make himself easy and indispensable. He'll feed your ego until you're addicted, then when he has control of the emotional side of the relationship, you'll see all that sweetness is not completely selfless. He's just as self-interested as you are, and to keep him around, you'll have to allow him the freedom to discover himself.

ARIES

(MARCH 21ST TO APRIL 20TH)

STEPHANIE MILLS, singer, actress	March 22, 1957
GEORGE BENSON, singer, composer, jazz musician	March 22, 1943
MAYNARD JACKSON, Atlanta mayor	March 23, 1938
DOROTHY HEIGHT, civil and womens' rights activist, institution builder	March 24, 1912
ARETHA FRANKLIN, rhythm and blues singer, the "Queen of Soul"	March 25, 1942
TEDDY PENDERGRASS, soul singer	March 26, 1950
MARCUS ALLEN, L.A. Raiders running back, Heisman trophy winner	March 26, 1960
DIANA ROSS, singer, actress	March 26, 1944
SARAH VAUGHN, jazz singer	March 27, 1924
BERNICE KING, social activist	March 28, 1963
PEARL BAILEY, singer, actress, comedienne, author	March 29, 1918
WALT FRAZIER, NBA star	March 29, 1945
NAOMI SIMS, model, entrepreneur, author	March 30, 1948
JACK JOHNSON, boxing hero	March 31, 1878
CLARA "MOTHER" HALE, child care specialist, founder of Hale House	April 1, 1905
GIL SCOTT HERON, musician, poet	April 1, 1949
ALBERTA HUNTER, singer, composer, nurse	April 1, 1895
MARVIN GAYE, soul singer	April 2, 1939

LUTHER VANDROSS, romantic balladeer	**April 2, 1951**
EDDIE MURPHY, comedian, screen actor	**April 3, 1961**
VERTAMAE SMART-GROSVENOR, culinary anthropologist, author	**April 4, 1938**
MAYA ANGELOU, Pulitzer Prize–winning author, actress, director	**April 4, 1928**
MUDDY WATERS, blues singer, guitarist	**April 4, 1915**
GENERAL COLIN POWELL, U.S. military officer	**April 5, 1937**
BOOKER T. WASHINGTON, educator, social activist, Tuskegee Institute founder	**April 5, 1856**
BILLY DEE WILLIAMS, film and television star	**April 6, 1937**
WILLIAM M. TROTTER, pioneering black businessman, social activist	**April 7, 1894**
BILLIE HOLIDAY, jazz singer	**April 7, 1915**
ROBERT JOHNSON, founder of Black Entertainment Television	**April 8, 1946**
KESHIA KNIGHT PULLIAM, actress ("Rudy Cosby")	**April 9, 1979**
PAUL ROBESON, singer, actor, political activist	**April 9, 1898**
MESHACH TAYLOR, television, stage, and screen actor	**April 11, 1947**
BABYFACE, singer, songwriter, producer	**April 12, 1958**
HERBIE HANCOCK, composer, jazz pianist	**April 12, 1940**
AL GREEN, soul singer	**April 13, 1946**
OLA ROTIMI, playwright, director	**April 13, 1946**
PEABO BRYSON, singer, songwriter	**April 13, 1951**
MAY EDWARD CHINN, first black woman doctor in Harlem	**April 15, 1896**
ELIZABETH CATLETT, sculptor, painter, printmaker	**April 15, 1919**
A. PHILIP RANDOLPH, labor and civil rights pioneer	**April 15, 1889**
BESSIE SMITH, blues singer, "Empress of the Blues"	**April 15, 1894**

MARTIN LAWRENCE, comedian, television and screen actor   April 15, 1965

KAREEM ABDUL-JABBAR, NBA star, actor   April 18, 1948

NATE ARCHIBALD, NBA star   April 18, 1948

LIONEL HAMPTON, jazz vibraphonist, composer   April 20, 1914

APRIL 21st TO MAY 20th

TAURUS

THE BULL
THE SIGN OF THE BUILDER

◆

STUBBORN, EASYGOING,

STABLE

◆

Ruled by Venus

COLOR: Blue

METAL: Copper

GEM: Sapphire

LUCKY NUMBERS: 1 and 9

FORTUNATE DAY: Friday

THE TAURUS VIBRATION

JANET JACKSON IS THE LATEST RULER OF "Rhythm Nation," which was the name of her extremely popular 1989 album. There have been rulers before her. James Brown, "The Godfather of Soul," comes to mind, because without a great singing voice, and certainly with no great gift for fancy lyrics, he rose to the top of music charts and shaped much of today's music on the strength of his earthy rhythms. Jackson and Brown were both born under the sign of Taurus.

Down-to-Earth is Taurus's middle name. And the rhythms of the earth are very important to the practical Taurean. Soon after we notice the deliberate, smooth cadence of even the Taurean's fastest motions, we notice the practical outlook that dominates Taurus's vision of the world.

Taurus is a solid vibration, more determined and persistent than Aries but nonetheless usually cheerful. If Aries symbolizes the awakening of the human spirit, then Taurus represents mankind's connection with the earth and the flesh.

In *Moon Walk* and in some of his statements to the press and friends megastar Michael Jackson describes Janet, the baby sister of the famous Jackson clan, as a perfect little Taurean child—always seeking harmonious relationships, gentle, kind, friendly, and a little lazy. Aldore Collier wrote in the September 1986 *Ebony,* "She has always been seen as pretty, quiet and somewhat shy."

Although their father, Joe Jackson, had a powerful impact on the Jackson children, Janet, like most Taureans, was influenced more by her mother. And Taureans are usually very obedient children who are slow to rebel against the mother's voice inside their heads. This can create a problem for Taurean children when they decide to express themselves, particularly if (as with Janet Jackson) the mother's viewpoint conflicts with their own.

If a Taurean rebels, it may be slow in coming, but it can be accompanied by a lot of rage. The insurrection is intended not for freedom, as it is with Aquarians, for example, so much as it is a war to establish control of the immediate environment, and mostly control of the self.

"It's taken me a good while to establish my own identity," Janet Jackson says in the *Ebony* article. And the songs on the album that followed after *Rhythm Nation,* many of which she wrote, were about her rebellion. The album was entitled *Control.*

When the search for mother love does not give them the sense of security they solicit, Taureans may seek security by acquiring material possessions. Those possessions can become a substitute for the emotional assurance they lack.

Presently on the American scene there is no one more interested in individualizing his identity than Dennis Rodman, the star forward for the Chicago Bulls of the National Basketball Association. The color of Rodman's hair changes regularly (it has been pink and green), he has tattoos all over his body, a ring in his nose, and has appeared on the cover of *Sports Illustrated* wearing women's clothes. His biography, *The Hard Way,* reports that his mother called him her most needing child— a "soft, painfully shy, passive child who listened to what anyone said and went along with the program." So when Taurus rebels, the rebellion is extreme.

Many astrologers have equated the Taurean desire to acquire possessions with an attempt at self-substantiation in the material world. The aim of the Taurus personality is reflected in this tale: Taurus and another bull were coming down a hill toward a herd of cows when the other bull said impatiently, "Hey, Taurus, why don't we run down there and make love to one of those cows?" To which Taurus replied, "Why don't we walk down and make love to 'em all?"

This is not to suggest that Taureans are disloyal or fickle or inconstant. Quite the opposite is true. The tale suggests that Taureans like to do a job slowly so that they can do it well.

People born under the second sign of the zodiac certainly prefer to take their time. And they often get more done than people who rush; they certainly do a more thorough job. The story further reveals that Taurus is a sensuous vibration, ruled by Venus, the planet of love. In mythology Venus, or Aphrodite, is the seeker after harmony, art, beauty, and affection. Love and earthiness is a powerful combination, which at its best produces sensuousness and eroticism. At its worst it produces jealousy and gluttony. The key words of the sign are I HAVE.

There is no better illustration of this than in *Beneath the Underdog,* the autobiography of Taurean Charlie Mingus, the great jazz bass player. The book is less about Mingus's life in jazz than it is about his tremendous appetite for food, and especially sex.

People born with their sun in Taurus have more fun than one would expect of such a conservative, earthbound vibration. In summary, Taureans are usually realistic in their thinking, reliable in their habits, firm in their values, affectionate and steady, but when they are not operating at their best, they can be boring, lazy, stubborn, resentful, and greedy.

Taurus is the most materialistic sign of the zodiac, which accounts for the Taurean's attraction to money; they love to handle it, to talk about it, to count it.

An ideal place for them is in a bank working as a teller. They love money and the things it can buy—fine homes, long cars, expensive clothing. Their single greatest ambition is to amass fine material possessions. Others might want money because it buys freedom or power, but not Taurus. Taurus is infatuated with money because it provides access to the comfort of fine places to eat and drink, and luxurious accommodations for sleeping and, yes, making love.

As an earth sign Taurus is a stable vibration, more cautious than adventurous. Since the sign is ruled by Venus, it gives Taureans a spiritual serenity that's often missing in the other earth signs; they are not as critical as Virgos or as cold and calculating as Capricorns. Certainly Taureans are less pessimistic than the other two. Still, they can be more resentful, grudge bearing, tightfisted, inflexible, and unknowingly tedious than other earth signs.

Some astrologers contend that Taurus is more than just one of the three earth signs. They claim that the sign is coruled by the Earth itself and that the rhythms of the sign are a mixture of the rhythms of Earth and Venus. When people speak of "solid as a rock," they're talking about Taurus. Seldom does the Taurean vibration transcend the flesh—their path is through the body. They exult in it and celebrate its rhythms and pulsations.

Not surprisingly Taureans excel at playing bass, an instrument that provides the rhythmical foundation of most jazz groups. Many of the best jazz bassists—Charlie Mingus, Ron Carter, and Ray Brown, for instance—are Taureans.

Taurus is one of the most musical of vibrations. It represents the throat of the Grand Old Man of the zodiac, and Taureans usually have very strong, smooth voices, perfect for speaking or singing. Taurean Ella Fitzgerald reflects the softer Venus aspect of the Taurus voice. This smooth, velvety tone is also apparent in the music of Duke Ellington—Taurus can be a very soothing vibration. But whether the tone is mellow and soft or rasping and rhythmic, there is an undeniable power in the Taurus voice.

Bulls have earned a reputation as raging, violent animals, but until provoked they are usually peace-loving creatures who are content to graze lazily and live life as it comes. They're violent only when goaded. It takes a lot to get them mad, but once they're angry, they can be totally destructive.

They have long memories and they do hold grudges. James Brown's popular song "The Big Payback" could easily be one of the theme songs of the sign. Taureans have committed more murders than the natives of any other sign, and their inclination toward physical confrontation is reflected in the careers of Taurean boxing champions such as Sugar Ray Robinson, Sonny Liston, and Joe Louis.

Clearly, even though Taureans are reasonably nonaggressive people, it's disastrous to push them beyond the limits they set. During the 1850s Taurean Martin Delany used his Pittsburgh home as a hiding place for escaping slaves. It was a known station on the Underground Railroad. Delany was a big, friendly man, but after the Fugitive Slave Law was passed, he warned, "If any man approaches that house in search of a slave—I care not who he may be, whether constable or sheriff, magistrate or even the judge of the Supreme Court—nay, let it be he who sanctioned this act to become law [President Buchanan] surrounded by his cabinet as his body guard . . . if he crosses the threshold of my door, and I do not lay him a lifeless corpse at my feet, I hope the grave may refuse my body a resting place, and righteous heaven my spirit a home."

This violent, raging aspect of the Taurean personality, however, is usually masked in the native of this sign. Their voices, as we've seen, are usually like dark silk, and there tends to be a rhythmical steadiness to their walk; it's surprising how often you find a Taurus lady wearing a silk blouse or a silk scarf. They like the feel of silk against their skin as much as they love fine food and wine.

Taureans are both industrious and lazy. Theirs is the sign of the day laborer. Nature fitted them well for manual occupations. They love to work with their hands. Once they start a task, they have the stamina, patience, and determination to work it through to the end; but once they decide to rest, they do that just as lovingly. They work hard and sleep hard. In fact they are among those rare people who can sleep straight through an entire weekend.

As Aldore Collier wrote in *Ebony,* Michael Jackson is an early riser. "Janet, however, hangs onto the pillow much longer." Since she is a Taurus, it's not surprising.

They are usually not easily ruffled by external circumstances. They go their way in their own style. Even when they're working hard, showing off, dancing frantically, or fighting, their movements are smooth, rhythmic, and flowing.

Smooth, yet stubborn as hell, the best way to get them to do something they don't want to do is with flattery. Push them and you'll get nowhere. Velvet-smooth Sugar Ray Robinson was born with Sun in Taurus. A friend said that Robinson was so stubborn, he forced a Chicago fight promoter to open a bank on Saturday to deliver $200,000 cash to his hotel room. It didn't matter that thousands of fans would be stranded at ringside and millions more stuck by their radios waiting for the second Sugar Ray Robinson–Carmen Basilio fight. Robinson wanted his cash, and he wouldn't budge until he got it.

Each element—air, fire, water, and earth—has its fixed, cardinal, and mutable sign. Taurus is the fixed sign of the most stable element, earth. Taureans, then, are the most steady, consistent, and persistent of all people. They are absolutely dependable and determined once they've promised to do something. But they can be totally inert once they've decided they don't want to deal with something; it doesn't even enter their heads to change. New evidence can bombard them, but they'll remain firmly in position.

Taurus is the least scatterbrained of the signs. Natives prefer to reason on concrete terms, thus many astrologers have assumed that they're the least intellectual of the signs. It's true that Taurus's intellectual achievements are usually the result of slow, methodical learning through research, long experience, or repetition rather than through quick deductions based on flashy insights.

The life of Malcolm X offers a fine example of Taurus's intellectual approach. His thinking was always keyed to the practical. He learned what he knew through hard experience in the ghettos and prisons of America, and then through the strict teachings of Elijah Muhammad. But once he had learned it, he was absolutely certain of it.

Finally, Taurus isn't as clever a sign as, say, Gemini. In fact Taureans are likely to regard clever people as too superficial or unreliable. On the other hand, Geminis and other air signs often think of Taureans as slow and even somewhat dull.

RELATIONSHIPS

It would seem that someone with Taurus's apparent good nature would like a lot of people, but this is far from true. Pleasure comes to Taurus not through extensive human relationships but through the senses. The greatest enjoyment comes from things that Taurus can taste, touch, see, hear, feel, drink, eat, or love. Taureans are rather reserved in relation to people. They control their emotions very well, so it's often not apparent that they're suspicious of people whose loyalties haven't been tested. Taureans judge people very harshly, and there's more than a little snobbery in the vibration. People of the second sign often erect barriers between themselves and others, and they watch from their side of the barrier.

The requirements for friendship are very high, but Taureans are definitely not loners. They enjoy the company of others. With people they've known for a while, they're extremely loyal and friendly; but for the most part, Taurean friendship is restricted to a small, closed circle.

In superficial social situations Taureans get along well with most people. They're not blunt, abrupt, or abrasive. People usually like them because they have pleasant personalities. They're more interested in harmony and peace than in competition and conflict. As a rule they're not boisterous or aggressive. In fact many of them aren't very talkative at all until they've gotten to know you.

Taureans are usually good with children because with children they can drop all their protective suspicion. They like to kid, play games, and forget about the complexity of adult human relationships. I know a Taurus mother who handles a houseful of children day after day without ever seeming to lose her cool. She keeps things running smoothly. She plays with her children, is strict with them, but is also very affectionate. She's seldom angry and she never seems flustered. She, like

Taurean Willie Mays in center field, makes even the spectacular look easy, and for her it is.

Because of their even temperament, Taureans are easy people to live with once their partners understand what to expect. The most common complaint from those who know Taureans is that they can be extremely insensitive and unreceptive to certain kinds of emotional appeals. Often they are without a great amount of compassion and sympathy.

In fact, unevolved Taureans have one of the heaviest spirits of any astrological vibration. Their imagination seldom soars above the mundane. Their conversation can be plodding, and their wit is not usually nimble. They tend to speak in monologues. Don't expect much easy give-and-take when talking with them. Interrupt them to express your views but don't expect a response, for when you are finished, they're likely to return to the same conversational line they were on before you spoke—they may even have ignored what you were saying.

LUCK, MONEY, AND WORK

As subjects of lucky Venus, Taureans are bound to be lucky people, but as children of the solid earth they are usually too cautious and security conscious to depend on luck. They usually know how to hold on to a dollar if it comes to them through hard work. Taurus is the sign of the steady builder. Natives of the sign value money once they've endured the long process of accumulation. But when money comes through a sudden windfall, they can spend it as fast as the nearest Libra.

Most Taureans think about money almost constantly. Theirs is not an idealistic sign, so they often fall in love and marry for very practical reasons—such as money. Not that they are gold diggers. Their schemes aren't usually so grandiose. They look for partners with good earning potential and good future security. Taureans love comfort and they're always searching for comfortable situations.

They make better businessmen than many of the more flashy types who chase get-rich-quick schemes. They seem to accept the fact that most businesses prosper because of good organization and careful squeezing out of percentages and fractions of percentages year after year.

Many of those hefty cooks in the town's best restaurants are probably Taureans, and many Taureans are successful artists, craftspeople, and carpenters. They work well at a great number of jobs, but they function best where things are organized and standardized, where there aren't a lot of rushed changes in plans and schedules. Routine suits them better than it does most people. They're good workers, not because they're quickly adaptable but because they are leisurely, uncomplaining people who don't mind giving a good day's work for a day's pay.

PHYSICAL AND MENTAL HEALTH

There's nothing at all fragile about most natives of the second sign. Even the thin ones are stronger than most people their size, and heavy Taureans are among the strongest people in the world. They are usually blessed with good health, although there is a tendency for them to put on weight in later years. Their mental makeup is just as robust as their physique. Taureans don't fly apart under pressure. They certainly know how to relax when they need to, and they escape most of the depression that plagues the other two earth signs.

But there is in the sign an unexpected susceptibility to small infections. A common cold is enough to incapacitate the best of them, and when they're sick, they certainly like to be waited on. Taurus rules the throat. Sore throats strike often, and it isn't uncommon for a Taurean to wake up with only a slight cold and find that he can't talk.

In addition there is a conflict between their normal restraints and an overactive physical appetite in the Taurean personality. Many natives of the vibration, for instance, have an uncontrollable sweet tooth and often complain about their great physical and psychological need to eat at the oddest of times. This problem can cause a great deal of anxiety. Before his death the late jazz bassist Charlie Mingus described what happened to him when he let his demons go. Besides recounting frequent occasions when he overindulged in eating, he claims to have made love to twenty-three women in one night. Even if his story is only half true, the book illustrates his problem of never being able to get enough. Many Taureans go on drinking binges or eating sprees, or they maintain fantasy lives full of orgies and feasts.

LOVE AND SEX

Taureans can do exactly as James Brown brags: "Stay on the scene like a loving machine." There are none better, and most aren't as good. Taureans like to wallow in sensuality. If Venus and earth are a good combination for music, they are an excellent one for love. The Venus influence softens the earthiness, and the earthiness adds weight to the romantic nature bestowed on Taurus by Venus, who, after all, is the goddess of love.

Venus adds charm and a pleasant nature to Taurean personalities. In love, they like romantic touches—the soft lights, the silks and satins, the flowers and perfumes, the wine and good food, the soft words and the soft music. But it doesn't stop there. Taureans add a great deal of physical stamina and the large sexual appetite for which earth signs are famous. It's not difficult for them to brush aside all the frills and get right down to the nitty-gritty. In fact after a while they may tend to do this too often for a more romantic or sexually playful partner, if that's whom they've chosen.

In love Taureans are protective, loyal, and extremely dependable, but inclined to be quite possessive. Crimes of passion are not uncommon among them. They love strongly and are stubbornly jealous at times.

Mature Taureans enjoy possessing and being possessed. For this reason there are not a great number of single people of this vibration. Men of the sign easily settle into comfortable love affairs. They are well fitted for marriage and domestic life.

Usually only in youth are Taureans likely to be sexual adventurers. Malcolm X lived a typical Taurean adolescence. As a teenager he enjoyed a loose and lustful life. He glutted his appetite for sensual experiences of all types. Charlie Mingus, on the other hand, maintained his lusty appetites until well into his middle-age years; he is a Taurean who never attained the sober, restrained adulthood that is customary for this vibration. He was self-indulgent to the end.

Taureans don't marry foolishly, for they're usually the kind of people who don't plan to marry often. A cycle of repeated marriages and divorces isn't normally appealing to so stable a temperament. They like to learn one partner's habits and have the partner learn theirs once and for all, if possible.

Because Taureans are creatures of habit and routine, marriage often gets a little boring; even so, the urge for excitement and sexual variety is very well controlled. I know a Taurean who has been married for fourteen years; during that time he has gone on four sexual lost weekends. But after each escapade he came back and, to this day, remains a dependable husband.

A married Taurus woman once told me that she has had a boyfriend for four years, but she has been so cautious and discreet about it that not even a hint of it has gotten back to her best girlfriend. She wants satisfaction and physical pleasure, but she doesn't call it love. "Love is where you live. All that other stuff is something else. I would be a fool to mess up my good thing for a few moments of pleasure," she said. Idealists might jump from one lover to another in a frantic search for the ideal love affair. Taureans know that nothing is very ideal. They can take the good with the bad as long as the situation is relatively comfortable and their sexual needs are met.

LOVE AFFAIRS

*(See the other chapters for love affairs between
Taurus men and women of other signs.)*

TAURUS WOMAN, ARIES MAN

A love affair between the two of you might stumble on for a while
because you each have a lot of what the other needs. He is exciting and
adventurous and you're patient and loyal. If you give each other plenty
of room, you might be able to make it work. But he's usually much too
unsettling and unsettled for you, and you're much too stubborn and
stable for him. He's likely to have a great taste for newness, variety,
and constant change while you usually prefer familiar people and places
and familiar ways of doing things. In fact, you often feel threatened by
that which hasn't been tried and tested, while he's often bored by that
which is too routine. He loves to argue and push, and your reaction
will be to nag and resist. With money he tends to be wasteful and risk-
taking, while you're cautious. He's an idealist who might seem foolish to
you. You're a materialist who might seem stodgy to him. You tend to be
home-loving, possessive, and jealous while he needs to be involved outside
the home. Innocent or not, these involvements are bound to arouse your
suspicions, and in the end the involvements might not be all that innocent.
The possibilities for arguments and conflict are boundless. The possibilities for happiness are contained in your mutual acceptance of the vast difference between the way the two of you see life.

TAURUS WOMAN, TAURUS MAN

This is bound to be a good old down-to-earth love affair. You each
know what the other likes and should have no trouble giving it. You
run a good home and you're probably a good cook, a careful shopper,
and a loyal, satisfying lover. He's probably a good provider, an excellent

father, a dependable husband, and a loyal, satisfying lover as well. What more could any two Taureans want, except perhaps some relief from their own practicality, inflexibility, and stubbornness? You may not be willing or able to lighten up and break the stalemate or free enough to encourage him to do so. There's a danger that you will hold each other too tightly in this situation that could use a little fresh air. But even you two can be bored by too much routine. True, you both enjoy a life that has a nice, steady groove—parties, music, dancing, familiar friends, good food, fine wine, choice possessions—but you must be careful that the groove doesn't become a rut.

TAURUS WOMAN, GEMINI MAN

For some reason this combination occurs often and, considering the differences in the pace at which each of you like to live, it works out surprisingly well. Even at first sight he's so different from you that you don't even expect him to act like you. You'll have to learn to accept the fact that he's so flighty and changeable, and he might come to see you as an anchor for his unstable, fickle nature. He might like the fact that you are so practical; it keeps him from having to be. You might like the fact that he's so excitable and impulsive; it keeps you from getting bored. Like you, he's not very sentimental. Your physical sexual appetite is likely to be stronger than his, but this might lead him to give more satisfaction than he needs or really wants, which is all right with you. Rabbits and turtles who respect each other make good companions; why not Geminis and Taureans?

TAURUS WOMAN, CANCER MAN

Two home-loving, security-conscious, socially cautious people like you are bound to have a lot in common. But there is more. You're both persistent, possessive, but relatively unaggressive people. He's likely to be more unstable, imaginative, impractical, and insecure, but good, steady Taurus love is just the thing to drive away those insecurities. He'll complain that you aren't romantic or imaginative enough in your approach to love, but he enjoys a little tension in his sexual relationships, and you're certainly sensual enough for him. He likes to provide, do for, and protect those he loves, and you don't mind that. You like to do the same. He would probably like you to be more verbal in your lovemaking. His feelings can be hurt as easily by what is not said as by what is said. But he trusts your stability, and you can make him feel wanted just by your loyalty. Whatever hurt you cause him might be just enough to keep him trying, and his dreamy, wandering quality that makes you angry can, at other times, make you feel needed.

TAURUS WOMAN, LEO MAN

There's bound to be a lot of initial attraction between a sparkling, regal nature like his and a gentle, receptive nature like yours. In most relationships Leo likes to be the star, and he might see a love affair with you as an excellent opportunity. Your charm is not as gushing and overwhelming as his, but in the end you may not be as responsive and enthusiastic as he likes a woman to be. At first he might try to impress you with his warmth and generosity, but later he might try to be domineering and demanding. At first you might be submissive and easygoing, but later defensive and resistant. He's egotistical and wants to have his way, even if he has to bribe and trick to get it. You can be so obstinate and suspicious that neither bribery, trickery, nor coercion will move you. When an intractable force meets an immovable object, there is usually an explosion.

TAURUS WOMAN, VIRGO MAN

It's not hard to see the two of you married for forty years or more. Through all the misunderstandings, it will remain apparent that you both see the world in pretty much the same terms. You are both patient, cautious people who don't marry for superficial reasons and don't divorce for superficial reasons either. Love for each of you is a matter of being dependable and giving and receiving service. It's neither sentimental nor overly romantic. It runs quiet, but it runs deep. You both enjoy home life, and both have a great desire for material security. There is an artistic streak in both of you that might make your social life center more on artistic or commercial entertainment than on constant involvement with people. In fact, both of you tend to be rather reserved in your relationships with anyone but the few people who compose your small, closed social circle. You both are rather jealous and suspicious. The sexual vibrations are excellent. Neither of you needs a lot of verbal stimulation, which is good since both often have trouble verbalizing tender feelings. Virgo men concentrate on physical satisfaction and that is what Taurus women most desire.

TAURUS WOMAN, LIBRA MAN

Libras like to flirt a lot. They need more freedom than you Taurean women like to give, but since there's a strong sexual attraction between you, you might be able to survive this difficulty. If he tries to curb his desire to be involved with too many people and you curb your tendency to be suspicious of everyone he's involved with, things might work out for a while. Libras are impractical and somewhat wasteful, but Taureans tend to like the things they buy—top-shelf clothing, wine, and food. Sexually Taureans are very physically demanding, but he might force himself to rise to the occasion for reputation's sake. Neither is very aggressive and neither enjoys confusion or confrontation. In the end, Libras like a little excitement and playfulness in a partner, and Taureans like a little more stability and practicality. This one could go along peacefully enough for some time.

TAURUS WOMAN, SCORPIO MAN

It's surprising that two practical, stable, cautious, and tenacious natures like yours don't get along better, but in most cases this is a difficult match, despite the fact that the sexual vibrations are not much short of excellent. Both of you have strong physical appetites and neither needs much mental or verbal stimulation to do your physical best. But outside the bedroom both of you have to be on guard all the time.

Scorpios are very demanding of themselves and consequently very demanding of anyone around them. Taureans are much more leisurely and tranquil. Scorpios are usually very critical of anyone with whom they profoundly disagree. They are fighters or naggers when things aren't going the way they want them. Taureans are peace-loving but can be very destructive when pushed. Both of you are likely to be good at clamming up, so fights might not come often, but when they do, they'll be large. Neither of you likes to back down and neither is gifted with a forgiving nature. A course or two in the power of positive thinking will be needed here.

TAURUS WOMAN, SAGITTARIUS MAN

Sagittarian men are very adaptable and they usually have good instincts for finding what is good for them. At times in his life he might think that a patient, practical, stable woman like you is just what he needs. You have a great deal to offer him and he might seem a very exciting man to you. But it may not be long before you start thinking he is much too careless about too many of the things that are important to you, and he may have already concluded that you are much too jealous and closed to new ideas for a free and easy soul like him. The sexual vibrations could be ever so good. In fact, they will be, since he's aggressive, passionate, and likes a sexual challenge, and you are sensuous and receptively able to deal with his best efforts and then some.

TAURUS WOMAN, CAPRICORN MAN

Capricorn men are ambitious, and you like that. He wants something out of life and he's willing to work harder than you do to get it. You can be strong and stable, a base camp for his forays into the world he wants to defeat. You two see the world in pretty much the same terms; thus your styles are similarly cautious, persistent, practical, serious, and security-minded. He likes the outward trappings of success, and you are a lover of nice things. His fits of depression are deeper than yours. You can cheer him up when he's down and reassure him if he ever begins to doubt himself. This seems to have been part of the role that Taurean Coretta Scott King played in the life of Capricornian Dr. Martin Luther King. Taurus and Capricorn is a good alliance for solid achievement. You're more steadfast than he, and more leisurely and unworried, but just as determined that he reach the goals he sets for himself. The sexual vibrations are excellent. Neither of you is sentimental, frivolous, or fickle. Your sex lives are dominated by strong physical hungers that need a lot of physical attention, as opposed to a lot of romanticism or superficial sweetness. There may be plenty of arguments, but your love can survive those. You might complain that he isn't amorous enough, but that's a small problem when you think of all you have going between you.

TAURUS WOMAN, AQUARIUS MAN

You Taurean women are creatures of strong physical passion. Most Aquarians have a playful attitude toward sex, but the physical need is a good match for yours. You're jealous, and Aquarians like a lot of freedom. You're self-centered, and Aquarians have a great need to be involved with other people. Aquarians are spenders, and you like to save for that rainy day. You're both stubborn and not very adaptable. What you have going for you is the ability to let each other alone without much trouble. Distant harmony is possible and preferred.

TAURUS WOMAN, PISCES MAN

This could be a good combination since each could benefit so much from the other's strong points. He needs someone stable like you with a good practical turn of mind. He might have a tendency to drift, and you can anchor him. He can be unsure of himself and you are full of steady self-confidence. You appreciate a creative, imaginative partner. His sympathetic and affectionate nature will bring out a side of your personality that will make you a warmer, more loving person. He enjoys the pleasures of the flesh, and despite your practicality, so do you. Good music, good food, good wine, and a strong sexual attraction could be the basis of your relationship. But you tend to dislike indecision and emotional confusion, and Pisceans are often surrounded by it. He could definitely broaden your interest and teach you to be more flexible, but you might feel more secure with a steadier, less sensitive emotional nature.

TAURUS

(APRIL 21ST TO MAY 20TH)

BYRON ALLEN, stand-up comedian, talk-show host	April 22, 1961
CHARLIE MINGUS, jazz bassist, composer	April 22, 1922
CHARLES JOHNSON, novelist, essayist, cartoonist	April 23, 1948
ALBERTA KING, singer	April 25, 1925
ELLA FITZGERALD, jazz singer	April 25, 1918
CORETTA SCOTT KING, civil rights activist	April 27, 1927
DUKE ELLINGTON, band leader, composer	April 29, 1899
SUGAR RAY ROBINSON, boxing champion	May 3, 1921
JAMES BROWN, "The Godfather of Soul"	May 3, 1933
JOHN LEWIS, musician	May 3, 1920
RON CARTER, bassist	May 4, 1937
KENNETH GIBSON, first black mayor of Newark, N.J.	May 5, 1932
MARTIN DELANY, ethnologist, physician, explorer, scientist, activist	May 6, 1812
WILLIE MAYS, legendary baseball player	May 6, 1931
JOE CLARK, educator	May 7, 1939
SONNY LISTON, heavyweight boxing champion	May 8, 1932
MARY LOU WILLIAMS, singer, musician	May 8, 1910
JUDITH JAMESON, dancer, choreographer	May 10, 1944

LOUIS FARRAKHAN, Islamic minister, social activist	**May 11, 1933**
STEVIE WONDER, singer, songwriter, composer, musician	**May 13, 1950**
DENNIS RODMAN, Chicago Bulls star player	**May 13, 1961**
JOE LOUIS, heavyweight boxing champ, "The Brown Bomber"	**May 13, 1914**
JANET JACKSON, singer, screen actress	**May 13, 1966**
ALVIN POUSSAINT, psychiatrist, expert on racism	**May 15, 1934**
JOHN CONYERS, Democratic congressman from Detroit	**May 16, 1929**
YANNICK NOAH, professional tennis player	**May 18, 1960**
REGGIE JACKSON, baseball star	**May 18, 1946**
MALCOLM X, social activist, civil rights leader	**May 19, 1925**
GRACE JONES, model, actress, singer	**May 19, 1952**

MAY 21st TO JUNE 20th

GEMINI

THE TWINS

THE SIGN OF THE
COMMUNICATOR

◆

VERSATILE, CLEVER, EXPRESSIVE

◆

Ruled by Mercury

COLORS: Silver and Gray

METAL: Quicksilver

GEM: Emerald

LUCKY NUMBERS: 3 and 4

FORTUNATE DAY: Wednesday

THE GEMINI VIBRATION

EMINIS ARE TALKERS; THEIRS IS THE SIGN OF
the chatterbox mind. Their minds are always active, and usually
so are their mouths. They live to express themselves. They
believe in, and worship, the spoken word. In fact Gemini represents the
point in the zodiac where the soul becomes enchanted with language.

Gemini is ruled by the planet Mercury, and in mythology Mercury
is the messenger of the gods. The key words of this sign are I THINK,
and its natives are driven to make connections or links between ideas
and reality. They can also become so obsessed with thinking that they
find it hard to turn their minds off to relax, watch a television show,
rest, or even to make love.

They are always noting their own impressions and compiling obscure
facts to be used later in some unique form of self-expression. And
because of their fascination with language some of our most inventive
poets are among their ranks. James Weldon Johnson, Countee Cullen,
Gwendolyn Brooks, and Nikki Giovanni are among them. So are many
of today's oral poets or rappers. Tupac Shakur, M. C. Hammer, and
Heavy D are all natives of the sign.

In the cycle of the zodiac Aries represents the awakening of the
human spirit and Taurus represents humankind's focus on material reality. Gemini, a dual sign, symbolizes *communication* between the spirit
and the material world. Its natives are the ones who are best at inte-
grating the two.

Nothing expresses this tendency more dramatically than the music
of the Gemini superstar formerly known as Prince. Nearly all of his
music revolves around the conflict between the enjoyment of sex and
earthly pleasures and the quest for religious or spiritual salvation. Although the X-rated lyrics in such suggestive songs as "Soft and Wet"
have gotten more attention from fans and critics, overall his music reflects as much religious fervor as it does sexual heat.

Gemini is the sign of the Twins, and natives of this sign usually display two noticeably distinct personalities. When the moody twin is showing its face, Geminis are extremely irritable. They want to be left alone. Nearly everything that anyone says will annoy them. In this state they can become extremely aggressive, touchy, and argumentative. They retreat into themselves, and when they emerge, they can be sarcastic or abusive. If left alone, they may become sullen and depressive.

But when the cheerful twin asserts itself, Geminis are not only among the most playful of the signs but also by far the most talkative. Sometimes they talk about themselves so much, they seem egotistical. And of course, as the lyrics of most any rap monologue demonstrate, they do tend to boast and brag. But they're much too analytical to be truly egotistical. When they analyze themselves, they find as many faults as strong points. Their own personalities finally become just one of many fascinating subjects for their curious minds. When they are fascinated with self, the fascination is total.

"I'm unreal. I am incredible. I am unbelievable to those who think on the limited conscious level of mind. I am God appearing as me, I am the Master Mind thinking as Me. I am the Divine Sweetheart of the Universe," asserted the Gemini evangelist Reverend Ike.

"I turned myself into myself and was Jesus . . . I am so perfect so divine so ethereal so surreal I cannot be comprehended except by my permission," Nikki Giovanni wrote.

For the Gemini, declarations such as these are often merely a way of mocking reality with words. Despite their assertiveness, they are not deeply infatuated with themselves. They can easily forget about self when they encounter a newer, more fascinating idea about something else. Since they have no trouble getting involved with things outside themselves, they have a great capacity for sustained cooperation with other egos, and they can easily subordinate themselves within organized groups. Truly egotistical people—like some of those born with their sun in Aries, Leo, or Sagittarius—have a difficult time doing this.

In summary, Geminis are generally regarded as adaptable, clever, and logical, with a great flair for language in speech and writing. They are usually open-minded. When they are not at their best, they can be restless, deceptive, superficial, and gossipy.

Because of their fascination with communication and their wide-ranging interest in various subjects, Geminis are often drawn to journalism. Robert Maynard, the first African American to own a major metropolitan daily newspaper (the *Oakland Tribune*), Clarence Page, a columnist for the *Chicago Tribune,* and David Hardy, who won a historic racial discrimination suit against the New York *Daily News*, are examples of Gemini journalists.

Power is not normally a major concern of Geminis. They are competitive but they'd rather outsmart than overpower. They would rather play mind games and predictably they have a great love for such games of skill as chess, bridge, or bid whist.

Geminis are not conventional people. In fact, like Aquarians and Leos, they enjoy being shocking or different. One look at Mr. T should tell you that he is probably a native of the third sign.

Many people think of Gemini as an intellectual sign because Gemini natives seem so bright. In fact, the sign does represent the soul's initial encounter with the intellect, but its natives are generally less *deeply* intellectual than they are exceedingly quick. They instantly pick up impressions from the spiritual and real worlds and they can communicate these impressions faster and better than any other sign.

Their knowledge comes more from interacting with people and life than from the study of books. Most natives of this sign are curious and restless. They move from one idea to another so rapidly because they are bored with mental inactivity.

This is why their remarkable brilliance doesn't often lead to true scholarship. They find it difficult to concentrate on one idea or concept at a time, and are often rightly accused of being superficial or merely clever. Geminis must guard against a tendency to be shallow and frivolous.

* * *

Geminis are sometimes called the grand imitators of the zodiac because of the way they copy ideas. If they see something done once or twice, they can do it themselves the third time, and they always add some personal touch to make it appear that they're doing something fresh and new.

Some astrologers characterize them as mental pickpockets because they are always taking and using other people's ideas. Of course all of us are guilty of drawing on ideas from various fields and sources; however, Geminis are criticized for this trait because they are more candid about it.

Nikki Giovanni's autobiography, *Gemini,* for instance, is a brilliant example of how the trait may be used creatively. She snatches ideas and perceptions from numerous sources and rearranges them to form fresh, often startling, insights. Geminis are walking collections of memory circuits, full of bits of information pulled out of one context to be combined and rearranged to make something new in another.

In less-evolved Geminis, of course, this fascination with words may produce barroom or barbershop philosophers who will rap for hours even if they know absolutely nothing about the subject. Afflicted Geminis can easily become illusionists, creating their own reality out of words. They're the world's best liars, masters of the half-truth and the misleading impression.

They're also among the best salespeople in the world. They can create a product out of words and sell it to someone who's never seen it. They question most of the world's beliefs and ideals because they know that illusions are created with words. Nothing is too sacred for the Gemini's probing, curious mind.

In this matter of creating a total self out of words, Gemini James Weldon Johnson was a master. In his novel *The Autobiography of an Ex-Colored Man,* he created a fictional personality that most people thought was a real but anonymous black man who had written a confessional autobiography. Not until fifteen years after publication did his readers realize that the "ex-colored man" was an illusion and that the so-called autobiography was really a novel.

Johnson's career also points up the versatility and restlessness of the Gemini personality. Not only was he a great novelist but he was also such an accomplished poet and lyricist that "Lift Every Voice and Sing," written with his brother, John Rosamond Johnson, was adopted as the Negro national anthem.

In 1898 he became the first black lawyer to pass the Florida bar exams. Until he was appointed as United States consul to Nicaragua and Venezuela in 1906, however, he and his brother formed a successful songwriting team whose music was featured in several Broadway shows. In 1916 he joined the NAACP and soon became its executive secretary. At the time he was killed in an auto accident in 1938, he was professor of creative writing at Fisk University.

Geminis are seldom content to pursue one thing at a time. Variety is a keynote of the sign; they like to spread their energy around. For afflicted or unevolved Geminis there's always the danger of being a jack-of-all-trades and master of none, or, more appropriately for this vibration, they can often be accused of knowing a little bit about many things but nothing substantial about anything in particular.

Since their minds are their chief means of understanding the world, they are often inventive, original thinkers, which is good because they can be quite lazy when it comes to physical labor.

RELATIONSHIPS

When they're not in one of their gloomy moods, Geminis love to be around people. Natives of this sign are likely to lead very active social lives. They're friendly and magnetic, and their sense of fun often makes them the life of a party. They are natural entertainers. Many of them aspire to sing. Unfortunately, despite the presence of Gladys Knight and Patti LaBelle in this vibration, most cannot. Still, they feel obligated to make people laugh or to otherwise entertain anyone in their presence.

They are also good companions—good conversationalists and interested listeners. But sitting quietly with friends is not their idea of fun. They prefer being active, and count it as a personal failure if they're not able to do so. I have a Gemini friend who won't allow anyone to watch television without his running commentary on what is happening on screen. And he can become quite sarcastic with anyone who doesn't respond to his efforts to keep things stirred up.

Natives of this sign make friends very easily, but they often lose them with equal ease. This is because there is an element of superficiality in most Gemini relationships. In comparison to most people, the word *friendship* for Geminis is not invested with deep feelings of loyalty, closeness, and warmth. People of this vibration don't cling and they don't like to be clung to. This is more than independence; it is detachment.

Their friendliness is often all on the surface and of the present moment. Deeply emotional people speak of Gemini as a shallow sign and—in comparison to Pisces or Scorpio, for example—it is. Some contend that Geminis aren't generous people, and in some ways this is true. Since many gifts—flowers, perfume, and so on, in fact *things* in general—have little symbolic value for natives of this sign, giving these things is meaningless. But Geminis are generous in giving away ideas and goodwill.

Geminis aren't emotional people. In fact, they sometimes seem coldly logical, and their love of argument might annoy others over a long period of time. Ultimately, however, this works out all right because they like to keep changing friends anyway.

LUCK, MONEY, AND WORK

If luck saw Gemini coming, it would probably run the other way. Gemini is not a lucky sign, and those born under it should avoid games of pure chance, but they are masters of games where skill and quick intelligence influence the outcome.

Geminis are adept at creating clever schemes for making money, and they're usually fairly good at holding on to it. But of all people, those born under the air signs, one of which is Gemini, are the least materialistic. Earth-sign people are most interested in material things; water-sign people are next; fire-sign people like material things because they help them show off. Air-sign people are materialists only to the extent that material things enhance their social creations. They are people-centered rather than object-centered.

This doesn't mean that the majority of Geminis are doomed to be paupers. They are often quite talented and successful. Although not naturally musical, the sign includes such gifted musicians as the jazz trumpeter and innovator Miles Davis, jazz organist and singer Hazel Scott, jazz pianist Errol Garner, and the songwriter and pianist Fats Waller, whose music and clever lyrics were featured in *Ain't Misbehavin'*.

Typically they are good performers and often have captivating stage personalities: Actors Lou Gossett, Jr., Hattie McDaniel, "Bojangles" Robinson, Josephine Baker, Morgan Freeman, and Cleavon Little; and singers M. C. Hammer, Leslie Uggams, Fats Waller, and Gladys Knight are examples.

Because they are persuasive communicators with a knack for the spontaneous, they make excellent public speakers and preachers. And combined with their love of language, the ability to grasp abstract ideas quickly usually makes them excellent teachers and writers. James Weldon Johnson, Gwendolyn Brooks, Nikki Giovanni, and Cornell West, and novelist John Edgar Wideman were all college professors as well as writers.

They love work that brings them into contact with a variety of people, so they're often drawn to careers in advertising, television, journalism, public relations, and linguistics. Roy Innis, a civil rights activist and Congress of Racial Equality leader, and Reverend Ike are excellent examples of Geminis who used their gift of gab and ability to deal with varying personalities and situations in order to fashion a successful and lucrative career. Geminis also make good salespeople of insurance, cosmetics, used cars, or any product that moves quickly.

Geminis usually don't excel as professional athletes. There are exceptions, such as football great Gayle Sayers, but most Geminis aren't physically aggressive, only verbally so. An inmate at a New York State correctional facility noted that Geminis are almost never convicted of crimes of physical aggression. He found that Geminis with criminal inclinations were drawn to "mental" crimes, such as forgery or embezzlement.

PHYSICAL AND MENTAL HEALTH

Geminis have a lot of problems with dry skin. Otherwise their physical health is good, but not robust or "hot" enough to throw off the various infections that afflict most of us. Geminis should always treat themselves with medicines or see doctors for colds and various other infections of the respiratory system.

And of course natives of this sign suffer a form of psychological claustrophobia. If they find themselves fenced in, they suffer more physical illnesses than can be accounted for on purely physical terms. Taureans, for example, do not suffer at all from "owning" or "being owned" in close relationships. A Gemini may well come apart.

Natives of this sign often have trouble assimilating enough calcium into their systems; thus they have particular trouble with their teeth and with bone breakage. Gemini rules the shoulders, lungs, and nervous system, and there's no doubt that the nervous system gives natives of this sign their greatest health problems. Of the physical problems that arise out of nervous disorders, indigestion, poor elimination, and migraine headaches are just a few.

Mental problems are often far more numerous and devastating. If the nervous breakdown had a ruling planet, that planet would be Mercury. People born under Mercury are prone to worry too much. The nervous system rarely gets a rest. They exist in a state of constant mental alertness. The mind is constantly receiving impressions, hearing and seeing things, abstracting and turning over ideas, worrying, anticipating, reasoning. An astrologer friend makes this point by saying that the Mercurial mind is turned on constantly like a cool, unshaded light bulb burning even in the middle of the night, allowing only the most restless and lightest of sleep. Geminis must teach themselves to relax and meditate with the mind completely blank. The best locations for them are high places, well above sea level—they seem to prosper better both in success and health in these areas.

LOVE AND SEX

When their minds are on love, Geminis can be enthusiastic and expressive lovers. They're full of sexual curiosity, and during intimate moments they're almost never inhibited. They find it easy to express the way they feel, and often even easier to express something they don't feel. Sexual satisfaction is only a minor part of the romantic games they like to play. Often the mental challenge of the chase is more important than the sexual act.

Because Geminis aren't very emotional, they're often accused of not being very loving. This is not true. They can be very affectionate when they want to be. But everything is ruled by the mind. They are seldom driven by any deep sexual hunger. In any long-term relationship friendship usually replaces romantic love as the major binding force. This friendship is often strained, because Geminis can be very moody and unfriendly at times, but they know how to patch things up when they come out of their gloom.

Despite the fact that Geminis don't usually make deep emotional commitments to any one person, they can be extremely faithful; when married, they often harbor some rather old-fashioned ideas. Geminis aren't usually very maternal or paternal, but many of them make very good parents because they're able to form close and respectful relationships with children as friends.

Because of the emotional detachment, Geminis are perfectly fitted for a love-'em-and-leave-'em lifestyle, and because they're not driven by overwhelming physical sexual appetites, they only love when the mood and mind are willing. Although Geminis aren't overly romantic or affectionate, they are clever seducers. They're very alert to the moods of others and they find it easy to believe in whatever role they have to play to get what they want. There's no large, cumbersome ego to get in the way. Geminis can be creatures of a million disguises. They can be innocently fun-loving or shrewdly calculating. Their reputation for sexual freedom and for a cold-blooded nature and tendency to sexual betrayal is well deserved, and it's all a part of the same character manifestation.

This emotional detachment may even be an asset when pure sex is the only goal. They're never completely lost in the act. At all times they know exactly what they're doing. Since their sexual drives aren't overpowering, they can forfeit their pleasure in order to give pleasure. Since their emotions aren't as deeply involved, they're free to watch the situation and play it for what it's worth.

It's not surprising that Geminis have so much trouble with their self-image. Theirs is a largely insubstantial world fashioned out of words and concepts; their restless movement from one idea to another reflects an ongoing struggle to connect their inner spirit with the outside world through the force of intellect. If they are ever to settle happily with someone as a lover and friend, to remain faithful to anyone, that lover or friend must share some of the impatient energy that rules Gemini's own airy, restless soul.

LOVE AFFAIRS

*(See the other chapters for love affairs between
Gemini men and women of other signs.)*

GEMINI WOMAN, ARIES MAN

This certainly couldn't be a boring love affair. Both of you like change, variety, excitement, and a very active social life, and each of you can supply plenty of mental stimulation for the other. It's likely that a Gemini woman like you will be much impressed with Mr. Aries's decisiveness, independence, and confidence, but even though he wants to be independent himself, he's not likely to allow a lover or a wife the same freedom. He's warm, friendly, and generous, but he can be dictatorial and aggressive. He's very impulsive and passionate. Soon he might argue that you're too cool or rather detached. For a while the sexual vibrations will be good, but soon he might discover that you aren't as serious as he is, or that you don't place as much importance on physical sexual satisfaction as he does. It's doubtful that he'll supply the kind of mental stimulation you require. This is an affair that will have to endure more than a usual number of arguments.

GEMINI WOMAN, TAURUS MAN

If someone were going to suggest a man for you to avoid, they would probably suggest a Taurus. He's proud of being stable, cautious, leisurely, materialistic, and sensuous, but you're likely to see him as plodding, stubborn, mentally lazy, inflexible, and very slow to adapt. It's true that neither of you are dominated by emotions, but his sexual appetite is much more physical than yours. And you need more excitement and sparkling conversation before you can perform your sexual magic. Taureans are often very artistic, and this will be a side of his personality that will interest you. And he will certainly admire you for your wit. This mutual admiration is enough for casual love if you don't have to live together. It is hardly enough for marriage or an everyday friendship. The difference between the two can account for some of the trouble between Betty Shabazz and Malcolm X. His single-minded dedication was bound to conflict with her desire for diversity and variety of social life. Opposites do attract, and this is what happens here. A lot of mutual understanding is needed.

GEMINI WOMAN, GEMINI MAN

Just because this one will always feel rather loose, that doesn't mean it isn't serious. Just because neither of you burn up with passion, wallow in jealousy, or go dewy-eyed when you're together, that doesn't mean it isn't love. Even the two of you might not know how much you love each other. There might be a lot of arguments, but you're the kind who can argue without bitterness. Unfortunately you both have so many up and down moods that you're likely to spend a good deal of time out of phase with each other. But when the moods come together, no one can understand Gemini better than Gemini. He's the kind of man you can relate to, and naturally your bright, sparkling personality is attractive to him. He understands how you feel when you want to be left alone. He feels that way sometimes himself.

GEMINI WOMAN, CANCER MAN

You'll find him easy to play with. He likes a love affair that's tight and tangled, and you might convince both him and yourself that that's what you're into. He's very emotional, and sometimes you can seem so. But in the end he'll find you too emotionally superficial, and you'll find him too jealous and clinging. His feelings are very easily hurt, and he's bound to think you're serious when you're only popping off. He's sensual, and you're manipulative. He might enjoy the little game of hurt-and-make-up. This can keep the affair interesting if it doesn't drive you apart. This love affair may be chaotic but not altogether unworkable.

GEMINI WOMAN, LEO MAN

It's not surprising when love happens between Gemini and Leo. This is not a highly magnetic combination, but it can grow together because as friends there's nothing much to push you apart. The love affair will last only as long as Gemini dances to Leo's tune, and that isn't easy for Gemini to do for long. Leo likes to court and shower affection, then sit at the center of the life he creates. He's willing to build a throne, but then he expects to be honored, catered to, fussed over, and all the rest as he sits on it. But you Gemini women aren't much impressed with the courtliness of the shower of affection, so you're not likely to pay tribute to anyone's ego for long. He has a tendency to be domineering and jealous and he won't understand your gloomy moods. He'll think they come as a result of something he did. You two can get along only if you give each other a lot of room.

GEMINI WOMAN, VIRGO MAN

Both of you have big appetites for art and ideas. You both like to analyze and criticize everything around you. You are both always thinking. You both have a lot of superficial charm, but underneath you're both very logical. A Virgo man can often supply some of the stability you need, and you can help him with that difficult task of understanding his complex self. With all this working for you, it's surprising that Gemini-Virgo is not an excellent combination. The problem is that a Gemini woman like you might find him too cautious, fussy, and unresponsive when you're in one of your lively moods, and too harsh and unsympathetic when you're gloomy. The sexual vibrations could be very good or very bad. Mr. Virgo is often looking for his real sexual self. He can be either very accomplished and offbeat or very prudish and uptight, depending on which self he finds.

GEMINI WOMAN, LIBRA MAN

He might think you're not as affectionate and romantic as he likes a person to be, but he'll stick around because he's probably not as deeply affectionate and romantic as he likes to think he is. You're both much more logical than emotional, much more mental than spiritual. Both of you enjoy a very active social life, and your lack of jealousy is equal. He won't like the way you're always analyzing him, but he'll have to admit you're right more often than not. He doesn't like a lot of arguments and confusion, but he's detached enough to leave you alone when you're in one of your famous gloomy moods. Each week you might threaten to leave each other, but your threats are often not serious enough to worry either of you. The sexual vibrations are quite good. You both need a lot of verbal stimulation. And you both can be very sexy when the minds are willing. It's advisable that you try very hard to become friends; this will make your light love affair more lasting than most of the heavy ones.

GEMINI WOMAN, SCORPIO MAN

Of course you love to express yourself, and you might think that he's more slow-witted than you because he doesn't express himself as freely. You'll analyze him and tell him what you find out, but don't think that because he doesn't talk about it as much, he hasn't analyzed you as well. By the time you discover he's not the man for you, he'll already know you're too unstable, independent, superficial, and public for a jealous, deeply private man like himself. He's the most suspicious of men, and he's not likely to trust you enough to fall in love with you. At first he might try to change you; when you won't allow that, arguments could get really bitter. You can easily forgive and forget, but he might find this much harder to do. On top of that the sexual vibrations aren't good. Your sexual appetite demands a partner of a more communicative nature, and he's certainly not the world's champion at pillow talk. He might want to make love in silence even after a big argument.

His sexual appetite will be largely serious even when playful, and yours will be playful even when serious.

GEMINI WOMAN, SAGITTARIUS MAN

This is an easy love affair for both of you to get into. Hazel Scott and Adam Clayton Powell, Jr., must have found it so. Gemini and Sagittarius can both be very easygoing people who are willing to compromise on almost anything except personal freedom, and a compromise on freedom won't be necessary since both of you need it and are therefore quite willing to give it to anyone you fall in love with. There's a great love of fun and conversation in both of you. People mean a lot to you both and you may have some trouble finding moments to spend alone with each other. You like to sample life in all of its variety. Neither likes to get bogged down in a search for security or material possessions, but you're both interested in finding some way to live a good life without working too hard. He won't understand your gloomy moods. You both love to argue, but neither holds a grudge for very long. There could be some problems in the sexual area since you Gemini women aren't very emotional whereas Sagittarius's emotions, although often momentary, are rather deep. He likes to "feel" and he'll want you to "feel" with him, but you won't always be up to the pretense.

GEMINI WOMAN, CAPRICORN MAN

Capricorn men are usually very involved with their careers. You're likely to be involved for a while, but your attention span is much too short. He's a persistent, serious man who's likely to find you a little too flighty and unstable, and you'll probably find him a little too cautious and nagging to have fun with. You can be quite critical, and he doesn't take criticism well. You forgive and forget quite easily, but when he's hurt, he broods for a long time. You're both subject to unpredictable fits of depression, and if one of these comes at the wrong time, you're bound to get on each other's nerves. You can both be quite ambitious, but your styles are very different. He's willing to work hard and long and unswervingly, while you feel that there must be an easier way for anyone willing to loosen up and take some chances. The sexual vibrations aren't the best. He doesn't supply the kind of stimulation you need in order for you to give the kind of heavy physical satisfaction that he needs.

GEMINI WOMAN, AQUARIUS MAN

Geminis and Aquarians see the world in pretty much the same terms. You benefit from the kind of attraction that must have pulled Gladys Knight and motivational speaker Les Brown, an Aquarian, together. Both Gemini and Aquarius are sparkling, friendly people who have their moments of moodiness. You're both guided more by your minds than your emotions. A love affair between you would be based on a basic similarity of outlook. Neither is very jealous, which is good since both need the freedom to come and go at will, and the freedom to be left alone when the mood strikes. Geminis like to argue, and Aquarians are sometimes rather quick-tempered. But neither one of you tend to hold grudges. The sexual vibrations are very compatible; in fact, they might be a little too compatible to produce the kind of tension that love often needs. You both enjoy the challenge of new love situations and are easily bored when things settle down to a dull routine. Other people might be able to keep their sex life active on the basis of physical sexual hunger alone, but both of you need mental stimulation as well. You must each work hard to provide this for the other, or each must be free enough to come back together without bitterness. Otherwise there is a great danger that your relationship will fall into the humdrum of two people who know each other too well to supply the "spark" of newness that you both need.

GEMINI WOMAN, PISCES MAN

Attraction is often based on admiration, so you two are often attracted to each other. It's certain that there will be times when you'll admire him because he's sensitive, gentle, emotional, and sympathetic.

At other times he'll be attracted to you because you're positive, sociable, playful, and aggressive. You each admire in the other what you find missing in yourself. But these same qualities could lead you to a lot of arguments. Geminis can be sarcastic and critical, and Pisceans can be withdrawn and secretive. If he really wants you, he could be long-suffering in his efforts to pull you into that deep emotional pool where he lives, and you'll be just as persistent in trying to pull him out into the logical realm where you feel life is most happily lived. The sexual vibrations might be very good for a very short while. In love situations you are not usually inhibited and you're usually not reluctant to say what the situation requires. He doesn't mind a woman who is aggressive enough to set the tone for a love session. He's emotionally very adaptable, but even if your behavior doesn't, his intuition will soon tell him that you're not as deeply involved as you say. You'll have to work at not seeming too detatched and unemotional, and he'll have to work at seeming less emotional and less in need of reassurance.

GEMINI

(MAY 21st TO JUNE 20th)

MR. T, Television star	**May 21, 1952**
FATS WALLER, blues pianist	**May 21, 1904**
NAOMI CAMPBELL, fashion model	**May 22, 1970**
GEORGE WASHINGTON CARVER, scientist, teacher, administrator, humanitarian	**May 24, 1864**
COLEMAN YOUNG, Detroit mayor	**May 24, 1918**
PATTI LABELLE, soul singer	**May 24, 1947**
HEAVY D, rap artist	**May 24, 1967**
LESLIE UGGAMS, screen and stage actress	**May 25, 1943**
JAMAICA KINCAID, novelist, essayist	**May 25, 1949**
K. C. JONES, basketball star and coach	**May 25, 1932**

BILL "BOJANGLES" ROBINSON, legendary entertainer	May 25, 1878
MILES DAVIS, legendary jazz trumpeter, composer	May 25, 1926
LOU GOSSETT, JR., stage and screen actor	May 27, 1936
GLADYS KNIGHT, singer, actress	May 28, 1944
BETTY SHABAZZ, political activist, wife of Malcolm X	May 28, 1936
GAYLE SAYERS, football star	May 30, 1943
COUNTEE CULLEN, leading poet of the Harlem Renaissance	May 30, 1903
PATRICIA ROBERTS HARRIS, Former U.S. Cabinet secretary, attorney	May 31, 1924
FRANKLIN THOMAS, Ford Foundation head	May 27, 1934
MORGAN FREEMAN, Academy Award–winning actor	June 1, 1937
REVEREND IKE, preacher	June 1, 1935
CLEAVON LITTLE, stage and screen actor	June 1, 1939
CLARENCE PAGE, Pulitzer Prize–winning journalist	June 2, 1915
CORNELL WEST, scholar, activist, essayist	June 2, 1953
JOSEPHINE BAKER, legendary dancer, entertainer	June 2, 1906
DR. CHARLES DREW, doctor, pioneer in blood plasma research	June 3, 1904
CURTIS MAYFIELD, musician, composer	June 3, 1942
SAMUEL L. GRAVELY, JR., first black naval commander in the U.S.	June 4, 1922
MARIAN WRIGHT EDELMAN, children's activist, Children's Defense Fund founder	June 6, 1939
ROY INNIS, national chairman of CORE	June 6, 1934
NIKKI GIOVANNI, poet, author, essayist, educator	June 7, 1943
PRINCE, musician, singer, songwriter	June 7, 1958
GWENDOLYN BROOKS, Pulitzer Prize–winning poet, novelist	June 7, 1917

HATTIE MC DANIEL, Academy Award–winning actress	June 10, 1895
HAZEL SCOTT, star on Broadway, radio, television, and film	June 11, 1920
JOHN EDGAR WIDEMAN, novelist, educator	June 14, 1941
ERROL GARNER, legendary jazz pianist	June 15, 1921
ROBERT MAYNARD, newspaper editor and publisher	June 17, 1937
TUPAC SHAKUR, actor, rap artist	June 17, 1971
JAMES WELDON JOHNSON, Harlem Renaissance writer	June 17, 1871
PHYLICIA RASHAD, actress	June 19, 1948
ANDRÉ WATTS, classical musician, conductor	June 20, 1946

JUNE 21st TO JULY 20th

CANCER

THE CRAB
THE SIGN OF THE PROTECTOR
◆
SENSITIVE, CHANGEABLE, PROTECTIVE
◆

Ruled by the Moon

COLORS: Silver and White

METAL: Silver

GEMS: Pearl and Moonstone

LUCKY NUMBERS: 3 and 8

FORTUNATE DAY: Monday

THE CANCER VIBRATION

A YOUNG WOMAN BORN UNDER THE SIGN OF Cancer said that she's had recurring fantasies in which she went out to work and came home each day with an armful of provisions for her husband and children. Such is the deepest Cancer urge—to nurture and protect, emotionally and materially, members of the family, especially the children, no matter how broadly family is defined.

Cancer is ruled by the Moon. In the mythology of many peoples the Sun is the father of the earth and the Moon is its mother. If motherhood itself has a ruling sign, that sign is undoubtedly Cancer. Cancerians are very involved with the mother figure.

This does not mean that Cancer is not a good sign for men to be born under. Men of achievement born under the sign usually fulfill their ambitions in ways that are traditionally identified with motherliness, and they work for what traditionalists would call motherly reasons. Cancerians of both genders are motivated by a chance to provide for others.

But if an entire group of people can have a mother, then certainly the prime candidate for the title of mother of African-American people would be Mary McLeod Bethune, who in 1904 founded Bethune-Cookman College almost singlehandedly and was eventually the adviser to five American presidents.

Writing in 1941, she said, "I am my mother's daughter, and the drums of Africa still beat in my heart. They will not let me rest while there is a single Negro boy or girl without a chance to prove his worth."

Or take Maggie L. Walker, who in 1903 in Richmond, Virginia, became the first woman of any race to found a bank. The bank grew out of one of the twenty-five "female benevolent orders" in Richmond at the turn of the century. These orders were women's communal efforts to create a storehouse for the money that the community needed to advance itself.

Even Cancerians who might be regarded as glamorous—Lena Horne or Diahann Carroll, for example—exude the soft, sheltering, affection-ate, tender, yet enduring and forceful side of this vibration.

As we've said, Cancer is also an excellent vibration for men. Cancer men are usually very resourceful, able, and forceful. Many famous ath-letes were born under the sign—Satchel Paige, Willis Reed, Carl Lewis, O. J. Simpson, Arthur Ashe, and Mike Tyson, to name a few.

But no matter how strong Cancer men are, there's usually a great need to show affection by fussing over and protecting those they love. A woman married to such a man reports that in public he's sporting and athletic. In fact, he's a defensive lineman in the American Football Conference. But in private he's a "mother hen." His wife calls him "Mother," and he doesn't mind. He couldn't change if he wanted to. He was born with both Sun and Moon in Cancer.

No wonder, then, that the man voted in public opinion polls as America's number-one dad in the 1980s and 1990s is Cancerian Bill Cosby. Cosby's fabulously successful television show was thoroughly steeped in the family-oriented values of its creator. According to an industry insider, despite numerous writers it is Cosby's values and his own unique variety of homespun humor that molds the show's character and has for years made it so attractive to a widely based audience.

The Cosby Show is nearly a perfect mirror of the Cancerian's desire to physically and emotionally nurture, support, and protect his or her family and loved ones. In fact, Cosby is an icon of the strong, successful Cancer man who embodies those traits.

Another quality for which the Crab is a fitting symbol is the Can-cerian desire to cling. It's said that once a crab gets hold of something, he would rather lose a claw than let it get away. This quality of tenacity runs through the Cancer personality and is manifested on many levels, such as in stubbornness when holding on to an idea, in persistence when holding on to a purpose, in retention when holding on to a memorable past perception. Cancerians cling to loved ones and grasp material objects. They refuse to let go easily.

They are patient people. This is why they succeed so often. They're usually content to work as long as necessary. Like the secretive, sensitive crabs that scurry and drift along the sandy ocean floor, without fanfare, in their own methodical way, Cancerians get what they want.

They possess among the best and most selective memories in the zodiac. They're the kind of people who can forget where they laid their hats but remember the smallest detail about their childhoods. The past is often as vivid to them as the present, and most of the memories of the past are pleasant ones. There is in the sign a tendency to romanticize the past. Romanticizing, in the broadest sense of the term, is a strong element in the poetry of Cancerians Margaret Walker, Alice Dunbar-Nelson, and Paul Laurence Dunbar, one of the most popular poets in American history.

Bill Cosby's best stories are largely romanticized images from his childhood in Philadelphia. It's surprising how often you catch Cancerians saying things like, "When I was a kid, we used to . . ." or, "Years ago down home we always. . . . "

They are natural collectors. The homes of many of them are full of things that they simply won't throw away, not because these things might prove useful but because they have a pleasant sentimental link with the past. Broken china, old appliances, high school term papers—all sorts of things that most other people would have thrown away long ago— are commonly squirreled away by Cancerians.

Of course this protective, deeply emotional sign has its bad points. Chief among them is a tendency toward self-pity. Cancerians often feel that they're misunderstood or unappreciated. Unevolved Cancers are subject to rapid changes in mood, and they expect others to follow them through these changes. If someone doesn't or can't accompany them, they feel that the person is being deliberately unsympathetic.

No one can be more hardened and outwardly independent than a native of the fourth sign who feels, rightly or wrongly, that others are ungrateful for his real or imagined favors or sympathies. No one can withdraw so completely. Self-absorption and pretended arrogance could become the operating principles, or the Cancerian might develop into a globe-trotter. There is in the sign a great deal of wanderlust caused by a feeling that what cannot be found at home might easily be found in some distant, vaguely perceived place, or with some new and untried person or situation.

In Cancer, the first water sign of the zodiac, consciousness and awareness turn inward. Whereas Gemini seeks to resolve the conflict between the spiritual and the physical by understanding the outer world through the mind and perception, Cancer seeks to probe the mysteries of feelings and the heart.

Stated another way, Cancer embodies emotionally what the previous sign, Gemini, grasps mentally. Intellectual awareness is transformed into emotional experience.

Those born under the sign of the Crab are driven to explore aspects of the inner life untouched by any of the previous three signs—no sign in the zodiac relies more on feeling than Cancer. But even as they pursue this inward course, like their symbol the Crab, Cancerians protect their own vulnerable feelings by erecting a hard outside shell. Cancer, then, while its primary thrust is toward feelings and the emotions, is a vibration that immerses itself and finds sustenance in the material world.

Like the other cardinal signs, Cancerians are initiators. They are good at getting enterprises started. They are active and energetic. But of the four cardinal signs, Ariens and Capricorns are more likely to act alone to realize their ambitions. Cancerians and Libras prefer to work in groups. They are good at inspiring loyalties in others and usually excel at promoting cooperation between members of the group.

Being cardinal, Cancers are more self-assertive than the other water signs, though not nearly so self-confident as Scorpios. Although they can be shy, Cancers are capable of overcoming much of the water-sign reserve in order to display a great talent for public speaking. The style is usually quite imaginative, and they are often good at adding new and exciting twists to old ideas.

Cancer is the personification of the common man. For no matter how high most Cancer natives rise, they seldom lose the ability and desire to communicate with people of all strata of society. Of all types they are the least likely to be snobbish or superior.

For example, despite the accomplishments of people like Mary McLeod Bethune, Louis Armstrong, Della Reese, Arthur Ashe, or the former Supreme Court Justice Thurgood Marshall, they never seemed to lose the common touch or the ability and joy of communicating with everyday people.

Cancer is an emotional and impressionable vibration, but there is much quiet ambition associated with it. Cancerians are achievers. As mentioned earlier, one source of protection for their extreme sensitivity is wealth and the security it affords; the industrious Crab, like Bill Cosby, may pursue that goal with fanatical devotion.

Operating at their best, Cancerians are sensitive, maternal or paternal, cautious, tenacious, persistent, and shrewd. At their worst they can be touchy and easily hurt, with a hard exterior protecting a moody, self-pitying, unforgiving nature.

Their greatest vulnerability is their extreme emotional sensitivity. A harsh word or a rude gesture is often enough to wound them deeply.

The rulership of the Moon gives to those born under Cancer a very changeable nature. Cancerians are more affected than others by the changing phases of the Moon. They're alternately happy and friendly, or cranky and pessimistic, depending on the Moon's influence. They're creatures of moods—steadfast yet changeable; withdrawn and independent, yet clinging and dependent; businesslike and methodical, yet hazy and indecisive. The Moon rules sensations, emotions, intuition, and the subconscious. The key words of the sign are I FEEL. Cancers are motivated more by what they feel than by what they think. For natives of this sign the feelings are more trustworthy than the power of reason. Intuition is one of their most valuable assets.

Cancerians make good businessmen and managers. They're especially good at organizing people because they have a very sharp insight into what each person is really like beneath the facade. But even the most businesslike Cancerian is likely to be a daydreamer. People of this sign like to imagine themselves in various ideal situations in which they can show the depth of their love by some grand, generous, or heroic gesture toward their loved ones. Cancerians may have the most active fantasy lives in the zodiac.

Cancerians are seldom revolutionary. When they are, the motive is likely not freedom or even justice but a desire to protect their loved ones. In the 1960s Stokely Carmichael's call for "black power" was for the purpose of protecting peaceful civil rights workers who were being attacked by mobs.

Ida B. Wells's life supplies an even more Cancerian example. During the 1890s Wells was a pioneer in the antilynching crusade. After the death of her parents and three of her siblings, Wells, at age sixteen, became "mother" and sole support of her five remaining younger brothers and sisters.

She took the three youngest to Memphis with her when she immigrated there from her birthplace, Holly Springs, Mississippi. Always concerned about providing for the community, Wells helped four young men found a store in Memphis. The store was so successful that the three men were taken out and lynched by associates of the owner of a competing white store. This horrifying incident drew Wells into a very personalized campaign to protect other black men from such injustice.

She became the most famous member of the antilynching movement. In her writings and speeches in the United States and England, she constantly referred to black men as "our sons." Despite the scope and critical importance of her work, she still remained an active mother to her own four children and two stepchildren. Others urged her to hire a baby-sitter, but instead she took her children on the road with her.

RELATIONSHIPS

Though many Cancerians pretend to be rather jovial and outgoing, they're not. They're cautious, reserved, sometimes even shy. They're fond of retiring into the privacy of their own emotions and imaginations. They get along well with people because there's a sincerity and warmth that draws people to them. Cancerians are safe people. They can be trusted, for there is very little deceit or cruelty in their nature. Under normal conditions Cancerians are willing to give generously in a relationship, assuming that the gift will establish an unbreakable bond.

Cancerians are willing and able to sympathize with, understand, and try to influence the emotions of others. This is why emotionally troubled people are drawn to them for advice and help. Cancerians love talking about complex ideas and emotions and giving advice. Since they don't trust people quickly, old friends are the real jewels of their lives. If wanderlust has taken over, however, they may lose contact with old friends and become social drifters. Then, after all their wandering, they must turn to their families as this is the only stable reservoir to which they can retreat for friendship. Mother, father, sisters, and brothers are always good choices for friendship anyway. With them, Cancerians can satisfy two contradictory urges: They can give while keeping their gifts in the family, and thus they can avoid really giving anything away. Generosity and thrift are both served.

Cancerians are enthusiastic participants in group activities. As a rule, people of this sign are easy to get along with. They may be moody and withdrawn at times, but they're seldom hostile. In fact they go to great lengths to be charming around people they don't know well. They're not bossy or dictatorial and they avoid confrontations unless they feel a direct threat to something or someone they love.

They sometimes act defensively because of deep insecurities, and this can make them more annoyingly self-centered than people who come by egotism naturally. Arrogance is a perversion rather than a natural expression of this sign.

Because Cancerians have such a great need to love and be loved, they often attempt to elevate friendship to love. And for them, *love* isn't too strong a word for the emotion that Cancerians tend to feel toward people with whom they become involved. Love, with its more demanding mutual obligations, is more congenial to the sentimental, romantic nature of the sign. Cancerians usually have three kinds of relationships: enemies (because they're famous for holding grudges), acquaintances, and loved ones. There's very little room for that half-love called friendship. This is why so many Cancerians end up as lonely seekers of the perfect relationship.

LUCK, MONEY, AND WORK

Cancerians are the hunch players of the zodiac. Some astrologers claim that Cancer is the luckiest of the signs. Others claim that Sagittarius is. But Cancerians have at least one definite advantage: When they get money, they're usually good at holding on to it.

Even though they're lucky, Cancerians aren't good at gambling. Theirs isn't the kind of luck that can be pushed. Luck works for them in other ways. They often find themselves in the right place at the right time for promotions and lucrative changes in careers. Good things happen to them because of intuitive decisions. When Cancerians are down to their last dollar, money always seems to turn up from somewhere, but married, relatively secure Cancerians are seldom down that far. Their maternal feelings make them thrifty. They like to keep a reserve of anything they might need to sustain life and comfort for those they love.

Cancerians can be as financially conservative and materialistic as Taureans if they are responsible for providing a home. They like to have three or four bank accounts into which they can put money away so that even they can't get at it except in a real emergency. What Cancerians do for loved ones, however, they seem unable to do effectively for themselves. Cancerians who are in emotional turmoil can be among the most wasteful people in the world. They tend to spend money searching for something money can't buy—love and emotional security—or they gamble, hoping that a little more money will satisfy their inner needs.

Cancerians are good in business because they have keen insight into what the public wants, needs, and will pay for. They are very successful in getting others to work for them. They can conjure up very vivid images of the commercial possibilities of an idea, and they can communicate this in the most dramatic of terms to other members of the organization. Their "mothering" attitude promotes a cohesion that's often missing within organizations headed by more egocentric personalities.

They make excellent teachers and preachers. Needless to say, women of the sign make good wives and mothers if they curb their tendency to hold their children too tightly. Natives of this sign have a fair aptitude for athletics, a fair aptitude for music, good potential as actors and actresses, and great abilities as writers and poets.

Cancerians are often very successful in politics because of their tact and their ability to keep an organization functioning with a minimum of internal friction. They're not aggressively ambitious, but they often find themselves in the right place at the right time to gain a measure of political power, and usually they wield this power with more fairness than most.

PHYSICAL AND MENTAL HEALTH

Although sensitive and subject to the fluctuations of the Moon, Cancerians aren't weak. When other people are depending on them, as is often the case, Cancerians will not allow themselves to be sick. They're often the center of a home or a business and they feel that their home or business can't run successfully without them. They can go from season to season without the slightest illness, but they love sympathy. After periods of neglect they might take to bed as a maneuver to gain loving attention. If it works, watch out. Cancer will use it again. Then we might have the not-uncommon spectacle of sick Cancer getting out of bed anyway to run the house or go off to work. Few things can fill the native of this sign with a greater sense of martyrdom than this: "No, I feel bad, but I'll fix breakfast." "I'm sick but I have to go to work."

Cancer rules the breast and the stomach, and the stomach is this vibration's weak spot. "Nervous stomach" is the scourge of the sign. Disappointment, hurt, worry, and loneliness strike first at the stomach. An unhappy home is the chief villain. Some men and women can toughen up to the extent that domestic problems aren't a constant concern. They can accept conditions and stay married, or refuse to accept and leave. Many Cancerians can do neither. They stay around, but they worry constantly. They hope, they bribe, they withdraw, they extend themselves, they plead, they reason, until bitterness or death takes them off.

There is in the sign a strong tendency to try to drown troubles in alcohol. There's also a strong attraction to prescribed or unprescribed stimulants.

Cancer's favorite room in the house is the kitchen. They love to eat; they have a strong tendency to put on weight, which they don't carry well since many of them are disproportionately large at the top— large round heads, large chest, breasts, and stomach—with small legs. These physical attributes are even more characteristic of those with a Cancer Ascendant. Staying slender is always a problem for them.

LOVE AND SEX

Cancerians are very romantic, but they often want more out of love than is possible. They tend to retreat to their vivid imaginations and make the love situation or the loved individual more ideal than real.

Thus Cancerians are often disappointed when they have to face the stark reality of a given situation or personality. They can be quite sentimental, often tearful, and they're very likely to feel that their partner has purposefully disappointed them.

Cancerians are sensitive and generous. Love is one of the things in their nature that doesn't usually respond to the waxing and waning of the Moon. Their love is constant and can grow until they're the most domestic, home-loving people in the world. But Cancerians (especially Cancer men) often learn not to show the tenderness of their feelings. There's too much fear of getting hurt. There's also an exaggerated fear of rejection. But it's impossible for them to love halfway. They don't know how. They may give too much one minute and too little of themselves the next. They're alternately extending and withdrawing their feelings in the most confusing manner.

Their physical sexual appetite is quite strong. Cancerians love to love. They're imaginative and sometimes experimental lovers. They're very concerned about giving pleasure since there is in the sign a great deal of sexual insecurity. "Am I pleasing you?" is a constant question in the Cancer mind, and they can be quite self-sacrificing in their efforts to get an affirmative response to that question. They can also be thrown into utter confusion if an affirmative answer isn't forthcoming.

As strong as the sexual desires are, Cancerians seek emotional communication more than physical satisfaction. Cancerians aren't natural sexual adventurers the way Geminis, Libras, or Sagittarians often are. There's no natural compulsion to dip and dab all over town. If a Cancerian becomes involved in extramarital romance, it's because he or she hasn't gotten the needed emotional reassurance at home; running around can be a manifestation of the same sexual insecurity that produces the tendency to cling. In this case the Cancerian begins turning from one partner to another to prove he or she is loving and lovable. This happens more often with the men of the sign. An unfulfilled Cancer woman may be lucky enough to have children to lavish her affection on if the man in her life doesn't work out.

LOVE AFFAIRS

(See the other sections for love affairs between
Cancer men and women of other signs.)

CANCER WOMAN, ARIES MAN

It's likely that you'll be attracted to each other because you each possess so much of what the other lacks. But it will take work for you to get along well over an extended period. His direct, straightforward, and simple approach to life is bound to come into conflict with your moody, complex view of the world. He can hurt your feelings without even noticing it, and you can dampen his enthusiasm by doing no more than voicing your normal Cancer sense of caution. His search is for excitement and adventure; yours is for security or emotional indulgence. You can each enjoy what the other offers, but it will take a lot of understanding.

CANCER WOMAN, TAURUS MAN

He could be the solid rock in the sea of shifting emotions. The sensual side of his personality will be very appealing to you. He loves to love in a physical sense, and you love to be loved. The problem is that he's not nearly as sentimental and sensitive as you like a man to be. You'll have to overlook the fact that it will be hard to take him along on one of your romantic fantasy trips, but he'll be dependably there when you get back. He loves home life and is usually easy to get along with; he's not aggressive or pushy enough to cause you to withdraw. He might wish that you were a little more practical and a little less moody, but he's patient enough to wait out your moods. But best of all, no man can give you a greater sense of emotional security.

CANCER WOMAN, GEMINI MAN

Both of you are moody, so all that has to happen is that you get out of phase with each other. Cancerians are very easy to hurt and Geminis can be very sarcastic without actually meaning to be. Cancerians are very emotional, and Geminis often like to play with people's emotions. Things that mean a lot to you will be no more than playthings for Mr. Gemini. He needs freedom and won't delight at all in your need to be close. When you give up in frustration and withdraw, his emotional attachment may not be strong enough to prompt him to pull you out of seclusion, and he may not be tender and sentimental enough to do it even if that's what he wants. The sexual vibrations might be good for a while. You both like to experiment and play games, but you'll have to learn how not to feel betrayed when you learn that you were really so much more serious than he seemed to be. He was serious in his way, but his way causes you a lot of problems.

CANCER WOMAN, CANCER MAN

If neither one of you has found a good sense of direction, you both could wander about leading each other down one blind emotional alley after another. This seems to be what happened to poets Alice Dunbar-Nelson and Paul Laurence Dunbar. A lot of time could be wasted in confusion. But if one of you has learned well how to deal with the outside world, the private part of your affair could be very beautiful. The complex emotional relationship could be satisfying to both of you. Hurting, nagging, arguing, loving, sharing, withdrawing, pouting, serving—all are enjoyable parts of the shifting mood of this relationship. A secure home for all of this to take place in is an absolute necessity for both of you, and your children will be the best loved and cared for children in the neighborhood.

CANCER WOMAN, LEO MAN

You're bound to be attracted to someone so warm, sociable, and apparently sure of himself. He's the Sun, you're the Moon. You'll enjoy being around him. That's how the Moon gets its light. Of course you'll be jealous of his tendency to want to shine on everybody, but for a while you can ignore that since he's likely to be very attractive and generous to you. He'll appreciate your talents as a homemaker and home economist. He knows that you can save him from a lot of his extravagances. The big danger is that after a while he'll feel smothered by your kind of love, or that you'll feel he's taking you for granted. You're not usually capable of asserting yourself against so overpowering a personality. You'll tend to drift off. He'll feel that this signals a lack of love. In such cases he can become quite a bully, or he'll become so easily offended that you won't be able to talk things out. This affair can work if each is very aware of the weaknesses of his own sign and is willing to compensate for them. This is not easy for anyone to do.

CANCER WOMAN, VIRGO MAN

This is likely to be a stable relationship. There's not likely to be an explosion, so even if you aren't head-over-heels in love with each other, you could hang together for a long time. Your two signs are often attracted to each other because each produces a reserved, cautious, unspectacular personality that promises a good sober, productive relationship. He's likely to be charming and intelligent, and you're usually gentle and considerate. But he's not much of an idealist or romanticist. He can be very realistic or critical at the wrong times. And you can be quite moody and withdrawn. You're often sentimental, and he's the least sentimental of men. He might be an excellent husband, you an excellent wife. That would be the main binding force.

CANCER WOMAN, LIBRA MAN

He'll certainly seem romantic enough, but his romanticism is not similar to yours. He likes harmony and companionship, but he seems to escape or shrink from the deep emotional ties that you enjoy. You're a complex emotional being, while he tends to be much more casual in his emotional relationships. He needs a lot of freedom, and you're likely to be very jealous. In the end you might give him that freedom, but only after you've withdrawn most of your deeper feelings. The big challenge will be for you each to hold on to the way you are while remaining close to each other.

CANCER WOMAN, SCORPIO MAN

Men like to boss; some women don't mind if the man knows how. For you Scorpio is the man who bosses best. He takes the lead, but he'll give you credit for the help you give. You can be so safe and supportive that you become one of the few people he'll allow to become indispensable to him. He understands you, so he'll trust you with some of those delicate feelings that he's extremely reluctant to show others. He doesn't go for a lot of foolishness. He takes his work seriously, and you're just the person to provide a comfortable home to which he can return. He can be sarcastic, but he knows how to make up. The sexual vibrations are excellent. He has the best sexual reputation in the zodiac, but at times you'll be just as passionate. Both of you are quite possessive and jealous. He's not likely to be as sentimental and imaginative as you are, but he's emotional and spiritual. He can take things as deeply as you want them to go.

CANCER WOMAN, SAGITTARIUS MAN

There may be a lot of attraction possible between the homebody and the traveler. Cancerians like to wander, too, but you're going to be more concerned about the home base than he is likely to be. Sagittarians can be very emotional and sentimental, but these moods are much too short-lived for a woman like you. He can be so blunt and tactless that he can hurt your feelings even when he is trying to soothe them. He has a rather large philosophical streak, but it comes more from the head than from the heart. He has a rather sunny disposition, and you're bound to be attracted to that, and he's bound to be curious about those deep spiritual and psychic vibrations that surround you. There are things you can give each other if you can hang together long enough to do that.

CANCER WOMAN, CAPRICORN MAN

Both of you can be quite moody and withdrawn, and each is cautious, reserved, and security conscious. Your ambitions are more indirect than his, but you'll admire the way he meets situations head-on. This won't be a bed of roses because you're both inclined to nag and argue endlessly, but there's bound to be a great deal of compatibility between your very maternal and his very paternal nature. His career may need to be the focus of your lives, but he'll appreciate your ability to run the kind of household he enjoys coming home to. You're likely to complain that he's not romantic or emotional enough, but he's a strong and permanent focus for your sexual expression. Your tendency to cling will make him feel needed, and his desire to be listened to and mothered will make you feel valued by him. This relationship will take a lot of work to iron out areas of friction, but both of you are patient workers when you know that you're working toward a secure and stable tomorrow.

CANCER WOMAN, AQUARIUS MAN

Aquarians aren't very emotional and they pride themselves in not being so. He'll reach out to you without reaching for your heart. You like to be reached in the heart. You'll reach out to him with your heart, and he'll want it all to make sense to his head. Heart and head combinations are great when there is a tremendous amount of mutual understanding, but you are not good at neglecting the impulses of your heart, and he is not good at doing anything that does not seem logical to him. You'll have to do a lot of enticing to keep his sexual interest as high as yours, and you'll be disinclined to do this when you see that his mind is constantly looking off, interested in something else.

CANCER WOMAN, PISCES MAN

This pairing may need a level, logical head to guide it, and you will probably have to supply it. Each of you can be remarkably effective when allied with someone of a better organized nature. This quality of personal organization might be present in either of your personalities because of other elements in your individual horoscopes, but Cancer as Cancer and Pisces as Pisces can make a rather muddled combination. But because of the strong emotional hookup, it is possible to move by intuition and instinct toward an effective means of dealing with each other and with the real world. In this case the great emotional compatibility should afford you a beautiful, erotic life full of the kinds of sensual indulgences that you both enjoy. There is still the danger here that self-indulgences can become so excessive that nothing gets done.

CANCER
(JUNE 21st TO JULY 20th)

HENRY OSSAWA TURNER, painter, photographer	June 21, 1859
ED BRADLEY, broadcast journalist	June 22, 1941
KATHERINE DUNHAM, dancer, choreographer, school founder, anthropologist	June 22, 1910
WILMA RUDOLPH, history-making Olympic athlete	June 23, 1940
CLARENCE THOMAS, controversial U.S. Supreme Court Justice	June 23, 1948
WILLIS REED, NBA star	June 25, 1942

JAMES MEREDITH, historic integrationist	June 25, 1933
BARBARA CHASE-RIBOUD, sculptor, writer, poet	June 26, 1939
PAUL LAURENCE DUNBAR, poet and novelist	June 27, 1872
STOKELY CARMICHAEL, civil rights activist	June 29, 1941
LENA HORNE, singer, actress	June 30, 1917
THOMAS SOWELL, economist, theorist	June 30, 1930
MIKE TYSON, boxer, "Iron Man Mike"	June 30, 1966
WILLIE DIXON, creator of the "Chicago Blues sound"	July 1, 1915
CARL LEWIS, Olympic track star	July 1, 1961
WALTER WHITE, social activist, founder of NAACP	July 1, 1893
MEDGAR EVERS, civil rights activist, martyr	July 2, 1925
AHMAD JAMAL, jazz pianist	July 2, 1908
THURGOOD MARSHALL, U.S. Supreme Court Justice	July 2, 1908
JEAN-CLAUDE DUVALIER, Haitian president	July 3, 1951
LOUIS ARMSTRONG, all-time-great jazz trumpeter, band leader	July 4, 1900
DELLA REESE, singer, actress, entertainer	July 6, 1932
SATCHEL PAIGE, legendary baseball player	July 7, 1906
MARGARET WALKER, poet	July 7, 1915
BILLY ECKSTINE, singer, bandleader	July 8, 1914
O. J. SIMPSON, football star	July 9, 1947
DAVID DINKINS, first black mayor of New York City	July 10, 1927
RICHARD HATCHER, Gary, Indiana, mayor	July 10, 1933
ARTHUR ASHE, legendary tennis star	July 10, 1943
MARY MC LEOD BETHUNE, educator, civil rights leader, adviser to presidents	July 10, 1875
BILL COSBY, actor, entertainer, comedian, author, businessman	July 12, 1937

MAGGIE LENA WALKER, first black woman bank president   July 15, 1867

FOREST WHITAKER, stage and screen actor   July 15, 1961

IDA B. WELLS-BARNETT, political and social activist, antilynching-movement founder   July 16, 1867

DIAHANN CARROLL, stage and screen actress   July 17, 1935

ALICE DUNBAR-NELSON, educator, author, journalist, social and political activist   July 19, 1875

JULY 21st TO AUGUST 21st

LEO

THE LION
THE SIGN OF THE KING OR QUEEN

◆

PROUD, GENEROUS, AGGRESSIVE

◆

Ruled by the Sun

COLORS: Gold and Orange

METAL: Gold

GEM: Ruby

LUCKY NUMBERS: 5 and 9

FORTUNATE DAY: Sunday

THE LEO VIBRATION

WHEN YOU LOOK AT WHITNEY HOUSTON, YOU immediately notice that there is something regal about her. It is not just that she is pretty. It's also that she's proud. There is the hint of something flamboyant, but it is styled down. If you know anything at all about astrology, you will guess that she is a fire sign—Aries, Leo, or Sagittarius.

The emotions are not as hot as those of an Aries vocalist like Aretha Franklin and they are not as cool as those of Whitney's Sagittarian aunt, Dionne Warwick. She's a Leo, you guess. Right! She's a Leo.

When Whitney sings that learning to love yourself is the greatest love of all, you might guess that this is something she doesn't really have to learn. It comes naturally to Leos.

You need to know even less about astrology to know Isaac Hayes is a Leo. Who else would appear on stage looking as he does—shiny bald head, dark glasses, bare chest draped with glittering gold chains. Self-confident, magnetic, the Leo vibration pours out of him. With him, the flamboyance is not toned down.

Emperor Haile Selassie of Ethiopia, the Lion of Judah, didn't tone it down either. There were things he might not have known, but he certainly knew how to be emperor. His court was one of the most lavish in the world, and he ruled Ethiopia for almost fifty years.

And how about Marcus Garvey, the leader of the great Back to Africa movement of the 1920s, riding in an open, horse-drawn carriage through the streets of Harlem in an admiral's uniform? He had to be a Leo. With all that pomp and love of pageantry he couldn't have been anything else. Only a Leo could have made the phenomenon a reality— and for Garvey it was.

The confidence that explodes from Marcus Garvey, Haile Selassie, and Isaac Hayes shines quietly from Leos like Vernon Jordan, the lawyer and civil rights leader, or Carol Moseley Braun, the first African-

American woman in the U.S. Senate, or Joycelyn Elders, the former surgeon general of the United States.

The vibration is not subtle. What at first might seem like subtlety in the music of Count Basie, the legendary big-band jazz man, is really quiet grandeur. Not subtle at all was Gloria Marshall, the first woman president of Lincoln University when she changed her name to Niara Sudarkasa. The name means "woman of high purpose." Leo's symbol is the lion, king of the jungle, and people born under it carry themselves as if they were the kings and queens of their world.

Whereas in Cancer, the last sign of the zodiac's first quadrant, the thrust is toward the inner depths of emotion, in Leo the movement is toward self-expression. Leos strive to create an external representation of the inner self. I WILL are key words in their vocabulary. More than any other sign in the zodiac, Leos live to express the ego in the present moment. Some astrologers contend that Leo represents the emergence of the individual in the zodiacal cycle, and indeed most of the Leo's energy is directed toward developing and establishing a separate, utterly distinct ego—to stand singly as a personality, even within a crowd. Their goal, finally, is to celebrate life and become open, spontaneous individuals who affirm the exuberance and freshness of the child—which, according to many astrologers, also symbolizes this vibration.

Leo is the middle sign of the trinity of self-assertion—Aries, Leo, Sagittarius. These are the fire-sign people: spirited, warm, optimistic, and friendly, but also aggressive, egotistical, and almost never retiring. They all live to express "the self," "the I or me." But neither Aries nor Sagittarius can do this with as much ceremony as Leo. Leo is a grand, extravagant vibration. The way its natives think about themselves shows in the way they walk, talk, and carry themselves.

They are proud and self-possessed, and although they may not be totally confident, most of them know how to appear to be. And since, in Leos, appearance and reality merge, they become confident in order to act confident. They dress to attract attention and walk with their heads held high, demonstrating the characteristic glow that gives them an unmistakable radiance.

Leos who for some reason misuse the qualities of the vibration can be about the most arrogant of all people. They can become thoroughly involved with their own high opinion of themselves. These Leos not only occupy the center of their own attention, they also want to shine brightest in any situation with which they happen to be involved.

People of the sign are usually very friendly, but the biggest mistake that anyone can make with them is to step on their pride. In cases where pride is involved, Leos are the most easily offended creatures in the zodiac. Their quick anger can expose a pettiness that is unexpected from people who usually conduct themselves with such generosity of spirit.

Leos are very emotional people who don't hide their emotions well. In fact, there's a tendency among them to overdramatize. Leo is the ruling sign of the theater and showmanship. Think of Melvin Van Peebles and his big, extravagant show, *Ain't Supposed to Die a Natural Death*. If you had the good fortune to see how big and spectacular it was, you probably suspected it must have been done by a Leo.

Leos love the spotlight, and their stage is their immediate environment. They are the performers of the zodiac, and they can go into a performance any time there is an audience.

Ira Aldridge, born in New York in 1807, was considered the greatest Shakespearean of the 1800s and one of the most enduringly famous actors of all times. A critic in Vienna in the 1850s wrote, "Ira Aldridge is without doubt the greatest actor that has ever been seen in Europe."

Other talented actors and actresses who were born under the sign include Wesley Snipes and Malcolm-Jamal Warner. For Leos, however, all the world's a stage, and those Leos who do not go into theater or television or film put on their own dramas in cars, bedrooms, kitchens, offices—anywhere they can find an audience.

Leo athletes, and there have been many great ones—Magic Johnson,

Rafer Johnson, Roberto Clemente, Wilt Chamberlain, Vida Blue, David Robinson, to name a few—certainly view athletic contests as dramas as well as competition. As the Leo Barry Bonds, arguably the greatest baseball player of the mid-1990s, said, "Why can't people just enjoy the show? And then let the entertainer go home and get his rest, so he can put on another show?"

Drama is central to their lives. Other people are often confused. What is drama? What is real? The truth is that there is no real distinction between their theatrics and their reality. Since Leos laugh or smile a lot, it's easy to forget sometimes that they are very serious.

Behind all the showiness, Leos are extremely dedicated people. In fact some of the best corporate organizers are Leos. They work well within systems. Leos find it easy to appreciate the qualities of all other types, and therefore they are good at asking from others no more nor less than others can actually give.

They are almost never militant radicals. They would rather rule it than run it, and they will work to make something better rather than overthrow it.

Leo is a fixed sign, and Leos are just as stubborn as natives of the other fixed signs—Taurus, Scorpio, and Aquarius. This doesn't surprise anyone who has tried to argue with a Leo. Leos can be quite smug and inflexible, even when sticking to ideas they themselves only dimly perceive. Once they've put an idea out for consideration, any attack on the idea is regarded as an attack on their ego. Leos can easily develop an oversensitivity to the smallest criticism.

One of the best ways of understanding the fifth-sign vibration's versatility is to observe how it's usually manifested among women. While the professional Leo woman will usually display all of the forcefulness and ambition that is characteristic of this sign, Leo women who have opted for a domestic life as homemakers normally aren't as openly aggressive; they're more likely to assume a queenly, regal posture.

Ambition doesn't surface as much because they're not inclined to make a drama out of running a household. In domestic situations Leos can become as protective and maternal as Cancerians or as cuddlesome as kittens. Their generosity of spirit makes them capable of a wide variety of roles.

Leo men also have plenty of ability to play a wide variety of roles, but they need to gain recognition for the roles they have chosen to play. When they don't get that attention, the natural dignity of the sign can turn to arrogance, pride can become conceit, forcefulness becomes despotism, impulsiveness becomes recklessness, flair becomes flamboyance. The taste runs to large, showy jewelry; flashy, overornamented cars; and loud colors.

Many Leos admit that theirs is not a sign of absolute confidence. Below the surface are a great many insecurities. Natives' of the sign may attempt feats of daring to try to hide their fear—even from themselves. This, some say, is why Leos need so much admiration and reassurance and why they are sometimes so willing to buy or bully to get it.

But no other sign has a higher sense of personal worth, and this, too, makes it easy for Leos to be generous with material things. They realize that material objects do not have much value anyway. What they keep is the "self"—which is, after all, most important. Nearly everything else, even service, they're willing and able to extend to anyone they like, love, or want to impress.

RELATIONSHIPS

Leo is ruled by the Sun, and the Sun wants to shine on everyone. Leos love popularity, and no personality is better fitted to get it. People like them because there is rarely anything petty about them. They are very open and trusting, and can be the most generous sign of the zodiac. They readily give goodwill to everyone. They are not as poor judges of others as Aries, the first fire sign, but they're often too optimistic to be suspicious or reserved or to take note of many of the subtle differences in people. They know, for instance, that evil exists in others, but it seldom alters their optimistic natures.

They love to entertain. They'll go to great lengths to see that anyone visiting their home gets the best they can afford. A male lion might spend next week's grocery money to buy the best Scotch for a friend who just drops by. If you come in the afternoon, a Leo hostess will probably insist that you stay for dinner, and she'll cook more than you can eat just to make sure you get enough. They are lavish, big-hearted people, who extend their warm glow to nearly everyone who falls beneath their rays.

Yet people who find it easy and necessary to merge with others are often dissatisfied in any close relationship with Leos. Leos seldom merge. The ego seldom fuses (as mentioned earlier, their ultimate goal is to stand alone and forge a separate consciousness). Leos impress. They attract, but they find compromise difficult. When their views aren't accepted, they tend to withdraw. "Be reasonable, do it my way, or we won't do it" is a common attitude.

Though they are sometimes impulsive, they aren't nearly as rash as their Aries cousins. They're surprisingly loyal and devoted to people when they form an attachment. And they find it easy to form attachments and aren't as socially restless as one would assume. As husbands they are good providers, but their need to be the center of attention may be burdensome to both children and wives. As wives they are a little too restless to be great homemakers, but they are eager to contribute to the career affairs of their husbands. They like to be involved. They are also very fond of children.

Leos are great at parties. They love to mingle with a lot of people, and though they are much impressed by wealth, they're very democratic in their choice of friends. They can enjoy the company of a beggar as much as the company of a superstar, unless the presence of the superstar will give their own social image a boost. But if the superstar doesn't acknowledge Leo, then Leo might prefer the beggar.

Many Leos like to avoid people of the same sex who would be

regarded as their social superiors. They feel uncomfortable when the center of attention is pulled away from them. They may have a great deal of trouble with authority figures in general. This is why so many of them have such severe conflicts with their fathers. Leo is heir to the throne, but often the father must die before they can wear the crown.

This is the drama that is worked out with such agony in the writing of one the most popular American literary lions, James Baldwin. In *Notes of a Native Son* he writes of his rebellion against his father. Baldwin admits quite frankly that he feared and hated him. Even after the father's death, Baldwin had trouble escaping his parental power. In all Leos the presence or absence of a father to emulate plays a more than ordinarily important formative role. Approval means more to Leos than to most types, and the fear of rejection by the father causes more anxieties. There is often an intense need to compete with him—an attempt to outdo or surpass him. Baldwin said of his severely disapproving father, "We had gotten on badly partly because we shared, in our different fashions, the vice of stubborn pride."

LUCK, MONEY, AND WORK

Anyone with Leo's self-confidence is bound to be a little lucky; in fact, their confident air can create situations in which things have to "go their way." Leos believe in themselves enough not to doubt their own hunches and intuitive judgments. They are gamblers who often don't play life as cautiously as perhaps they should; they're not as naturally lucky as Cancerians, Sagittarians, or Taureans. Things may not always fall routinely into place for them. But it's often hard to convince a Leo of that. After all, Leo is symbolically the Sun, and the Sun never doubts that tomorrow it will shine again.

Wise Leos teach themselves how to be a little more cautious with money than they are naturally prone to be. Natives of the sign are strong-willed and persistent, so they often overcome tendencies to be overly generous or extravagant. Despite their often carefree manner and rather chaotic emotional life, Leos are usually very well organized in their work. They're especially good at organizing the efforts of others, and this serves their ambitions well, for they are among the most ambitious of all types.

Leos love to be on top, and they try very hard to acquire that status. In fact Leos are sometimes criticized by other signs for getting farther with less talent than anyone else in the zodiac. But Leos realize that the charm, enthusiasm, and magic of their own personalities constitute a talent that no other sign possesses and few can hope to create. The large Leo ego may suffer a great deal when confined to a low or menial position, but despite this Leos usually make better organization types than natives of the other two fire signs. They do surprisingly well in well-structured bureaucracies. They can start at the bottom and work their way up, if that's what it takes. Of course they expect to get to the top more quickly than others, but they're not as impatient or childishly rebellious as many Ariens tend to be, or as disinterested or uninvolved as many Sagittarians are when stuck in some seemingly anonymous position at a large corporation. Being a large fish in a small pond is not bothersome to them; they can be quite satisfied exercising control in a specific, although limited, domain.

Their naturally authoritative manner inspires confidence, so they often make excellent bosses. They seem to know what each person is capable of and what each person needs as motivation. But among subordinates they tend to play favorites, giving preferential treatment to anyone who makes them feel good. Leo is king, not governor. Leos feel that it's their right to dispense favors among their subjects as they see fit. Unless they are wise kings, their rule can be quite arbitrary and uneven, being at one moment too severe or dictatorial and at another too lenient or tolerant.

Despite all the flash and flamboyance, Leos have very well-structured mentalities, and this is why they make such good lawyers. More renowned attorneys were born under Leo than under any other sign.

Vernon Jordan, the longtime civil rights activist and adviser to President Clinton, and Anita Hill, who became famous during the Clarence Thomas hearings, are examples.

This doesn't mean, however, that Leos are good with details. As mentioned before, they're often unconcerned about small matters. As educators they are not great at drilling students in crossing *t*s and dotting *i*s. They're more interested in inspiring their students to reach for the stars.

For example, Anna Julia Cooper, born in 1858, the daughter of a slave in Raleigh, North Carolina, eventually became principal of the famous M Street School in Washington (later Dunbar High School). During her tenure at Dunbar she inspired a larger number of African-American students to win honors and positions at America's best colleges than educators at any other high school in the nation.

Since Leos live so much inside their own egos, they are sometimes drawn to concocting fanciful schemes that have no connection with mundane reality. Some Leos pursue these schemes with all the enthusiasm that an optimistic personality can muster, often overcoming all obstacles and actually making their schemes work.

Characteristically fire-sign people don't have a conventionally realistic picture of the world; they see it as they would like it to be. Often this works for them. When it does, it enables them to live to a great extent on their own terms; when it doesn't work, they simply try to form another "idea" to impose on the world. Leo, as a fixed fire sign, is not as adaptable as the other two fire signs. Leos keep trying to see the world on their own terms, and they are honestly shocked each time the outside world does not conform to their image of it. An excess of naïveté and idealism is often apparent among certain unevolved Leos.

Evolved Leos make good partners for people of less fanciful temperaments, people who are willing to operate behind the scenes taking care of the nuts and bolts while the Leo assumes a more visible, creative position. Leos make good actresses and actors, salespeople, public relations people, or athletes, and of course they make fine preachers.

Nothing could please a Leo more than to be in the pulpit and to be shepherd to his or her own flock.

PHYSICAL AND MENTAL HEALTH

Leo men are usually robust and athletic, but they're susceptible to many minor infections. Surprisingly, Leo women can be extremely fragile. Colds and infections may come often and linger long. Leo rules the heart and spine, and natives of the sign are particularly susceptible to diseases affecting these areas. They like to live high and eat well, and this could put a strain on the heart. Excess weight is more likely to cause heart trouble among Leos than among natives of any other sign, and their tremendous energy can cause severe exhaustion and lead to stress coronaries. High blood pressure is also a danger for high-strung Leos, who are prone to overexcitement and temper tantrums.

But Leos often develop a great self-consciousness about health matters, especially diet. They want to look good and know that staying in shape helps them present a positive image. Personal well-being is one of their chief concerns, and they are among the most avid devotees of exercise classes and health foods.

Mentally Leo is a well-balanced sign, but severe depression is common to the Leo natives who overextend themselves and find that the world doesn't succumb to the magic of their charm, personality, or perseverance. When Leos convince themselves that they deserve a high or unusual place in life, it's hard for them to settle for something ordinary or run-of-the-mill. Leos aren't morbid people, but psychosomatic disorders sometimes result when the natives haven't achieved a feeling of personal significance.

LOVE AND SEX

In love Leos are very passionate and demonstrative. They seem to have little trouble expressing their feelings. Pride might hang them up for a while, but once that is mastered, there are few inhibitions to their warm and affectionately loving nature. Leos are very proud of their ability to make love. They live to express themselves, and lovemaking is one of the occasions when self-expression can become high art or drama.

Leos like to make an elaborate ceremony of love. In this regard, while they may not be as romantic as Libras, they are even more noble and chivalrous. They're naturally generous, but love accentuates this quality even more. No gift is good enough, and anything that Leo might think to buy is too embarrassingly small for king or queen Leo to give to a loved one. "Oh, my love, I want to give you the sun and the moon," Leo achingly feels.

They like to give their all in a love relationship. They're not the kind who can love effectively while holding back. They can be very self-sacrificing in love relationships. In fact, they can derive great pleasure from dedicating themselves to those who need their strength. If his wife holds him in high enough esteem, a Leo man can be one of the most generous providers. As long as he is boss, he will glory in the comforts of home. If the Leo woman feels properly adored, she is likely to be the most generous lover any man may have. Still, when in love they are extremely idealistic and more than a little sentimental; small tokens of love mean a great deal to them. They live for tributes, and anyone who hopes to get along with them will probably have to keep a constant flow of flattery aimed in their direction.

They're the kind of people who feel that love should make birds sing and bells ring. This idealism is one of the reasons why Leos aren't particularly fortunate in marriage. They tend to place the loved one on a pedestal or expect too much of the experience, and this leads to all kinds of disappointments and disillusionments when love turns out to be less than ideal. What Leo must learn is that everyone has faults and that love should be entered into with the eyes wide open.

But Leos have too much faith in the noble aspects of human nature to be good judges of people, especially when deep emotions are involved. They tend to impute to the loved one all the qualities that they long for in an ideal lover. When they discover finally that these qualities are missing, they often feel betrayed.

Leos also tend to have jealous natures. One reason is that they hate to be compared with anyone else. They want to be reassured that they are better than all the rest.

LOVE AFFAIRS

(See the other sections for love affairs between Leo men and women of the other signs.)

LEO WOMAN, ARIES MAN

Cynics say that true love lasts only for a short while. If this is true, then there isn't a better place for a Leo lady like you to spend her little while than with a courageous, ambitious Aries. And after that passion cools, the two of you make nice friends. He has many of the qualities you admire in a man. He's certainly bent on making a big success of his life. He's very active and likes to be involved with life in all its variety. He's fun-loving and friendly. He argues a lot, and each of you wants to have his own way—two spirited people like you are bound to argue a lot, but both of you tend to forgive rather easily. Both tend to be oversensitive when you feel that your pride is being offended, and in these cases both tend to be violent, aggressive, and temperamental. But if you learn a little restraint, fighting could provide a kind of diversion for two people who hate boredom more than anything.

LEO WOMAN, TAURUS MAN

Your instincts should tell you that Mr. Taurus is usually not Mr. Right for a Leo lady like you. Sure he's strong, sensual, often fun-loving and gentle, but he's also much too cautious, plodding, and not easily stirred mentally or physically. His ambitious nature may be as strong as your own, but he'll never understand how you intend to get ahead while remaining so idealistic, unrealistic, and visionary. And you might wonder how he plans to get where he's going while remaining so slow and unimaginative. The sexual vibrations might be good for a while, but basically he's a creature of a strong physical appetite, and you need your mentality and imagination stimulated as well. But the real trouble will result from you both being so stubbornly set in different directions. You are too emotional and he's too down-to-earth. When the fights start, you both are often too stubborn to give in. But if both of you make yourselves aware of each other's true nature, you can give each other time, and time cures a lot of things for people like you.

LEO WOMAN, GEMINI MAN

He's neither as passionate nor as emotional as you are. His sexual appetite is rather whimsical and short-lived. He's moody in very unpredictable ways. Sometimes he's the most sociable of all people and at other times he is among the most withdrawn. He can be extremely sarcastic and he's not very affectionate and romantic. When you argue, you really mean it; sometimes he argues just for the mental exercise. No other man can make you so furious, but few can stimulate you like he can. Giving pleasure is one of the games he plays. He's detached enough to sacrifice his pleasure to make sure that you get yours. He likes to manipulate people, and you don't mind being manipulated as long as it feels good. You are by far the more powerful of the two signs, but he will control the tone of the affair because he'll lose his head less often during lovemaking or during moments of discord. Still, you can be very jealous and possessive, and he's impossible to possess; he might need more variety and mental stimulation than you will give or allow.

LEO WOMAN, CANCER MAN

There is very little compatibility of outlook between you, but this combination often works well. When you stop looking for the ideal man, you might find that the Cancer man has more of what you need than you first thought. Sure, he's moody and withdrawn at times, but he's also romantic and sensitive. He doesn't display a lot of that masculine bravado that you sometimes admire, but he tends to idolize and cater to the woman he loves, and you certainly will enjoy that.

There are some problems, however. He might mother and smother a little too much for your independent nature. Although he's certainly among the most devoted of lovers. His ego seems to merge with the ego of anyone he loves, and he can be easily hurt by someone whose ego stays so shiningly separate and intact. He can give himself; you find it easy to give everything but yourself. He may want you to come closer than you can; you might want him to stop clinging so much. A lot of compromises might be necessary, but they're not impossible compromises for either of you.

LEO WOMAN, LEO MAN

Leo and Leo is bound to be a magnetic duo, but Leo and Leo might also be too much Leo for one love affair. This could be either an intense love or an intense hate relationship, or it could be both at the same time. There is bound to be intense competition for attention. You each need more admiration than either willingly gives. You're both likely to be aggressive, passionate, and easily offended in matters of pride. If you both maintain a sense of humor, you might be able to laugh at the fact that neither will back down. Because you do understand each other, love could be based on mutual respect for each one's determination not to be dominated by the other. This combination works better with two Leos who have busy careers and come together primarily for moments of friendship and companionship or for that dramatic but dynamic sexuality that you both enjoy. Your life together could become a glamorous ceremony. If it falls to less than that, you two might hurt each other in the trenches, where most marriages are worked out.

LEO WOMAN, VIRGO MAN

He's not much like you, but he has so much of what you need, and he can give so much of what you want. Never mind that he's critical, cautious, sometimes fussy, exacting, pessimistic (or at least realistic), unsentimental, and often unable to speak tender words during moments of sexual passion. What are words anyway? He can show by his actions that he's capable of more devotion than most jive talkers could ever manage. His jealousy will let you know how much he cherishes you as his "queen." He's intelligent and adaptable and might willingly suffer your fits of temper. His practicality and down-to-earth common sense might be just what you need. He's not always an inspiring lover, but when he gets started, he's even more enduring than you are. Leo women seldom find their ideal. They usually end up "settling," and this may be as good a place as any to settle.

LEO WOMAN, LIBRA MAN

Mr. Libra knows how to get along with you if he wants to. He knows how to use all those little romantic touches. He knows how to flatter and he'll deem it a pleasure to make you feel good about yourself. His sexual passions may not be as great as yours, but he knows more about the frills and trimmings of the sensuous life. He likes to play games, but if he's not too full of himself, he'll play them for your enjoyment also. If he's very vain, as many Libra men are, he'll be much too superficial for you. And you'll want more attention than he willingly gives. If he's an undirected do-gooder, his personality might be too vague for you to find something to hold on to. He hates ugly outbursts of temper, and you're very capable of these, and there's a strong possibility that he'll flirt too much for a jealous woman like you; but his eagerness to get along harmoniously might relieve a lot of problems that you would otherwise have.

LEO WOMAN, SCORPIO MAN

This is one that could prove that good sex doesn't always lead to happiness together. You two are among the most passionate creatures of the zodiac, but it will probably be very difficult for the two of you to get along in those other areas of your lives. Then, finally, you'll find it hard to get along in bed as well. You Leo women are generous, outgoing, idealistic, and often unrealistic. Scorpio men are usually stone-cold realists. You are both very magnetic. Your magnetism comes from the glow of your personality and from the impressive manner in which you carry yourself. His magnetism comes from something deeper. You will be drawn to each other, but a clash is likely to be the result. The struggle for dominance could be very intense. You can be explosive and hot-tempered; Scorpios can be sarcastic and menacing. The possibilities for disagreement are endless. But the sun signs are not the only determinants of character, and other aspects in the charts of each could make this one a powerful alliance.

LEO WOMAN, SAGITTARIUS MAN

For a lively, excitable Leo lady like you, Mr. Sagittarius could be your best shot. In love he's just as warm and generous as you are. He's just as egotistical, but he's also just as idealistic, perhaps more so. He loves to put his woman on a pedestal. You like that. You like to be courted. You like all those little courtesies that might seem like mere superficialities to some. You two can become good friends since your worldviews are very similar; both are optimistic and sociable. You both love a variety of activities. Since both of you have hot tempers, there are bound to be a lot of arguments, but you both tend to forgive easily. In most of the clashes, you'll win, since you're much more stubborn than he is. But even though he gives in, he's clever enough to lose and still end up with the prize—the loyalty, warmth, and sympathy you give to anyone who is strong enough to let you have your way without seeming weak himself. A problem might arise because you're jealous, and he might be one of those footloose Sagittarians who wants to have his cake and eat it too.

LEO WOMAN, CAPRICORN MAN

Only if you both are relatively successful and relatively career-minded can you find very much in common. Capricorn is a power sign, but there's nothing very regal about it. He can get along with you if being with you serves his ends. Otherwise he can find more faults than you can imagine. You are too unrealistic, impractical, wasteful, and ego-centric for him. He's too practical, suspicious, and pessimistic for you. You have a quick temper; he likes to nag. A million arguments could arise over money, as you like to spend to give yourself a pleasant lifestyle full of all the trimmings of the good life, while he likes to save and amass the kind of money that will give him power, security, and social standing. You're more interested in the present moment, while he's usually very interested in the future. The sexual vibrations aren't at all good. You Leos are quickly passionate and excitable. Because of their preoccupation with other things, Capricorns aren't in an amorous mood often. They have strong physical appetites, however, and you may not be able to satisfy them without the kind of mental and emotional stimulation he's unlikely to give.

LEO WOMAN, AQUARIUS MAN

Mutual fascination often brings you two together. You are astrological opposites. Leo as the fifth sign of the zodiac and Aquarius as the eleventh sign are 180 degrees apart on the astrological wheel. As character types, Leo and Aquarius are opposite and complementary. Leo is one of the most impassioned of all the vibrations, while Aquarius is about the coolest and most detached. Sexually and emotionally this often works out well. Aquarians are cool and detached enough to "operate" on passionate Leo until her passions are satisfied, and Leo can supply the spark that Aquarians often need to kindle a not-too-passionate sexual nature. One of the problems is that you're both very stubborn and tend to be rather quick-tempered. Another is that you each are rather self-involved. Leos can be jealous and domineering, while Aquarians desire a great deal of freedom and stubbornly refuse to be dominated. Both are prone to take impulsive actions to assert their sense of individuality.

LEO WOMAN, PISCES MAN

You'll like the dreamy sensitivity of his private moments, but you're likely to think that he's not as aggressive and sure of himself as a man should be. He's certainly among the most sympathetic and considerate of men. From your point of view the sexual life will be mellow. He might feel that you're a little too stiff and theatrical and that your passions are too short-lived. He likes the two egos to fuse in the act of love; you're usually always aware of "self" as an independent entity. It might appear that you control the love situation, but you should re-member that despite the tendency to be ambivalent, he has a great deal of emotional strength, and his rather unassuming manner of dealing with the world is often as effective as one full of pride and bravado. If his dreamy manner doesn't turn you off, and your aggressively egocentric manner doesn't cause him to withdraw, you two might find that you have a lot to offer each other. He needs a positive, independent type like you, and you'll be happy with someone who loves with a great deal of admiration and adoration.

LEO

(JULY 21ST TO AUGUST 20TH)

ASA T. SPAULDING, SR., pioneering businessman	July 22, 1902
GEORGE CLINTON, funk musician	July 22, 1941
HAILE SELASSIE, Emperor of Ethiopia	July 23, 1891

BARRY BONDS, San Francisco Giants star	**July 24, 1964**
KENNETH CLARK, social scientist, integration advocate	**July 24, 1914**
IRA ALDRIDGE, Shakespearean tragedian, "The African Roscius"	**July 24, 1807**
VIDA BLUE, legendary baseball pitcher	**July 28, 1949**
CHESTER HIMES, writer	**July 29, 1909**
GERRI MAJOR, journalist, columnist for *Ebony* and *Jet*	**July 29, 1894**
ANITA HILL, lawyer, educator, key player in sexual harassment debate	**July 30, 1956**
WHITNEY M. YOUNG, JR., Urban League director, economic mediator	**July 31, 1921**
WESLEY SNIPES, stage and screen actor	**July 31, 1962**
RON BROWN, politician, chairman of the Democratic National Committee	**August 1, 1941**
TEMPEST BLEDSOE, actress ("Vanessa Cosby")	**August 1, 1973**
C. C. SPAULDING, businessman, North Carolina Mutual Life Insurance founder	**August 1, 1874**
JAMES BALDWIN, novelist, playwright, essayist, cultural critic	**August 2, 1924**
EDWARD WILMOT BLYDEN, scholar, diplomat, journalist, educator	**August 3, 1832**
DAVID ROBINSON, San Antonio Spurs, NBA Defensive Player of the Year	**August 6, 1965**
ABBEY LINCOLN, singer, actress	**August 6, 1930**
MARCUS ROBERTS, jazz musician	**August 7, 1963**
RALPH BUNCHE, U.N. official and negotiator, Nobel Peace Prize winner	**August 7, 1904**
WHITNEY HOUSTON, Grammy-winning pop singer, actress	**August 9, 1963**
DEION SANDERS, football and baseball star	**August 9, 1967**
ALEX HALEY, author of *Roots*	**August 11, 1921**
CARL ROWAN, journalist, syndicated columnist	**August 11, 1925**

RENEE FRANCINE POUSSAINT, television anchor and journalist	**August 12, 1944**
JOYCELYN ELDERS, former U.S. surgeon general, pediatrician	**August 13, 1933**
MICHAEL WHITE, Cleveland mayor	**August 13, 1951**
NIARA SUDARKASA, first black woman president of a university	**August 14, 1938**
MAGIC JOHNSON, basketball star	**August 14, 1959**
VERNON JORDAN, lawyer, civil rights activist	**August 15, 1935**
CAROL MOSELEY BRAUN, first black woman in U.S. Senate	**August 16, 1947**
MARCUS GARVEY, black nationalist, early spokesman for Black Power	**August 17, 1887**
ARCHIBALD GRIMKÉ, antislavery activist	**August 17, 1849**
ROBERTO CLEMENTE, baseball star	**August 18, 1934**
MALCOLM-JAMAL WARNER, stage and screen actor ("Theo Cosby")	**August 18, 1970**
RAFER JOHNSON, Olympic decathalon athlete	**August 18, 1935**
W. WILSON GOODE, controversial Philadelphia mayor	**August 19, 1938**
ISAAC HAYES, singer, actor, musician, composer	**August 20, 1942**
COUNT BASIE, bandleader, composer	**August 21, 1936**
WILT CHAMBERLAIN, legendary basketball star	**August 21, 1936**
MELVIN VAN PEEBLES, filmmaker, actor, director	**August 21, 1934**

AUGUST 22ND TO SEPTEMBER 20TH

VIRGO

THE VIRGIN

THE SIGN OF THE CRITIC

◆

METHODICAL, DISCRIMINATING,

ORDERLY

◆

Ruled by Mercury

COLORS: Gray or Dark Blue

METAL: Quicksilver

GEM: Sardonyx

LUCKY NUMBERS: 8 and 4

FORTUNATE DAY: Wednesday

THE VIRGO VIBRATION

MAKING SURE THAT IT IS RIGHT—THAT IS how Virgos soon come to see their reason for being on earth. Virgo is the perfectionist. They may not do everything right themselves and they may not even be the neatest person in the house, but it is certainly true that their vibration is thrown into conflict when things are not as Virgo thinks they should be—ask the people who work for Virgo superstar Michael Jackson.

"It is his talent coupled with the star's hard work and often touted perfectionism, that has enabled Jackson to cross virtually every music line ever drawn," say the editors of *Contemporary Musicians*.

One of Virgo's main roles in the scheme of the universe, then, is to improve, and perfect what has been created. I ANALYZE are the key words. This is why Virgos are sometimes so difficult to please or so reluctant to venture out on their own, while they seem ever ready to criticize the adventures of others.

If Virgo and Libra enter a beautiful room, Libra's first comment is likely to be, "Hey, this is really nice," especially if someone whom Libra wants to impress is listening, but regardless of who is listening, Virgo is apt to say, "It's okay, but the picture over the sofa is a little off center." One of Virgo's strongest impulses is toward exactness and order brought about by concentration on the smallest details of a project. Something slightly wrong, something slightly out of place, can fill Virgo with uneasiness, like the young Virgo woman who sat through an entire Marvin Gaye concert with an almost uncontrollable urge to rush onto the stage and remove a small, dark smudge of makeup on the singer's face. The Sagittarian friend who sat next to her didn't even notice the smudge.

Virgo is the keeper of the standards, the scrutinizer; therefore Virgos excuse very little. "If it's not right, why not fix it?" Everything that passes before them is either secretly or openly examined for imperfections. Astrologers often contend that Libra is the judge, but she isn't—she is a mediator of competing interests. Virgo is the judge, a candid judge who will deliver the verdict regardless. If she were all powerful, she'd sit on a high bench and condemn all that was shoddy or imperfect, even within herself.

A good example is Constance Baker Motley, who was, in the early 1960s, the first woman to be appointed Manhattan borough president. In 1966 she was appointed federal judge. "Level-headed, lucid and sharp-witted and a persistent questioner, usually logical, direct and simple," say the editors of *Current Biography*. This is a description of the Virgo vibration at its best.

Astrologers also claim that Virgo's deepest impulses are likely to be conservative, methodical, dependable, and materialistic, with a very practical, down-to-earth approach to life; thus, they argue, Virgos make better businesspeople than artists. But these astrologers are looking at only one side of Virgo's personalities.

What the astrologers fail to see is that Virgo is a mutable or twin sign like Gemini, the dancing twins; Pisces, the two fish swimming in opposite directions; or Sagittarius, who is both horse and human. Virgos have two sides operating at the same time with no visible symbol of twoness. It might be easier to describe Virgo as two distinctly different people operating out of the same body at the same time.

Ever present is the conflict between a tendency to be severe, analytical, and critical and a tendency to be witty, charming, server of others, shy, and, above all, artistic.

Many ancient astrologers taught that Virgo was the most pleasing of all the signs. Virgos, they argued, are unassertive and alluring people who are dedicated to serving others. Perhaps this was true in ancient times, but the modern world is filled with the kind of chaos that Virgos are driven to make right.

If things are seriously wrong, Virgos are the severest critics in the world. When Virgos express themselves as writers, as we might expect, their work often reflects either their critical natures or their concern with the imperfections of society. The most seriously judgmental, most unforgiving writer in African-American literature was protest writer Richard Wright, whose novels and essays were blistering attacks on what was wrong with both black folk and white. This was the underlying theme of Eldridge Cleaver's work.

More Virgos would probably make their living as writers if they were not so self-critical that they find it hard to get sentences onto paper without going back over them dozens of times, becoming frustrated and never feeling satisfied enough to move on.

By making things right I do not mean that Virgos are dreamer-humanitarians the way Libras, Sagittarians, or Aquarians often are. They wish simply to make right those things that we come into contact with and that are essential to our lives on a day-to-day basis.

Even with all that is unjust about the African-American condition, Virgos are seldom revolutionaries. An Aquarian like Huey Newton might want to turn the world upside down to end injustice, but Virgo Jesse Owens would rather work through the system.

Owens, perhaps the greatest track athlete of all time, won four gold medals in the 1936 Olympic Games in Berlin, when Hitler and other Nazis were declaring that blacks were inferior, even in sports.

Even during the revolutionary 1960s Owens was conservative. "He kept his shoes shined when others wore sandals," his biographer wrote in *An Athlete Growing Old*. "He purchased expensive, smart suits; they donned dashikis and jeans. He kept his hair and mustache closely trimmed; they let their manes grow long, their beards shaggy. He liked jazz; they preferred rock and 'soul' music."

He was the picture of a conventional Virgo middle-class gentleman, and in his book, *Blackthink,* he agreed with the many prominent social observers who point out the African-American middle class is more puritan than the white middle class.

* * *

No one should argue that Virgos are not fighters for racial justice. Roy Wilkins, Judge Motley, Charles Evers, and congresswoman Maxine Waters are outstanding examples of the Virgo as fighter. However, the truth is that with few exceptions Virgos simply would rather do it in the most orderly, organized way possible.

The Virgo vibration would fit better guiding the National Association for the Advancement of Colored People, as did Roy Wilkins, Constance Motley, and civil rights leader Charles Evers, than coming up with a guiding vision for the Black Panther party.

Above all, Virgos are not likely to be idealistic. They don't view life through rose-colored glasses. They try to see life as it is; therefore in this world they usually see more bad than good. And what they see tends to make them more sober than cheerful, more burdened than charming.

In ancient lore Virgo was the gatherer of the harvest and the giver of corn and wheat. She's pictured as a virgin holding the sheaves of grain that are necessary for human life on earth. Typically, Virgos are practical, dutiful people, who emerge from obedient childhoods with a strong feeling for the necessities of life. Although they are materialistic, they are usually not so greedy that they would cheat for personal gain— they usually moderate their desires and satisfy themselves with what they can honestly afford. Nor are they egotistical enough or, usually, overtly aggressive enough to cheat for ego's sake. In fact there is a strong dislike within the sign for anything crude or vulgar.

Despite all of these fine attributes, sons and daughters of the sixth sign often find themselves wishing they were born under a less demanding star. It is difficult to be a Virgo because charm must so often be sacrificed to duty. It is as if, after all of Leo's concentration on the development of charisma and personality, the astrological cycle moves toward a new level—human fulfillment and improvement. And indeed, many astrologers contend that Virgo, which ends the first half of the zodiacal cycle, represents the culmination of the "perfection of the individual as individual." (The last six signs—Libra through Pisces—they argue, are concerned with the spiritual pursuit of merging the individual soul with the cosmic soul.) In Leo, personality is brought to its pinnacle; and in Virgo, that personality is subjected to harsh and unrelenting criticism in order to prepare the individual for the spiritual awakening that emerges in the second half of the zodiacal cycle.

Virgos are gifted with a fine sense of rhythm for music and dance. Not only Michael Jackson but also Branford Marsalis, Dinah Washington, Otis Redding, Cannonball Adderly, Jose Feliciano, Chico Hamilton, and B.B. King were born with Sun in Virgo, as were many other musicians.

The methodical, businesslike Virgo, then, has another facet—inside resides another creature, who is creative, imaginative, and full of yearnings for artistic expression in work and lifestyle. Jazz saxophonist Charlie Parker's inclusion in this vibration offers evidence of Virgo's artistic side at the extreme.

Parker, whose innovative approach to music helped create modern jazz, or bebop, in the 1940s, was not only born with his Sun in Virgo but also with his Jupiter (the ruler of luck and fortune), Saturn (the ruler of limitations, physical illness, and death), and Venus (the planet of love and beauty) under the influence of the sign of the Critic.

Since Mercury, Virgo's ruler, also rules the hands, Virgos are often excellent craftsmen. When craft rises to the level of art, Virgos are at their best. Virgo Romare Bearden, one of the most celebrated modern American artists, constructed many of his "paintings as a craftsman would using fragments of photographs cut out of magazines and newspapers, colored paper, pieces of cloth, strips of wood and other natural elements."

A second-grade teacher with a strong interest in astrology reports that the students in her classes who are best at line drawing and coloring are usually Virgo or Taurus children. Virgos tend to have wild, often unusual dreams and great imaginations. Only their daytime horizons are limited to the real. The night personality is truly artistic, providing a nicely balanced combination.

Virgo is the most deeply intellectual sign of the zodiac. Ruled as it is by Mercury, Virgo brings the intellect to bear on every situation. Hunches, emotions, and intuition might be acceptable to other signs, but even though Virgos do have a fine intuitive sense of what is right or correct, practical Virgo prefers thinking things through before acting. For this reason, Virgos are often regarded as plodding and self-doubting. Gemini is also ruled by Mercury, but as an air sign Gemini is known for the swiftness of its mental activity, while Virgo is known for its thoroughness.

Astrologers once believed that Virgo was not ruled by Mercury but by Vulcan, a planet that was said to exist between Mercury and the Sun. Some astronomers agreed that such a planet might exist but was orbiting too close to the Sun to be detected by a telescope. The name Vulcan was taken from the lame god of ancient mythology who was attracted to other lame people because he felt that healthy people might expect too much of him. This is an obvious reference to the fact that many Virgos suffer feelings of personal inadequacy.

Many Virgos suffer from inferiority complexes. One reason for this is that the root desire of the sign is to perfect all things and to criticize that which isn't perfect, including themselves. Virgo is undoubtedly the most self-critical of all vibrations. If this tendency isn't checked, blame, scorn, and the inability to forgive may start as self-hatred but radiate outward to the family, the nation, and the race in an ever-widening circle. One of the central lessons for Virgo personalities, then, is to learn to moderate self-criticism with self-acceptance even as they strive for honesty and perfection.

RELATIONSHIPS

Whether Virgos are businesslike and retiring or artistic and outgoing, they don't make friends easily. Both types are reserved and somewhat suspicious of people's motives. Most Virgos are very selective in choosing friends, although they are usually pleasant and courteously sociable. Most Virgos have very high standards, and usually they're immediately aware of anyone who doesn't measure up. They're forever noticing something about someone that turns them off. Nearly all natives of the sign have a hard time accepting their own faults and imperfections, so it is only natural that they often find fault with others.

Ironically, the businesslike Virgo is something of a social climber and is often more than a little status conscious. The natural tendency to be critical of themselves is reversed here. This Virgo likes the company of important people and can become one of the most unashamed worshipers of celebrities.

Virgos are very private with their own feelings. They're not prone to self-revelation, even to people who are very close to them. They tend to keep their deepest feelings and perceptions to themselves. Virgo is the sign of the recluse, the bachelor (of either sex), and the celibate. This is not because Virgo is independent in the same way that Scorpios or Aquarians are. They need people and, because of the amount of abuse they are sometimes willing to endure to maintain relationships they have selected as "right" for themselves, can become martyrs or even masochists. They may choose, however, to find satisfaction in substitute activities and avoid the messiness of illogical emotional relationships.

An interview in *Ebony* magazine with the late Roy Wilkins, former NAACP executive chief, is revealing of this aspect of the Virgo personality:

EBONY: Mr. Wilkins, do you have any close personal friends?

Wilkins: No.

EBONY: Why not?

Wilkins: I just don't have people that I call close personal friends. They might consider that they are close personal friends of mine, but they are not. I get unaccountably shy when asked to pick out a close personal friend. Maybe that's the reason I never get too close to anyone—the kind of person with whom you take down your hair and discuss off-the-record things. I don't know whether I'd ever be able to do that.

LUCK, MONEY, AND WORK

People who are mental and logical are usually not as lucky as people who are spiritual and intuitive. Logical people don't allow themselves to depend on luck. This is one reason why Gemini is not a lucky sign and why Virgo is even less fortunate with chance. Virgos therefore don't usually acquire money through windfalls or happenstance; it is almost always acquired through salaried jobs. Virgos are often good at managing money, but they are seldom fortune builders like Capricorns or Cancerians. Virgo Andrew Brimmer is a good example. He is the prototype of the money manager. He is an economist, and whoever selected him in 1995 as head of the District of Columbia financial oversight board picked about the best possible person for the job.

Virgos make about the most dutiful employees in the world. They're the kind who remember all the details that the boss forgets. They're quietly efficient with no great need to be in the spotlight. If properly appreciated and moderately rewarded, they're content to be the power behind the throne. Virgos tend to identify quite strongly with the company they're working for. The larger and more organized the company, the more contented and secure Virgos feel. They might be bored, but they'll find it hard to quit because of the health benefits, the retirement benefits, the paid vacations, and the relative certainty that a paycheck will be coming in every two weeks. Natives of this sign are more nervous than most when they don't know where their next meal is coming from.

Often the artistic side of the Virgo vibration leads to an erosion of the impulse toward order and stability and can encourage chaos. This manifestation of the Virgo personality can produce one of the most disorderly individuals in the zodiac (think of Charlie Parker)—even though they may retain the rigorous Virgo mentality. When this happens, the internal war that results is as great as that raging inside Gemini or Pisces, because the two personalities at war are more disparate than those in any other sign.

Virgo is the ruling sign of nursing, and many Virgos are attracted to nursing, since it is probably the best profession for providing affectionate concern in an impersonal way. Social work is less suited because it requires more involvement with the tangled emotional lives of the people being served. Virgos also seem to be attracted to the starched white uniforms and long, clean corridors of modern healing institutions. I know two Virgo nurses who say they prefer working the night shift because they love moving briskly through the empty antiseptic hospital hallways. The famous neurosurgeon Dr. Benjamin Carson is only one of the many doctors who have used their Virgo meticulous attention to detail to distinguish themselves in this serving profession.

Virgos also make good teachers, although they're sometimes quite impatient with smaller children. They will, however, be untiring in their efforts to make students learn what they must know to get along in what Virgo considers a hostile world.

Virgo men are good middle-level corporate managers. They take orders well and like to have things clearly spelled out to reduce the chance of error or inefficiency. They pay proper deference to superiors and can be fair but stern with subordinates. One side of Virgo may be wayward or artistic, but neither is aggressively rebellious. It is easy for Virgo to work within the system. Virgos are not engaged in an idealistic search for new horizons. They are more interested in a day-to-day struggle for order, survival, and progress in the imperfect world we have inherited.

PHYSICAL AND MENTAL HEALTH

Virgos aren't frail people, nor are they likely to ruin their health through excessive use of alcohol or addictive drugs. Virgo rules the stomach; thus many natives of this sign are fussy about what they eat, and there's a high incidence of indigestion among them. They are also prone to suffer from nervous headaches and insomnia because they worry too much about things they can't change. But most of Virgo's physical problems are mental, meaning that many of their illnesses are psychogenic. Hypochondriacs are more prevalent in Virgo than in any other sign. So overpowering is the mental activity of the sign that natives often "think" themselves sick. They seldom let their minds relax; the nervous system is constantly taking in impressions from the senses.

They aren't egocentric people, but they tend to be self-involved. And although they may seem unsentimental or emotionless, they are not; they are simply innately reserved and more mental than emotional in their affections. What they must be concerned with is a tendency to allow their inhibited emotional life to affect their health.

LOVE AND SEX

Despite the fact that Barry White, "The High Priest of Love" is a Virgo, Virgos are among the most selective when choosing to fall in love. People who depend on their emotions can do this easily by simply accepting the way a person makes them "feel." Virgos prefer to think about what they're getting into. They seldom fall in love easily; there are simply too many things to consider. And they weigh all these things before choosing to let go.

Barry White's birth date has been hard to find, so some astrologers have expressed doubts that Barry White is really a Virgo. He is something else, some think, and is hiding out among Virgos by giving a false birth date.

However, since Virgo is a dual sign, there is an artistic, expressive side to the vibration, and if the expression of love is good business, then Virgos are as capable as anyone of putting it out into the marketplace.

In this book we speak mostly of the more sober side of the vibration, which is seldom carried away by emotion. These Virgos are almost never chosen, wooed, and won by someone who has not passed some very logically established criteria. On the other hand, once Virgos have chosen the people they want for love or sex, they go directly after them and usually get them.

This is quite a pattern for a shy virgin, but it holds true. Virgos are charming but not very romantic or idealistic. They have very definite ideas about the people to whom they want to relate. Natives have very strong sexual appetites, but many also have very strong inhibitions, which make these appetites hard to satisfy. They sometimes loosen up sexually, but usually they prefer relating to one person.

Virgos are eager to do things for the person they love because they're reluctant to express their feelings verbally. Most attempts to force them will inhibit them even more. It is almost as if they are embarrassed to hear themselves saying something mushy.

Most Virgos have to teach themselves to be affectionate. Under affliction, they aren't enthusiastic about a lot of touching, kissing, or other forms of contact, and there is in the sign a certain reverence for purity and a fear of contamination. This standoffishness often gives Virgo a lot of trouble, so many of them make a conscious effort to "come on strong." Sometimes they erect an entire false personality atop the real one, which naturally prefers to stand back and scrutinize before becoming involved.

Virgos, like most others, have their sexual whims, but they're seldom carried away by them. A person usually has to have more than sex appeal to attract them—intelligence, social standing, money, or at least a good job. Astrologers often say that, like the earth, Virgo's sexual nature is slow to heat and slow to cool. Virgos are often overly sober and serious, but they can be intensely sexual and, like the natives of the other earth signs, quite possessive and jealous.

As a mutable sign as well as an earth sign, Virgos are much more faithful than the natives of the other mutable signs. But like Gemini, Sagittarius, and Pisces, Virgo is often unstable in affection. Virgos fall out of love just as easily as do the other mutables, but this rarely leads to sexual promiscuity. Usually Virgos adjust quite easily to a life that is not filled with a lot of romantic frills. There are many other reasons, practical ones, for staying in or moving out of relationships, they feel.

Some astrologers feel that Virgo women make the best possible mistresses, especially for married men who are "important." They are not anxious to have a lot of noisy, untidy children, and they tend to enjoy occupying the attention of men who are rich and famous. In fact, love for them is based primarily on admiration or respect. Being faithful is not difficult since they find it easy to be one-man women. They are also adept at suppressing their sexual urges when their lover is unavailable; they usually enjoy spending a great deal of time by themselves. But they're not so independent that they would resent having their bills paid. They're good intellectual companions and are usually excellent listeners. Perhaps best of all from the lover's viewpoint, they're discreet because they are very concerned about scandal and gossip. They are sensual, but most often they are willing to allow their men to establish the tone and level of their erotic life. When they decide to become involved, they can be as sexy and adventurous as their lover desires.

LOVE AFFAIRS

(See the other sections for love affairs between
Virgo men and women of the other signs.)

VIRGO WOMAN, ARIES MAN

You might be attracted by all that energy and apparent self-confidence. He's a doer, and you might see a million ways that you can help him do. But Ariens are full of excitement and enthusiasm that often translates to impatience. He'll want you to be quickly excitable and optimistic, too, and he may not understand how you can be so cautious and reluctant. He's a pusher. He's not the kind to leave you alone to be yourself. You're sometimes doubting and critical, and he hates to be criticized. He likes to argue and you hate to be argued at. He's quickly passionate, but because you are slower to warm up, the sexual vibrations will need adjustment in order for the two of you to mesh.

VIRGO WOMAN, TAURUS MAN

His view of the world is very similar to your own. He is not quite as pessimistic as you sometimes are, but he's certainly just as realistic. Like you he is patient and practical, just the ideal man for a good old down-to-earth love affair. Home life is important to both of you, and there is in each vibration a great love for material security. You are both usually very careful with money and rather reserved in your approach to social situations. You can be one of the best homemakers in the world for a man like him. His actions can show you how much he appreciates it. His stable personality can work a nice influence on your more erratic one. He is much more stubborn and opinionated, but you'll easily learn when to back off and stop criticizing his opinions. The sexual vibrations are likely to be good and strong. Neither is very sentimental, but neither needs or wants much sentimentality. You might need a little more mental stimulation than he gives, and he might need a little more sweetness than you give, but that's a small matter when compared with the good, steady physical satisfaction you can give each other.

VIRGO WOMAN, GEMINI MAN

Neither of you is very romantic or sentimental. You both can be very critical, and there are likely to be few sweet emotions to soften the harshly intellectual light you bring to shine on everything, including each other. The relationship will have to survive in this light, and that's tough. Your feelings are very easily hurt, and few people can be colder and more sarcastic than a Gemini in a bad mood. Your nature and your mental activity are slower, more cautious, and more thorough than his. His pace is faster, more superficial, and more adventurous. Your need for security and stability is much greater than his, and his need for variety and adventure are likely to be greater than your jealousy and suspicion will allow. In love he is quick, flirty, and changeable, while you are slow to warm but slow to cool. Both of you are reasonable, and love can be worked out on the plain of reason.

VIRGO WOMAN, CANCER MAN

Strangely, there are a lot of good things about this pairing. You are both rather cautious and reserved. You both enjoy spending a lot of time in a secure, well-furnished home. The financial side of the affair is likely to be quite good, since you both approach money matters with a great deal of common sense. A Cancer man, in fact, all water-sign men, are better than Taureans and Capricorns at opening up the emotional side of your personality. But this might throw you into confusion. You mistrust emotionalism in others and you are certainly frightened by it when you find it in yourself. You'll forever want to draw back and be logical; he'll accuse you of being too cold. He is a very sentimental man, and you are not sentimental at all. He needs a lot of encouragement, and you are not quick to give verbal reassurance. He is very demonstrative and you are not. Your tendency to scrutinize and criticize will bring out the worst of his insecurities, but working through the insecurities that both of you have could create a strong bond.

VIRGO WOMAN, LEO MAN

He might complain and lose his temper a lot because you keep throwing dirt on his fire, but if he's a wise Leo, he might sense that you are the perfect antidote for his big and often wastefully extravagant personality. If he's extremely ambitious, he might know that he needs some practical common sense behind him, and he's better off with you than he would be with either Taurus or Capricorn. You are more adaptable than either of the other earth signs. He enjoys the spotlight, and you don't really mind giving it up. You won't give his ego all the massaging that it needs, but he might find some public way to get that. If you have a career of your own you won't have the time to give him what he needs. If you're a housewife and he spends a lot of time away from home doing important things, you might be impressed by his public exploits and he might be impressed by your ability to keep him firmly anchored in reality.

VIRGO WOMAN, VIRGO MAN

This one could work out well. Two Virgos who use their critical faculties could spend too much time criticizing each other. If they are not careful, there will be little relief from the severe and pessimistic side of the vibration. But if both bring out the charming side of the vibration, this could make a good combination, full of mutual consideration. If only one has a stress-filled career, the other is probably quite willing to be the helpmate. You both enjoy quality cultural entertainment. In love neither is overly demonstrative, and both might be reluctant to verbalize tender feelings. But the physical part of the sexual relationship could be quite good. Overall, both can settle into an affair based more on logic than on passion, and more on intelligence than on emotion.

VIRGO WOMAN, LIBRA MAN

He's romantic and will surely be turned off by your realistic approach to everything, including love. He thinks that love should be playful, but love is very serious, even threatening, to you. He needs a lot of freedom, so he tends not to love deeply; but for you, if it isn't deep, then it isn't love. He'll share your love of art, music, pleasant surroundings, and friends who are involved in important things. Your periodic pessimism might confuse him, but few men are better at tuning it out. He enjoys an active social life. You are much more reserved, but you might not mind doing a lot of entertaining as long as you don't have to be the magnet that draws the people in. You find social contact stimulating. But after his friends go home, you might find that you have a lot of work to do keeping each other interested.

VIRGO WOMAN, SCORPIO MAN

This one might work out far better than most astrologers would normally assume. Sure, you two are very incompatible, but there are a lot of surface similarities. You're both realistic and you both tend to guard your feelings closely. You both approach life with a lot of caution and feel that patience and hard work are the best solutions to life's problems. He likes to dominate, but you might not mind this coming from the man with the best sexual reputation in the zodiac (that is, if he's as good as his reputation). He's emotional and uses his emotions to manipulate. Virgos are vulnerable to this because of much inherent emotional confusion. Both of you are sarcastic and critical, but you're also realistic enough to know that life and love must go on despite disagreements.

VIRGO WOMAN, SAGITTARIUS MAN

From far off you might admire his high spirit and optimism and he might dig your quiet charm, but you're far too pessimistic, cautious, and critical for him, and he's too careless and full of argument for you. You're perfectly designed to get on each other's nerves. He'll want to fly, and you'll wonder why he can't be more solid and down-to-earth. However, you're both very adaptable people, and a love affair requiring a lot of adaptation just keeps the interest high. You won't be bored because each will have plenty to do figuring out how anyone can be the kind of person that the other one is.

VIRGO WOMAN, CAPRICORN MAN

Sometimes when he sits down to talk, you might feel that part of you is speaking, the part that's practical, conservative, and realistic. You know why he wants what he says he wants and you approve of his way of getting it. He is patient and willing to work hard to achieve his goals, and like you he loves home life. He's the kind who gives a lot of advice and otherwise likes to manage or interfere with your life, but you can stop him from going too far. You can talk to him because you speak his language. And considering all the ways that you two are compatible, the sexual vibrations between you can't be anything but good and earthy.

VIRGO WOMAN, AQUARIUS MAN

He might seem a little fuzzy and confusing to you, and he's stubborn in what to you seems like disarray. It is not disarray. In his own way he is as logical as you are, but you are listening to the voice of everyday reality and he is listening to the voice from another place. He retaliates against criticism more quickly than almost any other sign. He is rebellious and you are set about by rules which you think must be followed to get from here to there. You can be quite sexually satisfying to each other, but you're going to have to have a lot of mutual understanding to get around the many differences in the way you see the world.

VIRGO WOMAN, PISCES MAN

There's an artistic side of him that will touch the artistic side of you, but the practical side of you isn't likely to know that a practical side of him exists. In truth, he can be rather persistent and methodical in pursuit of his goals, but you're likely to see only the emotionalism and indecisiveness. You can be indecisive, too, but indecisiveness bothers you more than it does him. He has more faith in the intuitive, while your faith is in the practical. The two can work well together if they can ever manage to make each other happy enough to stay together. You are not moved forward by emotions, and it will seem to you that emotions are the only things that really do move him forward.

VIRGO

(AUGUST 21st TO SEPTEMBER 20th)

DIANA SANDS, actress	**August 22, 1934**
JOHN LEE HOOKER, blues singer	**August 22, 1917**
ALTHEA GIBSON, tennis star, first black woman to play at Wimbledon	**August 25, 1927**
BRANFORD MARSALIS, jazz/crossover musician	**August 26, 1960**
RITA DOVE, poet, writer, educator	**August 28, 1952**
MICHAEL JACKSON, megastar of the music industry	**August 29, 1958**
CHARLIE "YARDBIRD" PARKER, jazz alto sax musician and jazz innovator	**August 29, 1920**
DINAH WASHINGTON, singer	**August 29, 1924**
ROY WILKINS, NAACP leader through the civil rights era	**August 30, 1901**
FRANK ROBINSON, Hall of Fame baseball player	**August 31, 1935**
ELDRIDGE CLEAVER, revolutionary activist and former Black Panther	**August 31, 1935**
MAXINE WATERS, congresswoman from Los Angeles	**August 31, 1938**
MARVA COLLINS, educator, inner-city school founder	**August 31, 1936**
ROSA GUY, award-winning writer	**September 1, 1925**
ROMARE H. BEARDEN, collagist, artist	**September 2, 1914**
JAMES M. NABRIT, JR., educator	**September 4, 1900**
FRANK YERBY, writer	**September 5, 1916**

JACOB LAWRENCE, painter of American history	September 7, 1917
RICHARD ROUNDTREE, stage and screen actor	September 7, 1942
RICHARD WRIGHT, influential author	September 9, 1908
SONIA SANCHEZ, award-winning poet and playwright, educator	September 9, 1934
OTIS REDDING, rhythm and blues artist	September 9, 1941
JOSE FELICIANO, singer, musician, composer	September 10, 1945
CHARLES EVERS, civil rights leader	September 11, 1922
RICHARD HUNT, sculptor	September 12, 1935
JESSE OWENS, legendary Olympic athlete of the 1920s and 1930s	September 12, 1913
BARRY WHITE, soul singer, bandleader	September 12, 1944
CLIFTON WHARTON, pension system administrator, educator, economist	September 13, 1926
ANDREW BRIMMER, renowned economist	September 13, 1926
CONSTANCE BAKER MOTLEY, lawyer, NAACP Legal Defense and Educational Fund official	September 14, 1921
JULIAN "CANNONBALL" ADDERLY, innovative musician	September 15, 1928
JESSYE NORMAN, internationally renowned soprano	September 15, 1945
HENRY LOUIS GATES, JR., scholar, author, essayist, cultural critic	September 16, 1950
B.B. KING, "King of the Blues"	September 16, 1925
ANDREW "RUBE" WALKER, Negro Baseball League great	September 17, 1879
BENJAMIN CARSON, neurosurgeon	September 18, 1951
ANNA DEAVERE SMITH, award-winning playwright, actress	September 18, 1950
GENERAL FREDERIC DAVIDSON, U.S. military officer	September 20, 1917

**SEPTEMBER 21st TO
OCTOBER 22nd**

LIBRA

THE BALANCE
THE SIGN OF THE ADJUSTER

◆

AMBITIOUS, AFFECTIONATE,

HARMONIOUS

◆

Ruled by Venus

COLOR: Pastel Blue

METAL: Copper

GEM: Chrysolite

LUCKY NUMBERS: 6 and 9

FORTUNATE DAY: Friday

THE LIBRA VIBRATION

LIBRA, SWEET LIBRA, ISN'T ONE OF THE SIGNS that people describe easily. Everyone has an illustrative story or two about impatient, egotistical Aries or sexy, secretive Scorpio, but as a rule Libras are thought of as gentle lovers of harmony, who are content to work behind the scenes. Libras are usually seen as not very aggressive or ambitious.

Then when people hear that Mae C. Jemison is a Libra, they try to think of her as an exception. Jemison, in her way, is a Renaissance woman. Winner of a National Achievement Scholarship, she graduated from Stanford University with a degree in chemical engineering but with enough credits for a degree in Afro-American studies as well.

After she graduated from Cornell University Medical School in 1981, she became a doctor. She worked in refugee camps in Thailand. She was a medical officer in the Peace Corps in West Africa; in 1987 she was selected by NASA to be an astronaut; and in 1992 she became the first black woman in space.

She looks and acts as gracefully as Libras are said to look and act. She has very graceful features and smiles a lot, but the list of her achievements will make people question some of their erroneous ideas about Libras.

Libra, like Taurus, is ruled by Venus, goddess of love, beauty, artistry, and refinement, which gives to Libras an easygoing side that is deeply romantic. Libras are also known to be diplomatic and refined, but Venus also imparts laziness, self-indulgence, evasiveness, flirtatiousness, vacillation, and a love of comfort and luxury. This is how people usually think of Libras.

Libras like cordiality and pleasantness. In fact, there are stories about Libras who will not talk to you unless you have something nice to say. There is a big urge in Libras to try to get along with everyone, and certainly they work hard to get people to like them; in fact, they are often thrown into confusion when someone doesn't. To this end, they are among the most intentionally charming and diplomatic of people. The key words are I HARMONIZE.

Libra's symbol is the scales of justice, and the scales represent Libra's central quest—the search for equilibrium and calm. The Virgo vibration moved toward the perfection of the individual, the "I," but the Libra vibration seeks a balance between the "I" and others, as well as a stable, unshakable inner harmony. For Libra, as an air sign, this harmony and balance must be achieved through communication with others. Thus Libras need harmony in the outside world to create and sustain stability and calm within themselves.

Disharmony and chaos upset Libra's carefully orchestrated, stable world, so Libras are driven constantly to attempt to rid their environment of ugliness and disorder. It is this determined, almost obsessional, struggle to create internal harmony that has established Libra's reputation as lovers of pleasant surroundings and agreeable company.

But from its reputation you might conclude that Libra is not a very complicated vibration—nothing could be farther from the truth. Libra's outward serenity is achieved through the paradox of engaging in a relentless, often nerve-racking, effort to assure their own inner harmony.

Friendliness is one of the most important resources for Libras to use in pursuit of their goals. To this end, they love popularity and are usually willing to do a great deal to stay in the good graces of all the people with whom they come in close contact.

They are very considerate of these people's feelings because they're very dependent on their approval. Usually when Libras sense that someone disapproves of them, even slightly, they become irritated and resentful. The Libra's major goal is to get along with people and to help people get along with each other.

In the grand scheme of things their role is to harmonize and bring people together for creative group efforts. But often, in pursuing this goal, they attempt to be all things to all people; they switch their own ideas and ideals to fit the immediate social situation. This is why the vibration has a reputation for being superficial. Confusion and frustration often result from their efforts to juggle old loyalties, moderate all extremes, and, if necessary, agree with the person nearest at hand.

This of course is primarily true among unevolved Libras, but all natives of the sign must beware of this danger, for in the deepest sense it is but one demonstration of how the Libra vibration deals with the real world.

Libras can be indecisive and vacillating, although not nearly as hesitant as the unevolved Pisces or not nearly so moody as the unevolved Cancer or Gemini. In pursuit of harmony Libras can assume a certain modesty even though they are in fact among the most self-admiring of all types.

An elegant physical appearance is extremely important to most of them. It was important enough for *Current Biography* to note that Libra Bryant Gumbel, the glib and quick-witted star of NBC's long-running *Today* show, "fastidiously coordinates his tie, cuff links, and socks."

If mirrors could talk, they would probably reveal that they've seen more Libra faces than those of any other sign—except perhaps Leo. Libras are usually extremely attractive people, with consistently pleasant faces and coordinated wardrobes.

Generally they are also witty people, who always seem to have the right words to handle any social occasion. They often give the impression that they focus their entire attention on the pleasure and comfort of others, but the truth is—like the other air signs, Aquarius and Gemini— they don't really like to become too deeply involved in the lives of other individuals. They are much more likely to get involved with groups, or ideologies about groups.

Libras are good talkers. Stokely Carmichael, head of the Student Nonviolent Coordinating Committee in the South during the 1960s, said when H. Rap Brown replaced him, "You'll be happy to have me back when you hear from him. He's a bad man." And hear from him the nation did. (Hubert Gerold Brown picked up the name H. Rap because his talk, or rap, was so strong.)

The gentle sweetness, although genuine, often covers a personality of great strength, determination, ambition, and cleverness. The romantic nature of the vibration, though genuine, often masks a mind that's extremely logical and opportunistic. Libras often have to agonize a great deal about it, but they usually insist on having their own way. Often Libra turns out to be an iron fist inside a velvet glove.

As a cardinal sign—like Aries, Cancer, and Capricorn—positive Libras are very enterprising. They love being leaders. They like to get things done, even if they have to get other people to do them. There is often an uncontrolled restlessness in the Libra personality that makes even the most sluggish natives disinclined to sit still for long periods of time or equally disinclined to focus on one subject for very long.

Libras often appear to be unambitious, but usually all cardinal signs are determined and aspiring. In Libra, however, ambition is in conflict with a love of moderation and tranquillity, which is also characteristic of this vibration. Moreover, it is a frustrating drive for many Libras since they prefer not to act on their own. Libra is the sign of partnership, and most Libras believe that authority originates not in the individual consciousness but in the group consciousness, the "we" consciousness. Libras usually prefer to act on behalf of "we": "We want this." "I'm going to do this for us." "We must have this." "We will not endure that." The effort is always to include someone else in their plans.

Since personal ambition and aggressiveness are usually much too crude and unbecoming for them to adopt as their own motivation, an important path to success for Libras is to find a "we" on whose behalf they may act.

There is no doubt that Jesse Jackson, for example, is personally very ambitious, but personal ambition is not his call to action. It seems that he has gotten the energy to climb higher by far into presidential politics than any African American has ever climbed only by constantly reminding himself and others that he is acting on behalf of the masses of exploited poor or black people.

Libras are rarely aggressive on their own behalf, but when acting for a group, a movement, or a loved individual, they can be as belligerent as Aquarians, though not so uncompromising. This is why the peace-loving sign of Libra has produced so many fighters for freedom.

Elijah Muhammad, founder of the Nation of Islam; Bobby Seale who along with Aquarian Huey Newton founded the Black Panther party; Jomo Kenyatta, founder and leader of the Mau Mau, the revolutionary group that helped drive the British out of Kenya—The list of Libra fighters for African and African-American freedom is longer than that of any sign, including Aquarius.

David Walker, whose *Appeal* was the boldest statement of the anti-slavery movement, wrote in 1829, "I will stand my ground. Somebody must die in this cause. I may be doomed to the stake and the fire or to the scaffold tree, but it is not in me to falter."

He may not have sounded much like the Libra he was, and we must remember that Nat Turner, who led the most famous slave revolt in American history, was a Libra. Among more modern revolutionaries, H. Rap Brown, as we have noted, and Dick Gregory were all born with the Sun in Libra.

Amiri Baraka, a poet, novelist, and playwright as well as a civil rights activist, offers a prime example of the seeming contradiction. He was born October 7, 1934, when both the Sun and Moon were in Libra; thus we would expect him to be a rather gentle, artistic man, which his friends insist he is when he's not fighting for his designated "we"— black people. Reflecting his more subdued side, in his poetry he often expresses a desire to leave the racial battlefield and return to a life of art and tranquillity: "I think about the time when I will be relaxed. When the flames of non-specific passions wear themselves away. And my eyes and hands and mind can turn and soften, and my song will be softer and lightly weight the air."

In a perfectly ordered world Libras would be dreamers. Dick Gregory would probably be just a comedian and a mystic; Jesse Jackson would be a lover or a preacher, anything but a warrior. Elijah Muhammad would have been the gentle lamb that his followers often assured us he was.

After his capture by New York City police and his incarceration, H. Rap Brown changed his name to Jamil Abdullah Al-Amin and turned inward to ponder the beauty of the human spirit. And Nat Turner, David Walker, and Jomo Kenyatta, despite their well-known acts of insurrection, were always seriously concerned with spirituality.

RELATIONSHIPS

The success of Libra's life can't be judged on the basis of money accumulated, prestige gained, or wisdom achieved. It must be judged on how well Libra has been able to establish successful relationships with other people. Libras are extroverts. They love to have people around them and are generally very easy to get along with.

They argue, sometimes vigorously and emotionally, but usually with open minds and conciliatory charm. They're very logical people who slide easily from argument to compromise if they're offered anything reasonable. They almost never hold a grudge, but they do tend to avoid people who consistently put them in a down mood.

They aren't good at ending relationships. The root desire of the sign is to bring people together, and it goes against the grain for them to have to separate. They tend to float from person to person, never really ending old relationships before surrendering to the fascination of new ones. Because they don't fight and make clean breaks, old friends and old lovers are always coming back into their lives. I know a Libra woman of forty who is good friends with all twelve of the men she has loved over the twenty years of her adult life.

First impressions are extremely important to Libras; they are usually neat and tidy, and tend to judge people on superficial things, such as their wardrobes or personal appearances. Libras are often more conscious of style than of content. Most Libras like to gossip, and one of the things they talk about most is how someone looked or what they were wearing.

They can be as faultfinding as Virgos, but they are usually more tactful at presenting their criticism, and unlike Virgos, who have a need to criticize no matter what, Libras usually save their critical observations to use them strategically in their efforts to gain advantages in social situations.

They love to occupy the center of attention almost as much as Leos do, but often pretend to be embarrassed by praise. "Oh, thank you, thank you, you shouldn't say that. No, not really." Libras will squirm under praise, but they don't want it to stop. Leos swell with pride; Libras tuck their heads and melt, or at least drop their eyes. They like to flatter others as well. Often this is their way of building friendships, thereby protecting themselves against isolation and loneliness; it also ensures that they get the support and social responses they need. Libras don't protect their sensitivity with hardened exterior shells as Cancerians do. Since they usually lack a strong defensive posture, they are nearly always exposed.

Libras hate rejection, even by someone who isn't really important in their lives or by someone who has every reason to reject them. They can go to extremes to reaffirm their acceptability. I know a Libra woman who occasionally gets dressed up and goes out to various night spots just to see how much attention she attracts. She flirts and tantalizes from afar. She doesn't want to be picked up or even approached. She simply wants to know she is attractive to other men. Thus reassured, she goes faithfully home to the real world of husband and children.

LUCK, MONEY, AND WORK

Venus is a benevolent planet, second only to Jupiter in its ability to bestow luck. Consequently Libras are fairly lucky people. They find it easy to attract money, which is good since many of them have expensive tastes. They are materialists to the extent that they wish to have the "proper" things—good food, fine wine, stylish clothing, and comfortable surroundings—in which they take sensual pleasure. Few of them have an appetite for hard work. Money most often comes to them through association with other people. Many use their charm to attract husbands or wives who are better off than they are. They're not gold diggers; they just seem to gravitate toward the pleasant life.

Libras tend to have very artistic taste. They're the kind of tactful critics who can criticize without alienating or discouraging. They like to encourage or promote the talents of others. For example, they make the best possible agents for a band or singing group. They're the perfect peacemakers when the inevitable wars flare up between members of the group. They're good at meeting people and singing the praises of "my" group, which is quite a good deal more acceptable to them than praising themselves. But they are, in their own right, musically inclined—the rock-and-roll innovator Chuck Berry and the versatile singer, composer, and band leader Ray Charles were born with the Sun in Libra.

Libras are the spendthrifts of the zodiac. If Libras make up one twelfth of the population, they probably possess no more than one hundredth of the money. Charge cards were made for them. They love to buy expensive things, but after they possess them, they can pout and find a million reasons not to pay the bills. Debt is one of the ugly realities they prefer not to face. Money doesn't represent power to them, and hoarding it is hardly their idea of fun. They believe that it was made to be spent, and they spend it with as much enthusiasm and taste as anyone.

If they have to fit in at all, Libras fit into the workforce wherever they can find a niche. Often they wander about changing jobs, even occupational fields, with great frequency. They're versatile and intelligent, but they're easily bored. They certainly never get excited one way or another about routine jobs, and they're almost never found working in dirty or unpleasant surroundings, or in places where a lot of physical effort is required.

Law is one of the best fields for their mixture of personality traits. They don't make efficient secretaries, but they're good receptionists.

They're not usually good artists, but they make excellent art directors. Surprisingly, they make very good mathematicians and scientists, but not surprisingly, poor bookkeepers and accountants. They're also good as salespersons, designers, decorators, teachers, and musicians. They make out better as instrumentalists than as solo vocalists, and some of the most inventive jazz musicians have come from their ranks—among them Bud Powell, John Coltrane, Thelonious Monk, and Dizzy Gillespie. They're usually just not egotistical enough to be a commanding presence when alone in the spotlight at center stage, although the placement of other elements in their chart—a Leo ascendant for example—may provide the needed push.

The Libra mind is very logical and analytical when it's not wandering and daydreaming. But Libras prefer to use it to make a living in some artistic, creative, or public-involved way. If they can't, they seek other imaginative outlets for their talents, such as decorating their homes in elegant ways, learning gourmet cooking, singing in the shower, and imagining they're writing poetry, dancing, or commanding center stage at the Apollo Theater or Radio City Music Hall.

PHYSICAL AND MENTAL HEALTH

Libra can be one of the most mentally balanced of all the signs. This balance is rather fragile and can be easily thrown into confusion. The physical health is somewhat frail also, and Libras are susceptible to minor infections. Libra rules the kidneys, and that is its native's most vulnerable area. By virtue of temperament and physique they seldom make good professional athletes.

When Libras don't take an active role and oppose injustice and turmoil in their immediate social environments, it can produce extreme forms of escapism in their personalities. Daydreaming, which is a common Libra trait, is a harmless form. Pretending to elegance is another form of refusing to deal with negative or ordinary situations. Some Libras aren't good at fighting battles with social circumstances that are close to them. In extreme cases they'll attempt to tune out much of the discord that might exist around them. They simply refuse to cope.

Unlike Capricorns and Scorpios, they don't usually use alcohol as a form of escape. Their kidneys couldn't stand it. They are more likely to retreat into illusion or, in rare instances, more serious mental disorders. Short of that, they may succumb to laziness or indifference. If unevolved Libras can't make the world pleasant, then they may refuse to exert themselves at all.

Most Libras don't need to be advised to get plenty of rest and relaxation. The influence of Venus assures that they will naturally appreciate the benefits of ease and idleness.

LOVE AND SEX

Considered the lovers of the zodiac, Libras like to flirt; romance is an enjoyable game to them. They truly enjoy playing at it. They often fool themselves into believing that they are deeper in love than their partner knows them to be, and when the partner acts on what he or she knows, Libra feels betrayed to the core.

In cases like this Libras can use their marvelous communication skills to take revenge. More than anything else this is what has made Libras Ntozake Shange, author of *For Colored Girls Who Have Considered Suicide/When the Rainbow is Enuf,* and Terry McMillan, author of *Waiting to Exhale,* high priestesses of the "he did me bad" school of writers.

Libras are not as obsessively jealous as Taureans can be. Neither are they as deeply passionate as Ariens, nor endowed with large sexual appetites as are many Virgos and Capricorns. Libras' love isn't fire but tinkling ice. They remain quite cool and in control, but no one is drawn to the thrill of the romantic game as much as they are. Libra love isn't syrup but light and bubbly champagne. Syrup is sweet but thick and sticky. Champagne flows easily, spreads thin, but evaporates when things get hot.

Libras often fall in love with love itself. Even when they know they're fooling themselves, they put on rose-colored glasses for the occasion. They're charming, gracious, and very demonstrative. They like subtle touches, such as sweet words, unexpected little gifts, candlelight, and wine. What is passion without all the trimmings? They respond very well to admiration and affection by showering their lovers with more of the same, but admiration and affection must come often if Libras are to remain faithful lovers. Otherwise, they're prone to seek love outside the home, or at least they begin to fantasize and dream about it.

One thing they can't stand in love is routine. They get bored quickly. Curiosity and adventure are at the root of their romantic drive, not the kind of raw sexual hunger that needs only regular intercourse in order to be satisfied.

Libras fall out of love very easily. All they have to do is take off the rose-colored glasses. In fact many of them can be downright fickle. "Can't we be friends?" they're likely to say when the feeling is gone. Friendship is a more enduring experience for them, and it is better because it leaves them free to expose themselves over and over again to the romantic excitement of a new love affair. But getting out of marriage is a little harder since Libras hate to separate from anything. They tend to hang around hoping that the situation will get better. Secretly they may hope their partner will break it up. If not, they put the rose-colored glasses back on and often succeed in falling back in love. They suffer, but not visibly, so if they can hang on, they may fool others as well as themselves. They are easy to live with even when they're not in love. Face-to-face maliciousness is very difficult for them. They usually find it very difficult to both maintain contact and remain hostile.

Libras are among the least sexually jealous of all people. They give freedom because they want it for themselves. Those Libras who aren't liberated enough to seek outside love in a physical sense live on crushes, flirtation, Platonic relationships, and dreams. Libra's theme song could be "I Won't Live in a World Without Love," of some kind. Often their craving for excitement, freshness, and romance is so impractical and wistful that the physical sexual act becomes nothing more than the seed inside a luscious piece of fruit. The buildup and foreplay are everything. Intercourse is almost anticlimactic.

As mentioned, Libra's physical sexual desires aren't overpowering. But this doesn't mean that Libras aren't good lovers. Often they're among the most skillful. They're imaginative, sensitive, willing to please, and willing to experiment. They're also capable of an emotional detachment that prevents them from losing themselves while making love. They're always aware of what is or is not satisfying their partners, and they're unselfish and manipulative enough to forgo some of their own pleasure in order to give pleasure. In fact, giving pleasure is one of their ways of gaining power.

LOVE AFFAIRS

(See the other sections for love affairs between Libra men and women of the other signs.)

LIBRA WOMAN, ARIES MAN

There is a great deal of attraction but not much compatibility between the two of you. The attraction stems from the fact that you're astrological opposites. Your signs are 180 degrees from each other on the astrological wheel, which means that you possess complementary personality traits. You Libra women are attracted to his decisiveness and self-confidence, and he knows that you can add some refinement and beauty to his rough, aggressive life. He's all impatience and enthusiasm, while you're cool and very logical. He displays his affection openly, and you'll love being the kindling in all that Aries fire. However, your love of peace and harmony stands in sharp contrast to his love of argument, conflict, and competition. His temper blows very easily and he'll have to control it if he hopes to get along with you. Your gentleness may bring out the most domineering side of his personality. Of course your gentleness is the velvet glove that sometimes covers the iron fist. You'll certainly frustrate all of his efforts to impose his will on the union.

LIBRA WOMAN, TAURUS MAN

He's gentle like you and sometimes he tends to be a little lazy like you. He's peace-loving and likes comfortable surroundings. There are a lot of superficial similarities arising out of the fact that both your signs are ruled by Venus. Of all creatures, you are the least likely to bring out the stubborn streak in him. You're seldom pushy or aggressive. There may not be many fights, but there is a good chance that you two will eventually begin recognizing some differences between your basic personalities. He's cautious, conservative, and materialistic. The way you handle money may irritate him, and on top of that you may be a little fickle and changeable for a man who likes life to settle into a predictable groove. He may see you as flighty and foolish, and you're likely to think he's heavy and unimaginative. Though both of you are very sensual, his physical sexual appetites are greater than yours, whereas your need for change and variety is much greater than his. There will be some areas of friction between a lady who's lyrical and playful and a man who's lyrical but inwardly slow and very serious.

LIBRA WOMAN, GEMINI MAN

The mental compatibility more than compensates for your complaint that he's not romantic enough for you. There's nothing very sentimental about a Gemini man. He does everything with eyes wide open and doesn't even own a pair of rose-colored glasses, but he does think like you, and he loves freedom, variety, and change as you do. He's logical and he can hold on to money better than you can. The practical side of his nature will be a blessing for both of you. He's moody, but you're just the one to leave him alone when he's not in a mood to be bothered. He likes to argue and can be quite cold and sarcastic, but when he wants to win you over, he can be just as detached, witty, playful, friendly, and helpful as you are. Your sexual appetites are very similar—quick and excitable rather than gluttonous and overpowering. Neither is very jealous or possessive, so there's sure to be plenty of room for each to do his own thing—whatever it is.

LIBRA WOMAN, CANCER MAN

This would be a romance between a rain shower and the ocean. You could sprinkle a few pleasant remarks that would ripple the surface, but it's not likely that you'll reach, or ever want to reach, the great watery depths of his personality. He may be too serious and insecure for someone as flirtatious as you. You could hurt his feelings a million times without knowing it until he tells you a week later. He'll want to pull you deeper than you care to go. He's cautious and you're rather careless. He's emotional and you're detached and logical. He's affectionate, thorough, and loves to love. For a while the sexual part might be the best part. You're both free and experimental and will love to play with each other's feelings until you learn that he's playing for much higher stakes.

LIBRA WOMAN, LEO MAN

Fire-sign people thrill you because you like to bask in all that heat and enthusiasm. They bring out the side of your personality that you're proudest of—the romantic side. You like being a jewel for Mr. Leo's crown. He's idealistic and often idolizes the woman he's in love with— you like that. You're just the one to massage his ego and make him feel good about himself. He loves flattery and you love to give it. The only problem here is that he tends to return much less of it than he wants to receive. You are ultrafeminine and he's supermasculine. You're often indecisive, whereas he has a lot of drive and usually a clear sense of direction. You'll have a lot of fun spending money on nice things, and you both have a touch of common sense that will assert itself every once in a while. Even though he is sexually more intense and jealous than you are, you're likely to be clever and adaptable enough satisfy him. He can be stubborn and domineering, but you're cool enough to wait him out unless he becomes violent, or in some way loses his cool. Then he might escalate things to the breaking point.

LIBRA WOMAN, VIRGO MAN

You're likely to be curious about each other because you are so different in so many basic ways. You Libras hate criticism, and his nickname is the Critic. You're practical sometimes, but even when he's being impractical, his mentality runs in a rather ordered, down-to-earth fashion. He's strict and severe, while your outlook is rather relaxed and flippant. He's materialistic and seldom likes to fly. You fly whenever you can. You have an easy time verbalizing your feelings, even verbalizing more than you feel, while he is often verbally inhibited when it comes to expressing tenderness. When it comes to sexual matters, his appetite is largely physical, while yours is mainly mental. He may not be romantic enough to inspire you to the physical level that he needs from the woman he loves, and he's sometimes too jealous to let you get your inspiration by flirting elsewhere.

LIBRA WOMAN, LIBRA MAN

The most pleasing thing for Narcissus to see is a mirror. You'll see in most Libra men many things that you like about yourself. You two make good friends, and for both of you that is the better part of love. The passion might be low since you're both playing the same kind of romantic games. The partnership could lack leadership and decisiveness. There could be a lot of laziness and softness to overcome if neither of you has trained yourself to take charge. You both might bring so much sweetness and romanticism into the relationship that it becomes artificial and boring. The glory is that neither is too jealous to allow the other to find outside excitement. There are likely to be plenty of outside people impinging on the relationship, and the mental compatibility might let you know that in many ways you were born for each other.

LIBRA WOMAN, SCORPIO MAN

You may have heard so much about his sexual prowess that you think he's exactly what you need, but you're a sexual kitten and he's a tiger. You're romantic, while he's strictly business in bed. He's more emotional than you are, but his emotions aren't often as flowery and romantic as yours. You are a dreamer and he's a realist. You like a life of comfort and harmony; he accepts the fact that it can't always be that way. He can thrive on discord and struggle. You might seem lazy to him and lacking in toughness. He might seem severe to you and lacking in softness. You're willing to compromise and try to make things better. His desire is to master and control things. He is very magnetic and domineering. You should be very sure before you get into something from which you won't be able to fly away as easily as you would some others.

LIBRA WOMAN, SAGITTARIUS MAN

This is an easy relationship for both of you to fall into. You're likely to like each other instantly. There's no reason why two optimistic, sociable, idealistic, and clever people like you shouldn't come in from the first date glowing. He'll seem to be a frank, open-minded man. You see a lot of things that the two of you could enjoy together. He'll like your rather cool and casual approach to life, but he's far more serious than he seems, and he's likely to be more egotistical than he lets on. He loves to argue and can be quite brutal with insults. He may not be as sweet as he appears at first, and he can be inconsiderate and selfish as well as supportive and generous. He gives, but it's usually on his own terms. Like you, his passion is short-lived, but there are times when it's so much more intense than yours. The sexual vibrations aren't bad, however; you each need a lot of stimulation, and both of you are equipped to supply it.

LIBRA WOMAN, CAPRICORN MAN

Chances are that you won't be attracted to each other in the first place. He's usually not a very romantic, dashing figure, and he'll quickly feel that your head isn't screwed on tight enough for him. He likes power, prestige, and position, but not for the same reasons that you do. He'll sacrifice a great deal to get where he wants to be; you're not that persistently ambitious. Most of his considerable charm he saves for the serious task of getting ahead in the world. With the people he loves, he can be petty, nagging, and interfering. He might play games for a while, but his real tendency is to get down to business in all matters, sexual and otherwise. You may need more inspiration than he's likely to give, and he needs more satisfaction than you can give without the proper romantic foreplay and mental stimulation. However, if you can teach him to loosen up and play more, then this one can work.

LIBRA WOMAN, AQUARIUS MAN

Even after this love affair gets very serious, it's unlikely that it will get very tight or syrupy. You are the kind who could be deeply in love with each other and choose to live in separate apartments just to preserve that freedom of thought and movement that you so prize. Jealousy or possessiveness is not a part of the nature of either one of you. Even if you live together, you might play it loose and joke a lot about this love affair that never seems to get very heavy or obsessive. It could be serious, though. You could love each other very much and still be playing games. The sexual vibrations are good. You both need a lot of mental stimulation, and each has a great need for variety. Neither is very inhibited nor, on the other hand, very sexually obsessed. Your minds work in much the same way, so one of you will have to force himself to take care of practical, everyday details. You both have a great deal of concern for your fellow man and a great need to be involved with a lot of other people. Mr. Aquarius has a quick temper and he can be far more stubborn than he seems. But logic and reasonableness will keep you together if indifference and lackadaisicalness don't start you drifting apart.

LIBRA WOMAN, PISCES MAN

It's surprising that two people so basically incompatible could have so much in common. It's the sugar-coating of Venus on that Libra personality that makes you gentle, sometimes sentimental, artistic, lyrical, romantic, affectionate, and cuddly. All of this Mr. Pisces will love, but he will sense that your emotional nature isn't as deep and all-consuming as his. Both of you can be indecisive, oversensitive, vacillating, nonaggressive, and easygoing. But you're both clever and very capable of duplicity. You need freedom, and he may not be willing to allow as much as you want. While you are rather breezy with your affections, he may be more serious and vulnerable. He'll often feel you're too superficial, and you'll feel he takes everything the wrong way. This one sometimes lasts because you're both rather adaptable, and even if it doesn't last, you two have the power to make each other very happy until it ends.

LIBRA

(SEPTEMBER 21st TO OCTOBER 22nd)

GEORGE C. WOLFE, playwright, stage director, producer	**September 23, 1954**
JOHN COLTRANE, jazz musician, composer	**September 23, 1926**
RAY CHARLES, singer, musician, composer, actor	**September 23, 1930**
CARDISS COLLINS, politician, first black congresswoman from Illinois	**September 24, 1931**
SCOTTIE PIPPEN, NBA star	**September 25, 1965**
BELL HOOKS, activist, author, essayist, educator	**September 25, 1952**

ALMA JOHN, radio and television personality	September 27, 1906
BUD POWELL, jazz pianist	September 27, 1924
DON CORNELIUS, *Soul Train* host and producer	September 27, 1936
DAVID WALKER, antislavery writer, author, and publisher of *Appeal*	September 28, 1785
BRYANT GUMBEL, cohost of NBC's *Today* show	September 29, 1948
JOHNNY MATHIS, singer	September 30, 1935
NAT TURNER, antislavery revolutionary, insurrectionist	October 2, 1800
CHUBBY CHECKER, rock 'n' roll pioneer, populizer of "The Twist"	October 3, 1941
DAVE WINFIELD, baseball star, batting great	October 3, 1951
H. RAP BROWN, civil rights activist, revolutionary in Black Panther party	October 4, 1943
LEE P. BROWN, New York City Police Commissioner	October 4, 1937
YVONNE BURKE, lawyer, politician, congresswoman	October 5, 1932
AMIRI BARAKA, poet, playwright, political activist	October 7, 1934
ELIJAH MUHAMMAD, former leader of the Nation of Islam	October 7, 1897
JESSE JACKSON, political and religious leader, Rainbow Coalition founder	October 8, 1941
NONA HENDRYX, singer	October 9, 1947
THELONIOUS MONK, jazz pianist, composer, band leader	October 10, 1918
BEN VEREEN, singer, dancer, stage and screen actor	October 10, 1946
DICK GREGORY, comedian, political and social activist	October 12, 1932

WILLIAM RASPBERRY, journalist, syndicated columnist	October 12, 1935
JERRY RICE, San Francisco 49ers star receiver	October 12, 1960
ALICE CHILDRESS, writer, actress, director	October 12, 1920
ANN PETRY, writer	October 12, 1911
SAUNDERS REDDING, historian	October 13, 1906
RAYMOND ALEXANDER, lawyer, judge	October 13, 1898
SHIRLEY CAESER, gospel singer, religious leader	October 13, 1938
BEVERLY JOHNSON, first black supermodel	October 13, 1952
LEON H. SULLIVAN, minister, entrepreneur, economic reformer	October 16, 1922
MAE C. JEMISON, first black woman astronaut, doctor, social servant	October 17, 1956
LERONE BENNET, journalist, executive editor of *Ebony*	October 17, 1928
JUPITER HAMMON, slave poet	October 17, 1711
WYNTON MARSALIS, composer, musician	October 18, 1961
NTOZAKE SHANGE, poet, playwright, performer, writer	October 18, 1948
TERRY MCMILLAN, novelist, editor, educator	October 18, 1951
CHUCK BERRY, rock 'n' roll legend	October 18, 1926
EVANDER HOLYFIELD, heavyweight boxing champion	October 19, 1962
JOHNETTA COLE, educator, first woman president of Spelman College	October 19, 1936
JENNIFER HOLLIDAY, Tony-winning actress, Grammy-winning singer	October 19, 1960
DIZZY GILLESPIE, jazz trumpeter	October 21, 1917
BOBBY SEALE, activist, cofounder of the Black Panther party	October 22, 1936

OCTOBER 23RD TO NOVEMBER 21ST

SCORPIO

THE SCORPION

THE SIGN OF THE INSPECTOR

◆

PASSIONATE, DETERMINED,

ENERGETIC

◆

Ruled by Mars and Pluto

COLOR: Dark Red

METAL: Steel

GEM: Topaz

LUCKY NUMBERS: 3 and 5

FORTUNATE DAY: Tuesday

THE SCORPIO VIBRATION

WHAT DO YOU WANT? PEOPLE BORN UNDER THE sign of the Scorpion think that they know. They might. They've probably studied you well enough. Scorpions like to study what makes people tick. They make excellent psychologists because in psychology they find work they can enjoy—delving into the human mind.

The Scorpio is the man or woman at the party with the deep-set eyes who seems always to be watching for something, waiting, observing deeply, examining. See if you can feel if he or she is secretive, even suspicious. See if there seems to be a lot of self-control of what would otherwise be a very emotion-tossed personality.

The Scorpio is the firm, determined doctor or researcher who moves with quiet dignity but obvious confidence in what he or she knows. The approach is almost religious with regard to the task at hand. The work is routine, hard, and wearisome, but no detail will be rushed. There is no foolishness. Nothing is taken lightly.

Or think about Dwight Gooden. Even at age twenty, when he began his major league baseball career, he amazed critics with his brooding seriousness. "He tries everything," one sportscaster said. "Nothing works. He keeps trying. He never loses his poise. Either he ain't twenty or he ain't human."

Or think about religion itself, think about Mahalia Jackson, whose songs the older generation always played during the joy or sorrow of transition. There is a knowingness in the songs and a quiet intensity.

I DESIRE are the key words of the sign, and it is in this vibration that emotional, mental, and physical desires reach their greatest intensity and focus.

The intensity of the desire produces the preference for secrecy, and the probing temperament has probably dug up enough evidence to justify the suspicions Scorpios have of most things and most people.

But the suspicions do not produce any primary insecurities as they often do in Pisceans or Cancerians. Scorpios can handle uncertainties because Scorpios themselves are so certain. Those born under the sign are usually very certain that they can come up with what is needed to handle whatever needs to be handled.

"We [African Americans] always have answered our oppressors with brave singing and dancing . . . the pith of the joy and sorrow in our unbreakable hearts. Ours is the truest dignity of man, the dignity of the undefeated" wrote Ethel Waters in her 1950 autobiography, *His Eye Is on the Sparrow*.

This dignity of the undefeated might not be the essence of the life experience for enterprising Capricorns or escapist Pisceans, but it is the badge that Scorpios are proudest of.

Scorpios have a firm sense of determination that can take on an almost religious intensity. Often their determination turns into a form of devotion to whatever it is they need to do to get what they desire.

Scorpios know what they want and they have the courage, willpower, and drive to get it, or the pride, self-control, and stubbornness to live without it.

Capricorn and Aries are also signs of great power and ambition, but Scorpios aren't simply seekers after a high place in life. They can settle at whatever they feel is their proper level. Scorpios know themselves. No other vibration is as relentlessly committed to facing reality, no matter how gloomy that reality might be. They know their own strengths and weaknesses, and they're not at all naive about what life requires and what it should reward.

There's very little self-delusion in the sign. Like everyone else, Scorpios may try to fool others, but they almost never try to fool themselves. They seldom overextend themselves. They sense exactly what they can and cannot do.

As the second water sign in the cycle of the zodiac, Scorpio, like the other water signs, Pisces and Cancer, is associated with emotional sensitivity. But whereas Cancer's extreme sensitivity forces its natives to protect themselves from the harshness of life, Scorpio plunges through the murky waters of the emotions to face life boldly, without fear or hesitation. That is the Scorpio goal, to unravel the deepest mysteries of the unconscious, to challenge any possible fears, and finally to make their actions correspond perfectly with their feelings. No other sign is as candidly introspective or conversely as unflinchingly aware of the gloomy aspects of the outside world.

As the sign of death and regeneration, Scorpios can destroy and create with the same intensity of passion. In this vibration all reality— even death—is felt and accepted unblinkingly. It is almost as if Scorpio natives have decided to live with an intensity based on their knowledge that any moment might be their last.

In Scorpio true self-confidence runs deeper than in any other sign. Scorpios might not brag or show off, because they don't have to. Anyone around them for a short time knows the deal.

People born under Scorpio are usually self-reliant and independent; they feel that others should be also. Therefore they are seldom soft-hearted or overly sentimental. Their natural metal is steel, and steel is a fitting symbol for their personalities. They feel that life is a difficult game in which they have to hang tough in order to win. The afflicted native can display an almost inhuman disregard for the feelings of others. No matter what the pain or suffering, the negative Scorpio often will offer little more than an unsettling silence.

But all this doesn't mean that individuals born with Sun in Scorpio are devoid of compassion. It does mean that when an abundance of sympathetic qualities are present, the explanation for them is likely to be found somewhere else in the individual's horoscope—perhaps their Venus or Moon is placed in a more compassionate sign, such as Libra or Cancer.

Scorpios often have a good sense of humor; they sometimes have fits of talkativeness—in fact they alternate between being silently watchful and overly chatty. When they are chatty, they are usually on the hunt.

They almost never play, that is, get involved with purposeless activity just for the fun of it. This does not mean that Scorpios are not fun-loving. It simply means that play is valued only when it is related in some direct way to the attainment of a particular desire.

Fun when it comes is intense, because it is almost always dedicated to the kind of rest, release, or relaxation that will enable the Scorpio to get back to the task. Scorpios are intense people who aren't happy unless they have some suitably interesting project to dedicate themselves to, some interesting activity that will absorb some of their incredible amount of nervous energy.

Scorpio, ruled as it is by both Mars and Pluto, is the most intense vibration in the zodiac. Many Scorpios fight a lifelong battle to master and control the explosive energy within themselves. They have an urgent need to discipline their strong desires, and because they have an equally strong will, they often succeed. But an unexplainable tension often re-mains—the visible evidence of their intense efforts at self-control.

Their powerful awareness of their own desires can make natives of this sign opinionated and stubborn. When their desires are not fulfilled, Scorpios can be the most jealous, resentful, vengeful, and relentless of all the signs. When Sagittarians don't get what they want, they might easily come to feel that something else is just as good anyway. Geminis might actually believe that they didn't really want whatever it was anyway. Even proud, purposeful Leos can rise above the frustration and the person who caused it, but Scorpios want revenge. Like the small noc-turnal, hard-shelled animal for which the sign is named, the Scorpio wants to sting whoever has frustrated it.

Scorpios are intuitive and inspirational, and very protective of the people to whom they are attached. Few parents are more devoted to their children than Scorpio parents. As a fixed sign Scorpio is very dependable and very prone to live up to any commitments that are honestly made. It is the most powerful sign of the zodiac, but in a world where power is often corrupt, it is easy to think about it only in negative terms and ignore all those Scorpios who control their power drives or use their power for the good of all who come under their protection.

In this regard a Scorpio can be as lofty as an eagle, which in ancient times was the emblem of the sign. Most natives of the eighth sign have eyes like an eagle's. No matter how happy, the eyes seldom seem to smile; they are always penetrating. The eagle sits and watches. No one knows what he or she is thinking, and he or she is certainly not inclined to volunteer the information.

Still, the eagle is among the most noble of creatures and is used in the flags of many nations to symbolize intense loyalty. Scorpios have great ability to inspire such feelings; therefore they make great leaders. Many people find it easy to follow them because of their single-minded commitment. The confidence they have in themselves inspires confidence in others. The eagle usually flies high and straight.

Their magnetism is hypnotic, and Scorpios often use their extraordinary sex appeal to help them establish and hold power. It isn't simply that they have a great capacity for sex; their power is more subtle than that. They have stamina, intensity, and control. When they're "there" sexually, they're all there. Whether engaged in sexual intercourse or not, their focus can be very unsettling. Insecure people feel drawn to them.

In the eighth sign there is also a fascination with drugs and alcohol. Problem drinkers and addicts are not unusual among Scorpios. Alcoholism and drug addiction are regarded by them as tests of will. Scorpios sometimes like to see how close they can come to destruction and still regenerate themselves. Other Scorpios, aware of this, refuse to drink at all.

Scorpio's relationship to alcohol and drugs is similar to his relationship to sex. For months he can overindulge, pushing himself almost to the limit; then he can cut it off and do without altogether.

These Plutonic themes—sex, death, and regeneration—are all captured in a scene in the novel *Blues Child Baby,* by Scorpio George Cain, in which a young woman apparently dies of an overdose of heroin. She is miraculously revived, however, when her boyfriend makes love to her. The power of his sexual desire brings her back to life. Seriously.

RELATIONSHIPS

The complexity of the Scorpio personality is well illustrated in the way Scorpios relate to other people. The investigation of this complexity is a long and wayward trip, but it reflects much about the influence— small or large—of the Scorpio vibration.

Scorpios are somewhat reserved, not out of shyness but out of a feeling that they don't owe anything to anyone and need not go very far out of their way to ingratiate themselves with strangers. This doesn't mean they're antisocial. They talk, they laugh, they joke, but not out of any real need to be thought well of by strangers. Their attitude is, "If you dig me, good. Here I am. If not, I won't go through many changes to get you to dig me, unless you've got something I want."

Scorpios' sense of authority doesn't come from what others think of them but from deep inside themselves. Often they're only barely conscious of whether other people approve or disapprove of them. Scorpios are secure enough not to worry too much about being disliked. Many of them live their entire lives without ever being vulnerable on the emotional level to anyone but the person they're in love with; and even in love relationships they're usually devoid of any posture that suggests dependence. Scorpios are often too proud to show that they need someone.

Often the Scorpio seems like a deep reservoir of emotions fed by underground springs, full of hidden currents and protected on all sides by high cliffs. There are no shallow edges, no places where a person can partially enter. You either stand outside and look or you come in all the way. If you enter, more often than not, you belong to Scorpio.

Since Scorpio is the sign in which self-control is most intense, it's only natural that Scorpios would feel urges to control anyone who belongs to them. They set high standards of self-discipline for themselves and extend those standards to the people with whom they're involved. Scorpios are severe judges and they can be quite contemptuous of people who are weak.

Many people think of Scorpio as an egotistical sign, but it isn't. Scorpios are goal centered, not ego centered. Pride is what people see and mistake for egotism. Being very goal oriented and self-contained, Scorpios are often very opportunistic. When they see their chance, they seize it, often forgetting about the consequences. No malice is intended. This is simply a natural expression of an aggressive personality. Scorpios' social relations are often marred by a tendency to argue or bicker, as well as by their habit of not opening up to many people, even the people they love.

LUCK, MONEY, AND WORK

Scorpio would be a hard-luck sign if Scorpios weren't such dynamic people. They thrive on adversity, which is good since they're likely to encounter more than their share of it. Scorpios aren't the kind of people who attract money; nearly every bit they get, they struggle for, but struggle they will because Scorpio is partially ruled by Mars, the god of competition and warfare.

Scorpios aren't overly materialistic, nor are they true lovers of luxury. They love power, but they seek only enough of it to satisfy their own goals. If the goals are modest, the power striving will be commensurate. Mars imparts a desire to work and earn and to judge one's worth on the basis of how many obstacles one overcomes. Scorpios hate to be outdone. They hate to lose. Therefore they are often excellent athletes.

Natives of the sign are careful with money, but Scorpio isn't a sign that promises great wealth. Wealth comes more often to people who think on abstract levels. Scorpios work hardest when they have a tangible material objective before them. When this is the case, they can be quite persevering and tenacious, with a great ability to stay on the job and perform well long after others have gotten tired, frustrated, or bored.

Scorpios can dedicate themselves to a single task for years; like a horse with blinders turning a grinding wheel, looking neither right nor left but straight ahead at the next step needed to get the job done. For instance the black mathematician and astronomer Benjamin Banneker, whom many called "The First Negro American Man of Science," lived most of his adult life alone on a farm, away from distractions. He was one of the primary architects who helped to lay out Washington, D.C. He worked methodically for years on his groundbreaking computation of the cycle of the seventeen-year locust.

In most Scorpios there's little desire to jump here, there, and everywhere in an unorganized, helter-skelter manner. Dedication and hard work rather than quick-witted adaptability are the keys to Scorpio's success. This is why Scorpios make good doctors, biologists, psychologists, chemists, and pharmacists.

Scorpios are advocates of force when necessary; thus they make good soldiers, policemen, corrections officers, private guards, and detectives. They also make ideal secret agents. If the CIA has a ruling sign, it is undoubtedly Scorpio.

Because they are decisive and thorough, they make good foremen, administrators, and supervisors; but they often have to curb tendencies to be too heavy-handed, bossy, and unforgiving. Scorpios like jobs with a lot of responsibility, but jobs like these aren't easy to find, especially for blacks. Although Scorpio is a powerful sign, there are fewer famous black people born under it than any other sign. Many Scorpios are undoubtedly too proud to take part in the psychological buck-dancing and shuffling that's often required for blacks to succeed in America.

Fortunately, some Scorpios can make themselves accept routine positions such as typist, clerical worker, bookkeeper, or keypunch operator. Discontent may boil beneath the surface for years, but these Scorpios will persevere—refusing to grin or "Tom" enough to reach the position his or her talent may deserve.

MENTAL AND PHYSICAL HEALTH

Scorpios don't fly apart easily. They take their troubles inside themselves and store them there. They're worriers, but it takes a lot of worrying to blow their minds. Danger, anxiety, boredom, fear, marital problems, and financial troubles don't drive them to high blood pressure as often as they do other people, Scorpios have means of escaping these pressures. They sometimes take flight into alcohol, drugs, or sexual overindulgence. They have an amazing ability to block out things they don't want to deal with and to keep on treading the mill until something good happens. Or they can relieve the pressure by criticizing others. Scorpio under pressure is even more critical than Virgo. Virgo criticizes to improve or perfect; Scorpio more often criticizes to wound or berate.

When Virgos see something wrong, they almost always speak out. But Scorpios can silently watch as things fall apart around them. They are often amused at others' foolishness and may gain strength from the knowledge that someone else is worse off than they are. This human tendency is great among Scorpios. In these instances the Scorpio assures himself that he's okay as long as the people around him are doing worse. If they endure, he will endure, for he is stronger and more unyielding than they.

Often Scorpios must escape their own brooding silence by using drugs or alcohol, but they have greater powers of regeneration than others. They can quit as abruptly as they start.

Scorpio is one of the most durable signs of the zodiac. The combination of energy and reserve assures a certain immunity to fatigue. Self-control and self-discipline allow them to reestablish their balance even after those periods of wounded withdrawal that are common to natives of the sign.

Physically Scorpios are robust people. They are, more often than not, slender but strong. Nervous energy burns up a lot of excess weight.

Scorpio rules the reproductive organs, and natives of the sign are susceptible to diseases affecting these areas. In fact most Scorpios have a lot of trouble with glandular infections.

LOVE AND SEX

If Taurus is the love machine, then Scorpio is her cousin—the sex machine. Libra knows more about romance; Pisces might display more subtle sensuousness and emotional responsiveness. Sagittarius knows better how to hunt and catch. But when it comes to well-focused sexual desire, Scorpio has no equal. But contrary to what most people think, Scorpio's sexual ability is not derived as much from the physical as it is from their emotional intensity. The sexual encounter, like nearly everything in a Scorpio's life, is addressed with total commitment to actualizing their feelings. Sex, which involves a tremendous amount of emotional energy, is brought to its pinnacle with Scorpio because no other sign is more in touch with its deepest, often darkest, unsuppressed emotions.

Scorpios have a great deal of animal magnetism. They provoke sexual curiosity. "I wonder what he's like," women ask about the Scorpio man. "I wonder how she'd be," men ask about the Scorpio woman. The answer to both questions is "good, passionate, orgasmic." Natives of this sign do not have to search very far for potential lovers. People are usually drawn to them. Scorpios are the most sexually secure of all the signs. They almost never doubt themselves in this area; thus both male and female Scorpios attract more than their share of partners who are sexually confused.

Still, most Scorpios would rather settle the sexual side of their lives by finding that rare someone with passions equal to their own. They'd like to have this done with so that they can dedicate their energies to other things. For them sex is a stimulus and inspiration for creativity in other fields. They want to be about their life's work.

Love may be a game for others. A Libra, for example, often finds love a pleasant pastime full of humor, flattery, and romance. Libras might enjoy a little teasing and/or flirting, but with Scorpio love is most often an intense, tightly bound relationship with no cheating, no games, and no flirtation. Passion and emotional commitment are the key words, not playfulness.

In genuine love Scorpios are supportive, loyal, dependable, and dedicated. They expect their partners to match them. The legal ties of marriage are extremely important to them. Home and family life mean a great deal. They make good parents, even though they may be a little too strict at times. Although they're a bit difficult to live with, they make good husbands or wives. They are eager to trust deeply so that they can start planning some ambitious joint project, but they quickly draw away from anyone they feel they can't trust. They often come to need more reassurance than anyone can easily give. They can be tender and affectionate only if they're very, very sure that they're not being fooled. They're often reluctant to show too much love for fear that the would-be lover might be secretly laughing at them.

Obviously they would come to distrust sentimentality. They become suspicious of too much mush and tenderness. In love, as in all other areas, they're extremely realistic. They're often accused of being inhibited about displaying the romantic conversation or gestures that others may expect in a relationship. They're also accused of being more interested in sex than in emotional attachment. Neither charge is quite accurate, but it is true that in many circumstances jealousy, caution, or suspicion is the emotion that dominates the relationship.

In this world full of game players, it's hard for serious Scorpios to fall in love. Sometimes they have to become game players themselves, which is dangerous because they are very good at it. They can be sly sexual manipulators. They find it easy to turn their passions on for someone they don't love if that is in some way useful, such as the doctor in Seattle who was supported through medical school by a woman he said he didn't love. "She knew I didn't love her. She kept hoping and going to work every day bringing money home. Sometimes in bed she'd ask me if I loved her and I couldn't say I did. I wouldn't say anything. Those words mean a lot."

The woman is now his wife. He says he doesn't know what love is, but he's not thinking of divorce—she's good to him.

LOVE AFFAIRS

(See the other chapters for love affairs between
Scorpio men and women of other signs.)

SCORPIO WOMAN, ARIES MAN

At last a man whose passions and ambitions are equal to your own. He would be great if you two could get along better. If you were teamed together fighting for something, you would be almost unbeatable. What he lacks in perseverance and patience you can supply. What you lack in optimism and idealism he has in abundance. The sexual vibrations are not bad either. You both enjoy a lot of good physical lovemaking. Actions mean more than words. Physical satisfaction is more important than sensual stimulation. The big problem is that you both are aggressive, domineering, and quarrelsome. You both like to interfere in the life of anyone you fall in love with. You will try to make him more stable, thrifty, and patient, and he'll want you to be more adaptable, affectionate, and forgiving. When the battles come, they could be big ones. You should avoid them at almost any cost.

SCORPIO WOMAN, TAURUS MAN

Often Taurus men are a little too lazy and easygoing for an intense, energetic woman like you. But sexually there could be no better match. Both of you enjoy the physical side of lovemaking, and no two people are more likely to overindulge. Taurus likes to take the romantic approach, but he is not foolishly sentimental. He plays love games, but he is loyal and steadfast enough to let you know that he is also very serious. You bring drive and ambition to the relationship and he brings sensuality and artistic taste. But there is a strong jealous streak in both of you, and no two people can be more violently stubborn. Both of you are very goal oriented, so it would be better if you were working together toward a goal; that would also provide excitement for a relationship that could easily get dull and bogged down. If the relationship were to become too unchallenging, you might get quarrelsome and critical, not caring that he can't stand to be criticized.

SCORPIO WOMAN, GEMINI MAN

It won't take the two of you long to discover that you weren't made for each other, but you can both make yourself over to fit. Gemini men are often attracted to challenges, and Scorpio women often like to be someone's challenge. Do it if you can. But no two people are better designed to drive each other crazy. Scorpio women are jealous and possessive, and Gemini men need freedom. Scorpio women like a nice, settled life, and Gemini men are bored by routine. He is not deeply romantic, but he says a lot of romantic things. If you happen to believe any of them and find out later that he was only playing games, you'll be aching for revenge, but if he can do what is necessary to make you believe him, you'll love his serenade. You must remember that it may not be that he is lying, it's just that he changes from one day to the next. His is a quick, risk-taking, mental vibration. Yours is a cautious and secretive emotional one. But there is a lot of benefit that you both can get from staying in the relationship and giving each other a lot of distance. It is tough, but it can be interesting for someone who is quick, curious, and emotionally superficial like he is to be in love with someone who is steady, emotionally deep, and passionate like you are.

SCORPIO WOMAN, CANCER MAN

He's the kind of man who might annoy the hell out of you and you won't be able to figure out why you love him. But of all men, he is the kind you could probably love most deeply. He shows all of that emotionalism that you hide, but after a while you'll feel safe in showing yours too. He seems dependable and gentle enough. Yet he is strong, and he loves to be deeply involved. His feelings will be a little too easy to hurt, and you are just the lady to hurt them. But he is patient and loyal enough to wait for you to open up and show your vulnerability. You might be more passionate than he is, but he has the kind of sexual imagination that should make the lovemaking better than good.

SCORPIO WOMAN, LEO MAN

This one could start off well. Both of you have a lot of natural magnetism, and Mr. Leo can be very affectionate, generous, and romantic when the affair is new. He really wants to be loved and appreciated, and he will go all out, but if you are not as enthusiastic and responsive as he thinks you should be, he might try to be bullying and overbearing. And you know that won't work. We need to hope that he learns it too. You each can be proud, domineering, and stubborn. You can be somewhat critical, and he hates to be criticized. You are cautious by nature, and he is forever gambling with life. A lot of arguments could arise over money. Leo men like to be served, and you are the kind who can cater to a man if he also caters to you. But Leo doesn't do it naturally. He must teach himself to give as much as he gets in this department. He certainly can be generous with things, and you like that. The challenge is for two stubborn people not to be stubborn with regard to each other, and to get all of that synchronized.

SCORPIO WOMAN, VIRGO MAN

This could turn out to be a good, solid, security-conscious love affair. The two of you are very much alike, yet different enough to make life interesting. First of all you are both practical, realistic, cautious, and patient. You are the kind of people who know that life is not a bed of roses, so you won't expect love to always be a dewy-eyed experience. You won't blind yourselves to each other's faults. You both tend to analyze and criticize, but you both hate to be analyzed and criticized. This could be the cause of innumerable arguments. Of course the Scorpio woman will win almost all of these, but most Virgo men don't mind giving in after they've had some time to pout. Scorpio is a much more passionate sign than Virgo, but most Virgos will go out of their way, extending themselves to the limit, to please. Though Virgo men are not overly emotional, they can be masters of technique and they can be very physically satisfying. Virgo fussing and worrying over Scorpio won't always make her happy, but it can serve to assure her that she's loved.

SCORPIO WOMAN, LIBRA MAN

Libras like to play at love, but even though playing, they're really in love. That's the meaning of love to them: It is related to fun. You like to have fun in love, too, but you are much more serious-minded about matters of the heart. Libras tease and flirt, but this kind of playing might start jealous Scorpio to playing, and when Scorpio plays, she's serious. She will put malice in the game. This is only one of the differences between a Scorpio woman, who takes life so seriously, and Mr. Libra, who is likely to be rather casual about many things. Be careful, he does know how to flee. He's easy to get along with, not passionate, but he can be very sexy in his way. At times he might seem somewhat lazy and indecisive but very accommodating. On balance he will probably think that he's a pretty good catch, so he won't understand if you fluctuate so much between jealousy and unconcern or why you are so often discontented with him when he so often comes to you well groomed, pleasant-tempered, and smiling.

SCORPIO WOMAN, SCORPIO MAN

Not that there won't be fights. There'll be plenty of those, but fighting never broke up a love affair between two people who think that strife is a necessary part of life. If mutual recrimination does not drive you apart, mutual suspicion might keep you each in line. Of course, the other things match as well. You are both very careful with money. You are both rather reserved about meeting new people, but very loyal to tried-and-true friends. You are both either very ambitious or very self-controlled and dependable. But there is a tendency toward over-indulgence from which neither will be able to save the other if it ever gets out of hand. Drinking, drugs, sex, or pessimism could become excessive. But deep love and high achievement could also result from the wedding of Scorpio to Scorpio.

SCORPIO WOMAN, SAGITTARIUS MAN

Ruby Dee and Ossie Davis know that this one can work. It worked for them for over thirty years. Curious Sagittarius wants to know what's inside that hidden well of emotions. For this reason he might find you an interesting woman at whom to fire his arrow and gallop in for a good time. You enjoy a good time, but not an in-for-some-fun-and-out-again love affair. "No, make up your mind," you'll say. He'll make up his mind, but he has trouble keeping it made up in the same way. Periodically the sexual vibrations will be good, and you will find it a challenge to try to change his in-again-out-again style. He loves that style and does not mean to be insulting. He rebels against anything confining. He dislikes jealousy, and his restless nature will get on your nerves almost as quickly as his careless attitude toward money. In fact he is careless about a lot of things that you are serious about. He loves to argue, but he is not stubborn enough to win many arguments against you. When you withdraw into icy silence, his first impulse will be to grab his coat and ride, and it will be up to you to welcome him back, for many good reasons, or to tell him to keep riding.

SCORPIO WOMAN, CAPRICORN MAN

This is the kind of relationship that could work out even after you've discovered how different you two are. Each of you is very ambitious and you're each likely to admire that about the other. Both can be very headstrong and aggressive, but Capricorns know how to back down if it serves their own best interest. You both will have to curb tendencies to nag and mess with each other. If you both have separate careers, you won't have much time for a relationship, since each is very inclined to live a career-centered life. But as housewives you Scorpio women are well suited for aggressive, ambitious husbands like Capricorn men are likely to be. You are very supportive and love to be involved. Capricorns are very good at taking the kind of good, practical advice that you are good at giving, and you often have a better understanding of the nuances and subtle meanings of situations than he has. You can save him from a lot of career snares that he is not intuitive or complex enough to see. Both of you have strong physical sexual appetites. Neither is lighthearted enough to lift the other out of a bad mood, but your natural talent for seduction will make him feel wanted and needed. You will feel very much in control of the emotional side of the sexual situation, and this will increase your ability to arouse his strong physical potential. This one could work out quite well.

SCORPIO WOMAN, AQUARIUS MAN

The fact that you are different wouldn't matter half as much if you both were not so stubborn. Fortunately there is usually very little initial attraction between you. You are likely to see Mr. Aquarius as rather dryly playful, coldly logical, detached emotionally, or, to your mind, needlessly rebellious. He may even be something of a bohemian. None of this really appeals to you. He is likely to see you as a rather closed, secretive person who is too possessive and jealous and too restricted in outlook for a free spirit like himself. Both of you are quick-tempered and love to fight. Aquarians are seldom controlled by consuming sexual passions. Friendship is often more important. But they are often sexually free since sex is not so important that it needs to be confined to one partner. Scorpios are passionate and think that sex is very important and should be confined. This may be the rock that the relationship either steps over or upon which it stumbles. If each gives the other a lot of room, there could be a very enduring relationship.

SCORPIO WOMAN, PISCES MAN

Both of you are rather curious and probing, so you're likely to know a lot about each other before you get into a love affair. And there's a lot about each other that you won't like. A Scorpio woman won't understand why a man can be so indecisive and unsure of himself, as Pisces men often are. And a Pisces man will be hurt by someone who can be as blunt and sarcastic as you can be. But sometimes he enjoys a little sting as much as you enjoy stinging. You might have to take charge of family finances because he is likely to be somewhat careless with money. And you might have to give him a push every once in a while because of his tendency to procrastinate. However, Scorpio Shirley Graham Du Bois, who was a playwright and activist, seems to have had a most successful marriage to W.E.B. Du Bois, the great Pisces scholar. "One of the reasons I married him," she said, "was because I knew he needed help . . . to carry on the work that he was doing. . . . Whatever I was doing seemed so insignificant compared to what he was doing that I let it all go so I could devote myself to him and his needs." How much more can anyone want than that?

SCORPIO

(OCTOBER 23RD TO NOVEMBER 21ST)

PELÉ, Brazilian soccer star	October 23, 1940
MAHALIA JACKSON, singer, "The Gospel Queen"	October 26, 1911
EDWARD W. BROOKE, U.S. senator, Massachusetts	October 26, 1919
EMANUEL CLEAVER, mayor of Kansas City, Missouri	October 26, 1944
RUBY DEE, actress, social and political activist	October 27, 1924
LEN WILKINS, basketball star and coach	October 28, 1937
MELBA MOORE, actress, singer, comedienne	October 29, 1945
ETHEL WATERS, singer, dancer, actress	October 31, 1900
SIPPIE WALLACE, blues singer, songwriter	November 1, 1898

IKE TURNER, musician, creator of *The Ike and Tina Turner Revue*	November 5, 1931
SHARON MCPHAIL, lawyer, National Bar Association president	November 6, 1948
THEODORE BERRY, Cincinnati mayor	November 8, 1905
JAMES MC GEE, Dayton, Ohio, mayor	November 8, 1918
BOB GIBSON, baseball star	November 9, 1935
BENJAMIN BANNEKER, mathematical wizard, inventor, lay astronomer, essayist	November 9, 1731
DOROTHY DANDRIDGE, actress, singer, nightclub entertainer	November 9, 1922
MICHAEL SCHULTZ, director	November 10, 1938
SHIRLEY GRAHAM DU BOIS, political activist, writer, playwright, composer, director	November 11, 1904
WHOOPI GOLDBERG, award-winning actress, comedienne, social activist	November 11, 1950
LAVERN BAKER, singer	November 11, 1929
BERT WILLIAMS, banjo-playing balladeer, comedian, entertainer	November 12, 1874
YAPHET KOTTO, screen actor	November 15, 1937
YOLANDA KING, civil rights activist	November 17, 1955
WARREN MOON, football star	November 18, 1956
HOWARD THURMAN, theologian, minister, author	November 18, 1900
ROY CAMPANELLA, legendary catcher for professional baseball	November 19, 1921
TEVIN CAMPBELL, pop singer	November 19, 1978
AHMAD RASHAD, sportscaster, NFL player	November 19, 1949
EARL MONROE, basketball star, "The Pearl"	November 21, 1944

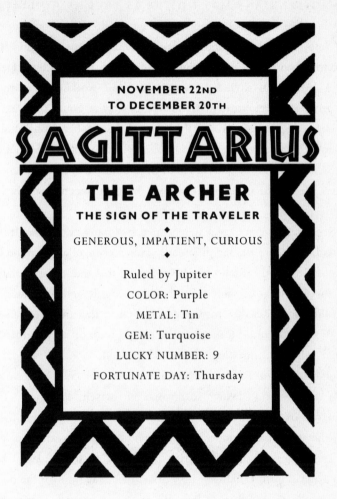

**NOVEMBER 22ND
TO DECEMBER 20TH**

SAGITTARIUS

THE ARCHER

THE SIGN OF THE TRAVELER

◆

GENEROUS, IMPATIENT, CURIOUS

◆

Ruled by Jupiter

COLOR: Purple

METAL: Tin

GEM: Turquoise

LUCKY NUMBER: 9

FORTUNATE DAY: Thursday

THE SAGITTARIUS VIBRATION

SAGITTARIANS MAY NOT BE AS FREE AS AQUARIANS, but they are usually prouder of their freedom. An Aquarian might know that she "cannot be bought and will not be sold," but a Sagittarian like Modjeska Simkins loves to say it. Simkins, born December 5, 1899, kept an independent voice while working in more than fifty progressive reform organizations in her native South Carolina.

Unbought and Unbossed was the name of the autobiography of Shirley Chisholm, who made her way up through the clubhouse politics of Brooklyn in the 1950s and 1960s to become the first African-American woman elected to Congress. Chisholm kept an uncompromisingly independent voice.

Sagittarians seem to seek independence of mind rather than freedom of mind, and there is a big difference. True seekers of a free mind enjoy being alone and they don't like being bound to a quest. Sagittarians are very social, yet at the same time they are more bound to a quest than any other sign. Still they manage to hold on to their independence.

Who can think of a more independent group of women than Tina Turner, wife of controlling Scorpio Ike; Eslanda Goode Robeson, wife of dominating Paul Robeson; Dionne Warwick, the cool, haughty songstress who seems to belong to no one but herself; and Cicely Tyson, the actress in Hollywood who has more consistently than any others of her generation turned down roles she simply did not wish to play?

Then there are the Sagittarian politicians, such as Adam Clayton Powell and Ronald Dellums, who worked their way through the political clubs in their own districts but still came out accurately announcing themselves as mavericks.

Sagittarius is the sign of the independent mind bound to the endless search for the meaning of life. This search will take them to faraway places on the globe or into the mysteries of human psychology or spirituality.

Sagittarius can be the most optimistic sign of the zodiac. People born under it forever try to look on the brighter side of life. They always expect the best, but even when the worst happens, they usually suffer disaster with short-lived sadness and quickly resume their cheerful outlook. They tend to see people in an idealistic light even when they should know better. They're straightforward and direct to the point of being tactless, and this makes them justly famous for saying the wrong thing at the wrong time, for insulting people without even knowing they've done so, and for speaking impulsively without thinking about the consequences. Sagittarius is the truth seeker, and whether the individual Sagittarian has found the truth or not, she or he will certainly say what has been found.

For all their seeking of truth and independence there are few true revolutionaries among Sagittarians. Sagittarians are teachers who urge others to find freedom and independence within whatever social structures already exist.

The key words of the sign are I SEE. For Sagittarians the ongoing quest is to see what is over there, or in there, or out there. They seek to expand their consciousness through the gathering of experience, to move ever closer to the truth and to mold those truths into meaningful principles. No sign in the zodiac bases its actions so definitively on its own principles.

And when they perceive what they take to be the truth, no sign is more determined to make others aware of it. They're poor at keeping secrets but good at giving advice, even when it is not asked for. In fact many of them have the tiresome habit of insistently telling other people how to run their lives.

Sagittarius is in many ways one of the most adaptable of signs. It is self-adjusting because nothing is really all that important except the quest. It is self-compensating because it seems to know instinctively what is good and bad for the quest. Sagittarians could live fairly healthy, tension-free lives if they weren't always trying to determine what is right for others.

They are helpful, generous people with great sympathy for the underdog. They often assist many people without ever expecting anything in return, but they can also take from many people and return nothing since their relationships with any specific people can be quite casual.

Self-acceptance is one of Sagittarian's most prominent traits—they are usually quite fond of themselves. This is why many Sagittarians can seem so conceited, opinionated, and egotistical. Most of them are in a lifelong struggle to live their lives on something approaching their own often egocentric terms. When Sagittarian Sammy Davis, Jr., sang "I did it my way," he was singing the theme song of the sign. And although we may not always agree with what he did, you have to admit that no one did it with quite as much self-satisfaction.

Sagittarians do not like to take orders or to be supervised, and when they're locked into situations that are too confining, they can become extremely rebellious and disruptive. There is a great deal of wanderlust in the sign, making natives restless and eager for travel and change. But their need to wander can degenerate into a desire to escape all responsibility.

In these cases marriage and parenthood can become little more than burdensome impositions. Sagittarians will often withdraw from any relationship in which they can't have their own way. "If you want me around, you have to let me be," their actions seem to say.

Sagittarius is a dual sign like Gemini, Pisces, and Virgo. That's why people who know them often complain that they never know what to expect. One day nothing offends them; the next day they're quick-tempered and combative. They may argue or fight over something that wouldn't have fazed them two weeks before. Sometimes they're open-minded and tolerant; at other times they're the world's greatest nags. They may love everyone on Sunday and by Tuesday not care about anyone.

The Sagittarian comic genius Richard Pryor not only reflected the sign's bold, straightforward approach but also mirrored the striking duality of the Sagittarian personality in his brutally honest stage humor. Described as "crass but sensitive, streetwise and cocky but still somehow diffident and anxious," Pryor used both his rebellious, extroverted side and his vulnerable, introspective side in his comedy. He slipped easily from direct insult to sly innuendo or candid self-acceptance, warts and all.

A similar dichotomy is found in most Sagittarians. One side is fiery, extroverted to the point of boisterousness, freedom-loving to the point of rebelliousness, and always on the go; the other is quiet, philosophical, and fond of learning and teaching. This duality is reflected in the sign's symbol—the Centaur—which is half human, half animal.

The human is a wise man pointing his arrow toward the heavens seeking wisdom and knowledge; the animal is a frisky pony who wants, more than anything else, to romp freely in life's pastures. This is why the Sagittarian personality can seem so contradictory—even-tempered yet restless, cautious yet carefree, concerned about the future yet wasteful and extravagant. They seem not to want much for themselves, but often they are poised to exploit any situation for their own advantage.

Astrologers sometimes wrongly suggest that the Sagittarian woman is the quiet one while the Sagittarian man is the footloose extrovert. This is not true. All Sagittarians reflect this duality. Beneath the quiet exterior of the most domestic Sagittarian housewife beats the heart of an adventurer; beneath the buoyant exterior of the Sagittarian adventurer and roadrunner is a philosopher.

Sagittarius is the sign of the teacher or counselor, and Sagittarians are often their own best pupils. They know that they tend to be impatient, so they teach themselves patience. They know that they like the finer things in life, but they can train themselves to enjoy the "simple pleasures"—sunshine, fresh air, and good friends. A Sagittarian man or woman who tends toward the quiet side loves nothing better than puttering around the house, thinking and socializing with friends. They may be sages who love study and philosophical inquiry, but they are not intellectuals in the sense that Virgos are, nor are they as logical as Aquarians. They seek not intellectuality but wisdom, the fruit of learning applied to living a pleasant life. This is the side of the personality that produces a genuinely affectionate, sentimental, honest, and devoted nature. Self-control and self-adjustment are the personal keynotes.

Their rebelliousness often leads them to think of themselves as social reformers, but the most discussed aspect of this vibration is the extravagant or philandering side—the Sagittarian who is the fire-sign cousin of flamboyant Leo and aggressive Aries. This is the side reflected by brash, outspoken, clever, independent, blunt, and sarcastic, but generally good-intentioned people such as Adam Clayton Powell, Jr., Shirley Chisholm, Redd Foxx, Flip Wilson, and Richard Pryor. These Sagittarians love politics, show business, and all public occasions. Nothing pleases them more than a chance to talk in front of a large crowd. They're alert and quick, so many become public speakers, comedians, or politicians. They are usually not especially musically inclined, but many of them become singers because they are excellent at phrasing—Sammy Davis, Jr., Dionne Warwick, Lou Rawls, and Tina Turner are examples of Sagittarians who can turn a song into a meaningful story of truth.

RELATIONSHIPS

Sagittarians like to think of themselves as the friendliest creatures of the zodiac. They're usually quite talkative and cheerful. They love to mingle. They like to stroke others and to be stroked. They lose track of time when they are enjoying a social occasion. They genuinely like people and assume that people like them.

They take things to a personal level very quickly. They are often nosy and tend to pry into other people's personal lives, and they're not at all reluctant to reveal very personal things about themselves. They're almost never secretive, and they are impatient with people who refuse to open themselves up to their vast Sagittarian curiosity.

Sagittarius is among the most democratic of the signs. This is why its natives, who are often so narrowly determined, may seem so open-minded. They enjoy socializing with people from all strata of society and they have very little snobbery or elitism on a social level. They often disregard the differences of caste and class and treat everyone with impartiality. They like to rub shoulders with the high and mighty, but they're not deeply impressed by rank—unless it's their own, and sometimes not even then. In short, Sagittarians are hard to impress but very eager to be impressive.

There is a casualness of speech, dress, and manner that endears Sagittarians to many but that signifies to others a looseness, even sloppiness of character. Although they're easy to know casually, it's often extremely difficult to tie them into any close relationship. These children of the universe easily cooperate with others as long as their own interests are being served. They enter relationships for the simple joy of sharing, but they're quick to recognize any potential personal value in all they encounter. They're generous people, but not selflessly so. They are extremely giving, but they don't like to owe too much of themselves or too much of their time to other people. Of all the signs only Aquarians are more resentful of authority.

At heart Sagittarians really are reformers. They want to sweep away the old ways of doing things and start a new system under which all people will be free and equal. Adam Clayton Powell, Jr., the great congressional reformer who seemed to have too much fun being a reformer to be taken seriously, and "unbought and unbossed" former congresswoman Shirley Chisholm are typical examples of this Sagittarian trait. But no matter what the system they were reared under, they would probably challenge it. The point is, they despise systems because systems seem to constrain people.

For all these reasons Sagittarians are not as easygoing and friendly as they like to believe they are. They can be aggressive, pushy, and inconsiderate of others. But they are generous enough to almost never find themselves friendless.

LUCK, MONEY, AND WORK

Sagittarians have every reason to believe in luck, for they are among the zodiac's luckiest people. They are gamblers. They like to play hunches because their intuition is usually good. They often seem to take a devil-may-care attitude toward money and life, but most of their risks are well calculated, and there is a great deal of hidden caution behind the carefree facade. Though they often seem to be giving more than they get, or to waste more than they save, they are usually very aware of how much will end up back in their own hands.

The ruling planet of the sign is Jupiter, which is called "The Greater Fortune." It's said that if Jupiter is for you, then no one can prevail against you. Sagittarians are the kind of people who go to the racetrack knowing nothing about horses and win the biggest daily double of the season. They're forever finding themselves in the right place at the right time. Theirs is a money sign—not in the way that Taurus is, but a money sign nonetheless. People born under Taurus are better at saving money and investing it in homes and real estate. Sagittarians know how to make it faster, but they can also think of a million ways to throw it away. They are opportunists. Many of the world's great fortunes were made by Sagittarians. Sagittarius is the sign of daring, active money.

Because of their skill in handling people, their broad vision, and their natural sense of authority, they make good executives. Although they can be somewhat lazy and careless when working at lower-salaried jobs, they have amazing amounts of energy and endurance when working for their own profit. They do not accept hard work as the fate of mankind. They'll work very hard if there's a chance that they won't have to work long.

Sagittarians like working outdoors if the job doesn't require heavy manual labor. They are people who don't normally like to work with their hands. Few of them are good craftspeople. They like working with words and ideas. A traveling-salesman job is ideal. They are fascinated with faraway places. Many of them find their way into some branch of the travel industry.

They like office work only if they are given plenty of freedom to work in their own disorganized but effective manner. They are attracted to the public relations field and to the clergy. They make good teachers in the free and experimental school systems. They make good journalists, lawyers, and social workers, and excellent promoters because they're intrigued by get-rich-quick schemes.

If they end up in jail, they're seldom guilty of crimes of violence. They are more likely to commit mental crimes, such as fraud, misappropriation, and forgery. They're not as slick as they think they are, and when they lie, the only people they consistently convince are themselves.

PHYSICAL AND MENTAL HEALTH

Sagittarians are very active, healthy people. They love the outdoor life and often excel at sports: Bo Jackson, a star in football and baseball, and basketball superstars Oscar Robertson and Kevin Johnson, are fine examples. They are not callous either in actions or in temperament. Often, like Aquarians, they demonstrate a blending of many secondary sex characteristics. For example, Sagittarian men often have soft, feminine eyes with naturally curly eyelashes and a softness of disposition, which they try to hide behind a rough, aggressive, supermasculine facade. Good-looking Sagittarian men are often cute or even pretty, but they're seldom ruggedly handsome. Many women of the sign are boyishly handsome rather than lovely. They have firm, athletic bodies, but are seldom superfeminine. They often seem more at home in jeans or tailored suits than in dainty little dresses. As children many of them were tomboys.

Sagittarius rules the thighs. Consequently in middle years Sagittarians have a great tendency to put on weight in the thighs and buttocks.

A good exercise program is therefore very important for them as they approach their middle years.

Most Sagittarians have a great need for fresh air, sunshine, and a lot of space. This need is as much psychological as it is physical because they are prone to suffer claustrophobic restlessness if they are mentally, physically, or emotionally penned in for a long period of time. In fact Sagittarians are not good at dealing with sustained emotional pressure. It affects their stomachs and nervous systems. Ulcers, high blood pressure, and nervous disorders are common among those Sagittarians who find themselves locked into situations from which they cannot escape.

Still, footloose Sagittarians are seldom depressed for very long. A more common mental problem is dissociation from reality. They are so eager to appear untouched that they refuse to see situations as they are. They want everyone to think that they are doing fine. They doggedly continue to believe that things are really happening for the best. The latter part of the career of Congressman Adam Clayton Powell, Jr., reflects this trait. Refusing to admit that his power base among black people had eroded and that racists in Congress had succeeded in destroying his reputation, he left for Bimini. He took along a beautiful woman, surrounded himself with comrades, and appeared before photographers smiling, enjoying himself, and apparently unconcerned about his political problems. He pretended to love Scotch and milk, but the milk was there to soothe his eroded stomach. This escapist pattern is common among Sagittarians. They can easily lie to themselves and others to make things seem better than they are. They keep their spirits up even when life is falling down around them.

LOVE AND SEX

The quiet side of Sagittarius produces good lovers. They're "friends and lovers, too," as Sagittarian Dionne Warwick sings. During long love affairs Sagittarians seem to slip from passion into an easygoing familiarity with their mates. The relationship takes on more of the elements of friendship than of sexual love. They are tender and affectionate. They're usually quite conventional in their lovemaking and in their attitude toward all sexual matters, but they're warm, generous, protective, tolerant, and supportive. They can be quite sentimental, romantic, and demonstrative at one moment and gone the next.

Sagittarians are often almost foolishly idealistic, especially when young, and if the love they find approximates their ideal, they can be among the most faithful lovers in the zodiac. But love is seldom ideal, and most of them are disappointed very soon. This produces a subconscious fear of romantic attachments that can last a lifetime. It produces emotional insecurity that is often worked out by openly seeking many sexual conquests. Sagittarians have the kind of easy charm that makes them great at getting in and out of one superficial relationship after another. They flirt, they love, but they are seldom caught. The minute a relationship begins to mellow, they become restless. They begin searching for faults in their partners, and they find good excuses to be off like frisky ponies in search of other fields to play in.

This is only when the pattern is taken to extremes, but it is surprising how many Sagittarians do so. The world becomes a big sexual playground for them. They are often accused of emotional superficiality at best and dishonesty at worst. The truth is that they do mean what they say when they're saying it; but when they're whispering the same sweet words to another lover, they also mean that.

These Sagittarians will stay married only as long as they are given freedom to come and go as they please. The sex drive of the sign is really not as strong as many Sagittarians want others to believe. Quiet Sagittarians readily admit this and settle into cozy love affairs, while the others philander and make sure everyone knows about it. They like to pretend to be doing much more than they're actually doing. Many of them have a strange compulsion to tell one lover about their other lovers; it is not a compulsion to confess but a clever way of bragging. As it must be for those Sagittarians who have made their multiple love affairs very public—Sammy Davis, Gordon Parks, Adam Clayton Powell, Tina Turner, Richard Pryor, and Berry Gordy, just to name a few.

This is part of the legacy of the ruling planet Jupiter. Jupiter is the planet of expansion. His most restless sons and daughters are forever trying to expand their horizons, to enlarge the areas of their experience. The animal half of old Sagittarius keeps moving, while the human half is forever aiming his arrow toward ever more distant objectives. Sagittarius can be the sign of the endless romantic quest, like the character in the Sterling Brown poem who says,

> I laks you' kin' of lovin'
> Ain't never caught you wrong,
> . . . .
> (But it's) Jes my name and jes' my habit
> To be Long Gone

LOVE AFFAIRS

*(See other chapters for love affairs between
Sagittarian men and women of other signs.)*

SAGITTARIUS WOMAN, ARIES MAN

This sexual hookup may be the best that can be found for a frisky woman like you. He is more romantic than you but a little less passionate. Like you he is warm, generous, and responsive, and both of you are idealistic and very much interested in a rich and varied social life. The best part is that you two see the world in pretty much the same terms. He is more openly ambitious than you, but he'll be delighted when he finds out how steadfast in your purpose you can be. This seemed to be what happened between Arien Paul Robeson and his wife, Sagittarian Eslanda Goode Robeson.

Sagittarian women can save Arien men from many mistakes brought on by impatience; you can lift his spirits when things do not go as well or as quickly as he thinks they should. He is fascinated by new ideas, so there is no better fellow adventurer for an adventurous woman like you. He can be a little domineering and possessive, and both of you like to argue. But you are both quick to forgive. The arguments and fights will be many, but the sweet times can be as sweet as either of you have any right to expect.

SAGITTARIUS WOMAN, TAURUS MAN

The initial attraction is likely to be quite strong, and the lovemaking might be good for a while. He is slow, sensual, fun-loving, comfort-seeking, and easy to get along with. He'll like you because you're fresh, energetic, full of good ideas, and very adaptable at first. You might try hard, but you can never be as serious and practical as he is about all the things that he thinks a person should be serious and practical about. After a while your restlessness will annoy him and his love for stability will bore you. He is methodical and likes life to slow down to a nice, leisurely pace. You like to keep things moving. He likes regularity and you like variety. Though he is a romantic, he can enjoy sex without a great deal of mental stimulation, while you like a lover to fire your mind before he gets to your body. You may soon need more inspiration than he gives if you are to be ready for the sexual weight he'll put you under. But the adjustments needed in this affair can be very good for both of you if you can hang in there.

SAGITTARIUS WOMAN, GEMINI MAN

This is a kind of mental relationship that must thrive on novelty, excitement, and freedom if it is to thrive at all. It is what, by all accounts, Cicely Tyson and Miles Davis found in each other during their long on-again, off-again romance. The fact that both Sagittarians and Geminis hate to cling or be clung to is a big plus. Cicely did say that because Miles wanted her to quit her career as an actress and go on the road with him, she chose not to marry him during their first four-year-long courtship. Later she reluctantly consented, but they broke up; however, the mental attraction pulled them back together again. With Gemini the meeting of the minds is usually never a problem and neither is the meeting of bodies. He is quick, sexy, experimental, a little detached, a little fickle, and quite uninhibited, like you. But to you his moods may seem to swing unpredictably from optimism to pessimism. He is always analyzing and dissecting himself, which is all right. But you'll resent it when he starts analyzing and dissecting you. You are sentimental, and he loves to attack anything that sounds like sentimentality. Both of you are moody, blunt, sarcastic, and quick-tempered. You don't like to fight, but you love to argue and insult. The saving grace is that neither of you carries a grudge very long.

SAGITTARIUS WOMAN, CANCER MAN

This is one of those attractions of opposites that sometimes works. Often Sagittarian women like to swim around in deeper emotional waters, and an affair with Mr. Cancer can be as deep as they come. He is sensitive and devoted, but he can be jealous and clinging. He'll find you romantic and sensitive, but you can also be superficial or fickle. He loves home life, and you get bored very easily with domestic routines. Sexually he is much more intense, serious, and stable than you are, so you might find him easy to manipulate. If you do it well enough, he is the kind who'll enjoy the game. If you're clumsy at it, he may withdraw into that famous shell, and you certainly don't have the patience to wait for him to come out. You both like travel. This is a good money combination if he can control your extravagant habits. But ideally he likes a woman he can protect and "mother," and you certainly aren't the type to let yourself get smothered that way. Ideally you like a man who lives free and easy. But there is often enough of an attraction between two people like you to keep you loving and testing each other for a good long while.

SAGITTARIUS WOMAN, LEO MAN

This love affair will have a lot of physical and verbal warmth. You both like to compliment others and have nice things said about you. You love to court and conquer. You find it easy to express yourselves, and both enjoy gifts, poems, music, fluttering hearts, and loads of sentimentality—fire to fire can result in infatuation and strong dramatic sexual attraction. He struts like the most masculine of men, and you can be the most understanding, supportive, and generous woman to the lion who has caught your fancy. The only danger here is that it might burn itself out too rapidly, and then he'll turn out to be far more domineering than you thought, and you'll probably be less subordinate and selfless than he thought. But because your views of the world are so similar, and because you are basically optimistic people, your long-term affair could survive a lot of clashing of egos and flare-ups of temper.

SAGITTARIUS WOMAN, VIRGO MAN

Even the Virgo who is an artist and a wanderer may not be loose enough for you. His rigid personality structure may seem too much like a straitjacket. You can't see why he's wearing it, and you certainly won't let him saddle you with it. He cares very much about order, structure, and details, and you can be among the most unstructured person in the world. He can be affectionate and charming, but he hates mushiness and sentimentality, and you thrive on these. He often has difficulty verbalizing his feelings, and you thrive on sweet words. He is cautious, critical, optimistic, wayward, and often nonchalant. Your relationship will have to survive getting on each other's nerves a lot. Still, this attraction of opposites may work on the sexual level; the tension between cool but secretly sexy Virgo and romantic, aggressive Sagittarius can keep things interesting. You Sagittarian women like challenge, and Mr. Virgo certainly is that.

SAGITTARIUS WOMAN, LIBRA MAN

If friendship is the better part of love, then you two are made for each other. You make great friends. He is not hard for you to understand, and though he's not much like you, you can understand him without much trouble. You both need a lot of freedom, so you are willing to give a lot. You are both attractive, optimistic, and extroverted people who want nothing more than an easy, uncomplicated life. You might have to call in outside help to keep the checkbook balanced and the bills paid on time. There had better be a lot of money coming in, for there certainly will be a lot going out. Libras hate discord and disharmony close at hand, and Sagittarians sometimes stir up trouble just for the excitement of it, but the sexual vibrations are good. You both think that love should be a lighthearted romp, full of good times, sweet words, playful sex, and music, but not too much jealousy and brooding.

SAGITTARIUS WOMAN, SCORPIO MAN

This affair can run smoothly only as long as you do not insist on being yourself, for your real self will surely bring out the worst in a Scorpio male. Then it might become open warfare. According to Tina Turner and others, this is what happened between her and husband Ike. When she started to assert herself, the conflict began. The Scorpio man will not feel confident with you unless he can bring you under control. He usually needs to dominate before he can freely love. He is always passionate and sexual, but he usually does not show a great deal of tenderness and affection to someone unless he is absolutely sure of them. He is cautious, suspicious, secretive, and competitive if you don't belong to him, and you are not the kind who really ever "belongs" to anyone. He is emotional but not sentimental or romantic. He can be sarcastic and critical; if you start an argument with him, he'll never back down, and he always finds it hard to forgive and forget, but you can. The weight in this regard is on you, but there are rewards if you take it.

SAGITTARIUS WOMAN, SAGITTARIUS MAN

Because you so thoroughly approve of yourself, it is natural that you'd approve of someone else who is also optimistic, cheerful, idealistic, and interested in life in all its variety. You will approve of his need for freedom because you have the same need. He is, like you, generous, affectionate but a little detached, clever, restless, and romantic. The two of you will enjoy a hectic social life. The family budget may never be balanced, and between two sarcastic, blunt, argumentative people there is bound to be a lot of breaking up and making up. But the real danger to this Sagittarian love affair is more subtle than that. The problem is that both of you can be too self-revealing. You may be too frank and open. You might honestly discuss each other's weaknesses and strengths. You might say too much about past loves and present fantasies until pretty soon you've talked the love to death. Love often needs a little mystery and illusion about it. You might become too close as friends to make successful lovers. Sagittarians often get bored when there is nothing more to discover about a love, when there are no more secret corners to look around.

SAGITTARIUS WOMAN, CAPRICORN MAN

There is usually very little compatibility between you and someone as realistic and free of illusions as Mr. Capricorn. He is too serious and pessimistic about too many things that you are careless and optimistic about. Capricorns like a lot of stability in a woman, and you like a lot of flexibility in a man. He loves to argue and so do you. There is likely to be a strong initial attraction between you if you catch him in one of his gay and playful moods, but you'll feel doubly betrayed when he later sinks into the deepest depression. He likes to run his home, which is all right until he tries to run you. He likes to face life's problems with both feet planted on solid ground, which is all right, too, until he tries to get you to be more cautious and practical. But both of you are opportunistic, and you're bound to see each other as fantastic "opportunities."

SAGITTARIUS WOMAN, AQUARIUS MAN

The two of you have a lot in common—your love of freedom and your friendly, generous approach to life. There is a bohemian streak in both of you that could make you the best of friends and the warmest of lovers if you meet at the right time in each other's life. But there are times when Aquarians can be too detached, stubborn, and self-absorbed for you, and times when you can be too sentimental and interfering. You both have quick tempers, and you both like to argue. The emotional vibrations are not good. Aquarians are kind and affectionate but surprisingly unemotional. Sagittarian emotions might be short-lived, but they do run very deep. Sexually things are somewhat better. You are both free and uninhibited. An affair between you is a good risk to take. It might be fun, and even if it doesn't work out, you each can walk away from it with a minimum of emotional strain.

SAGITTARIUS WOMAN, PISCES MAN

The best part is the emotional part. Sagittarians are periodically very emotional people, and Pisceans are almost always that way. The sexual vibrations are also very good since both of you like a lot of sentimental and psychological stimulation before, during, and after the physical part. You are both sensualists. You like to feel, and both of you are likely to have rich fantasy lives that each will nourish for the other. Sexually you fit together very well, but a little past that the harmony may end. Pisceans may want an emotional closeness that you will resist. You enjoy independence, but if you take too much of it, he can become extremely withdrawn and secretive. His personality tends toward secretiveness; while you are open, frank, and direct. You are an optimist and you are likely to see him as an indecisive pessimist. You are both rather careless about money. Neither is very practical, but both are good schemers. This is bound to be a complicated relationship, but often a good one.

SAGITTARIUS

(NOVEMBER 22ND TO DECEMBER 20TH)

HARRY EDWARDS, sports and social activist	November 22, 1942
GUY BLUFORD, first black space-shuttle astronaut	November 22, 1942
RONALD DELLUMS, U.S. congressman from California	November 24, 1935
ART SHELL, football star and coach	November 26, 1946
TINA TURNER, Grammy-winning singer, actress	November 26, 1939
JIMI HENDRIX, electric guitar virtuoso	November 27, 1942
BERRY GORDY, founder of Motown Records	November 28, 1928
ADAM CLAYTON POWELL, JR., congressman, social activist	November 29, 1908
DAVE BING, businessman, basketball star	November 29, 1943
PEARL PRIMUS, pioneer in development of black dance	November 29, 1919
OSCAR ROBERTSON, basketball legend, businessman	November 29, 1938
ROBERT GUILLAUME, stage, screen, and television actor	November 30, 1927
SHIRLEY CHISHOLM, first black female member of the U.S. Congress	November 30, 1924
GORDON PARKS, SR., filmmaker, writer, photographer, composer	November 30, 1912
BO JACKSON, football and baseball star	November 30, 1962
KURT SCHMOKE, mayor of Baltimore	December 1, 1949

LOU RAWLS, singer, social activist	December 1, 1935
RICHARD PRYOR, comedian, actor	December 1, 1940
JOHN A. WILLIAMS, author, essayist, educator	December 5, 1925
JIMMY SMITH, blues musician	December 6, 1928
CAROLE SIMPSON, broadcast journalist	December 7, 1940
WILLIE B. BARROW, religious leader, Operation PUSH official	December 7, 1924
SAMMY DAVIS, JR., actor, singer, dancer, entertainer	December 8, 1925
FLIP WILSON, comedian, actor	December 8, 1933
JUNIOR WELLS, singer, musician	December 9, 1934
CARTER WOODSON, historian, "The Father of Black History"	December 9, 1875
REDD FOXX, comedian, actor	December 9, 1922
ESLANDA GOODE ROBESON, intellectual, writer, activist	December 12, 1896
JOE WILLIAMS, singer, "Emperor of the Blues"	December 12, 1918
DIONNE WARWICK, Grammy-winning singer, social activist	December 12, 1940
ARCHIE MOORE, professional boxing champion	December 13, 1916
JOHN E. JACOB, president of the National Urban League	December 16, 1934
BRUCE WRIGHT, New York State Supreme Court justice	December 18, 1912
GENERAL BENJAMIN O. DAVIS, groundbreaking U.S. military officer	December 18, 1912
OSSIE DAVIS, actor, activist	December 18, 1917
CICELY TYSON, award-winning stage, screen, and television actress	December 19, 1938

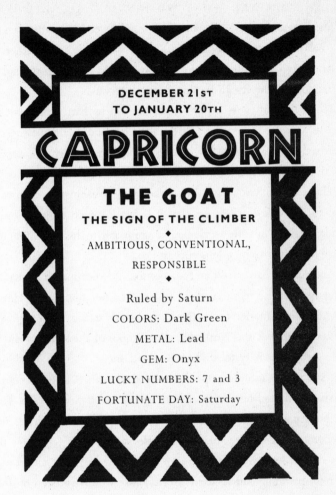

**DECEMBER 21ST
TO JANUARY 20TH**

CAPRICORN

THE GOAT
THE SIGN OF THE CLIMBER

♦

AMBITIOUS, CONVENTIONAL,

RESPONSIBLE

♦

Ruled by Saturn

COLORS: Dark Green

METAL: Lead

GEM: Onyx

LUCKY NUMBERS: 7 and 3

FORTUNATE DAY: Saturday

THE CAPRICORN VIBRATION

NO MATTER WHAT WOMEN SAY, DENZEL WASH-ington is not just another pretty face. No matter what the fellas think, Debbie Allen is not just a pretty face either. Both got to the top of their fields by hard work and careful planning. Capricorns don't think it can be done any other way.

It is true that most people reach the top by hard work, but many of those who get there might have waited on God or their associations, or devised clever schemes, or come up with cosmic insight, or depended on love or luck. Capricorns usually do not strongly believe in luck.

Those in Hollywood who've worked with Washington, who won an Oscar for his role in *Glory*, say that it is not his good looks or even his abundant talent but his workmanlike approach to his craft that is responsible for his tremendous success.

And Allen's hard work and no-nonsense dedication to her craft are legendary. Because of racial discrimination in her home city, Houston, as a child Allen traveled to Mexico City to study dance. After high school she was rejected at the North Carolina School of the Arts, so she went to Howard University to study acting and speech, but in Washington, D.C., she found another opportunity to study dance, and after graduation she continued her study of both acting and dance in New York.

She is now world famous as a dancer but also as an actress, singer, choreographer, and director of a hit television series, *A Different World*. None of this seems to be the result of a lucky break. It all grows out of careful planning and focused effort. Those who have been on the set of *A Different World* say she is a workaholic.

Astrologers write that Capricorn is realistic, reliable, slow, and not a particularly joyful vibration. Capricorns are usually too serious and not spontaneous enough to be good mixers, unless they must mix to get something they want. Otherwise they would just as soon be alone somewhere making plans. Sagittarians plan by expecting the best, while Capricorns plan by preparing for the worst.

Capricorns are capable of great devotion and intense concentration of mind and will; they are farsighted but secretive. They may seem narrow because their minds are usually set on one thing at a time.

Both male and female Capricorns are like the mountain goat who keeps climbing. It's almost impossible to completely discourage Capricorns once they have their minds set on a goal.

Most astrologers agree that the last four signs of the zodiacal cycle—Sagittarius through Pisces—represent the final phase of astrological evolution: the phase in which mankind attains a clear, far-reaching vision of the Cosmic Whole. In Sagittarius that vision was directed toward the gathering of knowledge, the expansion of awareness beyond the self, and the establishment of meaningful principles.

In Capricorn it is directed toward the relentless quest for the integration of the inner self with the external world and one's public identity. Capricorn represents the peak of *individual* human achievement on the earthly or material level. Natives of this vibration use their cosmic vision to accomplish worldly tasks.

Capricorns are driven to seek worldly success and power. Their worldly identity and their spiritual essence are one and the same. Carving out their unique niche in the world is not usually just a vain quest for glory. It is their willful attempt to make visible and concrete their inner convictions and beliefs. Capricorn, more than any other sign, symbolizes integrity, and in its most evolved manifestation there is little or no pretense.

Not surprisingly, then, Capricorn is considered the success sign of the zodiac. Capricorns aren't more talented than other people. They're simply more ambitious and determined to reach whatever goals they set for themselves. They thrive on the kind of hard work that brings practical results, and they're not easily discouraged by obstacles.

Once they start, they work steadily without a thought of giving up. Whether the goal is as lofty as that of Dr. Martin Luther King, Jr., or as ordinary as establishing a successful marriage and properly rearing children, Capricorns have the ability to put one hundred percent of their talents into the service of ambition.

They achieve a high degree of success in almost every field imaginable. This isn't because they're excessively quick-witted or flexible. Many other signs are more naturally adaptable, but none of them can keep plugging away with the determination that Capricorns can muster. Capricorns persist because their greatest fear is the fear of failure.

No sign is more miserable in failure. Yet Capricorns are realistic people. They don't all aspire to anything as large and influential as, say, owning both *Ebony* magazine and an insurance company, the way Capricorn businessman and publisher John H. Johnson does, but few signs are more single-minded in the pursuit of high worldly achievement.

Under the rulership of Saturn, Capricorns develop very firm mental images that keep them from wavering in times of personal crisis. The only thought is, *How can I get past this personal thing so that I can march forward?*

Madame C. J. Walker, one of the more famous entrepreneurs in American history, is a good example. Born Sarah Breedlove on a Delta, Louisiana, cotton plantation, she was orphaned at age seven in 1874 and had to work to support herself.

In 1905, with $1.05 in savings, she started a hair-care business. With hard work, dedication, and great administrative talent she expanded the business into the Walker Hair Culture Union of America. By 1916 the Walker Company claimed twenty thousand agents in the United States, Central America, and the Caribbean, and Madame Walker became one of the nation's first self-made women millionaires.

Discipline and dedication likely accounts for the great number of Capricorns who have become heavyweight champions of the world. Floyd Patterson, Muhammad Ali, Joe Frazier, and George Foreman are all born under the sign.

Capricorns may have less extravagant ambitions, but they almost never value pleasure more than achievement—achievement *is* pleasure.

For them life's goal is not primarily enjoyment; accomplishment is the purpose of living. A night of fun is not out of the question, but they know that the next day duty must be served.

They enjoy exercising authority over others and can display deep respect for those who have, to their minds, justifiable authority over them; they prize order and structure. Often they are also susceptible to an overwhelming and uncritical admiration for the successful, and they can be among the zodiac's most eager social climbers. There is a great deal of status consciousness in the vibration.

The central irony and most troublesome problem for Capricorns is that their drive to pursue worldly success is based on a deeper need to confirm their inner convictions. Therefore, while they are driven to establish a position among the high and mighty, they are truly content only when that position reflects their own inner principles. They don't spurn adulation for the tremendous efforts they make to reach their goals, but praise and applause from others is not the barometer of their success.

The nagging Capricorn need for a clearly defined goal was apparent in the career of civil rights leader Martin Luther King, Jr. "He had the constitution of a bull," said Andrew Young, King's primary lieutenant. "He could go on and on and on when things were going well. It was when he did not have a clear sense of direction that he got very tired."

Obviously there are many Capricorns who lack King's integrity. And when distracted by outside influences, their awesome ambition can become very destructive, and self-destructive, because it is so intense. Capricorn is the sign of the "terrible father."

Unevolved Capricorns may court success and power so vigorously that they become ruthless, cunning, selfish, and totally unprincipled. The key words of the sign are I USE, and negative Capricorns will use anyone or anything to get what they want.

Anyone who has experienced it will agree that you have never been flattered until you have been flattered by a Capricorn who wants something you've got. They are generally not charming people unless they have to gear up the charm in order to get something they want. In such cases they can be irresistible.

The comments of poet Langston Hughes about Capricorn novelist Zora Neale Hurston are indicative: "In her youth she was always getting scholarships and things from wealthy white people, some of whom simply paid her just to sit around and represent the Negro race." She was also an anthropologist, and Hughes wrote that "nobody else could stop the average Harlemite on Lenox Avenue and measure his head with a strange looking anthropological device and not get bawled out for the attempt." Some astrologers call Capricorn the sign of the diplomat.

Even highly evolved Capricorns feel that "getting the job done" is the only goal, and if someone gets used, then that's often justified, especially since it is Capricorn's conviction that most people are not doing anything useful with their lives anyway.

Evolved Capricorns feel strongly protective toward whatever group they belong to. If Cancerians feel motherly toward their group, Capricorns often feel that they are the father, the father in fact of some usually irresponsible, frivolous people, starting with their own family and extending outward to race, nation, and mankind—in that order.

Capricorns always see their work as most important, and very often it is because it is work that anchors a vision about the group in the material world. For Capricorns this is often a prideful vision of the race.

There are certainly many examples of Capricorns who have been quite willful at making visible and concrete their inner convictions and beliefs—John H. Johnson, for example, who in *Ebony, Negro Digest,* and *Jet* established in concrete form (print) the social reality of the race.

Earl Graves, publisher of *Black Enterprise,* did something similar for black business aspiration. Little Richard makes a justifiable claim for being the architect of rock 'n' roll.

Alvin Ailey did a great deal to establish an institutional setting for African-American dance, which is exactly what John Hope Franklin did in history, Zora Neale Hurston did in folklore, and James Cleveland did in gospel music. Other people have visions but often do not have the determination, or the need, to express spiritual enlightenment in structures that can be organized and administered. If there is a little fun along the way, well, then, maybe that's all right, but generally they think that fun is just distraction.

Capricorns also have a great urge to be of service to mankind and to be recognized for that service. They willingly forgo personal considerations in order to advance the thing they believe in. There is something of a martyr complex among them, which makes them stubbornly determined to go to the wall rather than give up. In addition to Martin Luther King, Jr., two of the relatively few Americans who very early risked everything to oppose the Vietnam War were Capricorns Julian Bond and Muhammad Ali.

Often Capricorns are conservative and patriotic, but among black Americans these traits are usually expressed through racial loyalty. Novelists John Oliver Killens's prime criterion for judging the worth of a black person was that the person had an "undying love for black people."

Still, Capricorn is not a rebellious vibration. Its natives like to see things done the "right" way. They're seldom openly eccentric or different. They have principles that reflect the traditions of family and nation. They make up more than their fair share of the responsible citizens of the world because they're very much concerned about moral standing in the community.

The pull between internalized moral principles and the practical requirements of success, between personal ambition and the desire to be of great service, is responsible for the much-discussed Capricorn depression. Capricorn is a fatalistic sign, not a happy-go-lucky one. Libra might feel that life is a fast skate across thin ice—if you don't slow down, you won't fall through. Capricorns also know the ice is thin, but they believe you should walk carefully, picking each step with a great deal of caution. Capricorns are opportunists. When the chance comes, they know how to make the most of it.

Saturn, the planet ruling Capricorn, governs the organization of matter as well as society, and is considered the father figure of the zodiac. Consequently, in order to be content, many Capricorns need to be around children or younger people whom they can groom, teach, and prepare for life. Otherwise they tend to meddle in the lives of those with whom they work or live. The father-teacher instinct must be indulged. If no other pupils are available, they work on themselves.

Capricorns are sober and reserved, but they can teach themselves how to loosen up; they're self-interested, but they often teach themselves how to be helpful to others. It's difficult for them to escape being materialistic. Much of their inspiration comes from a strong desire for material things, but they can teach themselves concern for improving the material base of life for those around them.

They love power, but they can learn how to share it. They learn to be helpful by curbing tendencies to be jealous and envious of people who outdo them. They must also teach themselves how to lose without bitterness.

Balanced Capricorns are, in truth, self-made women and men. They are iron-willed people who control their impulses and allow very little spontaneity in their lives. They have strong physical appetites, but they can suppress them; personal satisfaction must be sacrificed for ambition and achievement. For the evolved Capricorn these attributes are beneficial for themselves and for society, but for unevolved natives too often this end justifies any means.

RELATIONSHIPS

Capricorns don't make friends easily. They often seem to be outgoing, but they aren't. Capricorn is the sign of the jovial introvert. Despite the superficial friendliness, Capricorns are inclined to rely on their own counsel. They resist depending on other people and usually are suspicious of the motives of people whose loyalties haven't been tested. They're proud and competitive, and they hate to give away a competitive edge by letting others know too much about them.

Although often reserved, Capricorns are (when need be) much too socially aggressive to be considered shy. In fact they thrive on confrontations of all sorts. Harmonious social relations are often too indirect for them. This is often true even in love—like the Capricorn woman who calls her husband "Mouse" simply because he refuses to confront her or anyone else in a forceful manner.

Once made, a Capricorn friendship is very durable. Capricorns are team players. There's a great deal of clannishness associated with the vibration. If a Capricorn chooses you as a friend, he is likely to be very jealous of your other friendships and may even try to break them up so that you'll be his friend alone. Certainly you'll never be his friend *and* the friend of someone he doesn't like.

Capricorns tend to "disapprove" of a great number of people, sometimes for the oddest of reasons. Though they're not likely to be rude, they will avoid people they disapprove of.

Natives of the tenth sign tend to be very moody, and not everyone can understand or tolerate their bouts of depression. Often their loved ones are the only victims of the discontent that grows out of their depression. Sometimes an ironic reversal takes place: Capricorns remain congenial to people they don't know well, but are quite irritable with people they love. If they're not careful, strangers benefit most from their considerable charm, while loved ones see a great deal of sourness and bad temper. The irony of this is that Capricorns may not even like the strangers to whom they are congenial. Libras, Aquarians, and Sagittarians might develop easy sympathies for the weak, the lazy, or the unambitious. Capricorns don't. They believe, with few exceptions, that most people get exactly what they deserve in life. Their sense of justice is very severe at times, and more than anything else, this accounts for their vindictive treatment of anyone who has wronged or opposed them.

Another irony of the sign is that in a certain sense Capricorns do *need* people, because finally it is within the social environment that they seek success. They are ship captains who are weakened considerably without a crew and, for that matter, a stormy sea to navigate. Ultimately, although they must have solitude to replenish and reaffirm their inner convictions, they are not well equipped to work in solitude for any extended period of time. Several of the more gregarious signs, such as Leo, Aquarius, and Sagittarius, are better at walking a lonely road to success.

LUCK, MONEY, AND WORK

Capricorns deserve to be proud of anything they accomplish because they usually attain it through their own hard-earned effort, with little help from luck. The planet Jupiter, ruler of Sagittarius, is called "The Greater Fortune." Saturn, Capricorn's ruler, is called "The Greater Misfortune." Saturn, Old Father Time, represents limitations, disappointments, sorrows, setbacks, and privations; but this teaches his subjects the value of hard work, patience, and perseverance.

Still, Capricorn is one of the real money signs of the zodiac. Even though not lucky, Capricorns make good gamblers. Whatever the game—cards, craps, love, or life—caution and patience are often better allies than luck. Natives of this sign like to make sure before they bet. One of their finest talents is the ability to learn lessons quickly and translate them into simple formulas for success. When it comes to going after what they want, few are more pragmatic than Capricorns.

They're usually very good with details and are therefore good as secretaries, accountants, bookkeepers, doctors, lawyers, and businessmen. Even when their work involves the philosophical or inventive, their practical mental approach is evident.

Most of them enjoy working on something concrete rather than something totally abstract. They make better artisans and craftspeople than artists, better promoters of projects than originators of ideas. There's nothing very avant-garde about the vibration; even in matters of artistic expression Capricorns prefer the conventional and proven to the experimental. They're neither pioneer nor poet. They're the leaders and builders on the middle ground, where everyday life is lived.

PHYSICAL AND MENTAL HEALTH

Adult Capricorns are strong and sturdy people who usually excel at sports and activities that require a lot of stamina. They're often well disciplined, and to prove that mind can control matter, they're seldom sick when they have something important to do. Though they work hard, they're seldom troubled by fatigue. Capricorn is a self-charging battery but, like Taureans and Virgos, they lapse into periods when they may sleep for days.

Most earth-sign people have this inertia. When they're rolling, they like to keep rolling, and when they're resting, they like to remain that way. When a job is unfinished, when there is something "not taken care of," Capricorns find it hard to relax. The mind is constantly occupied, working out plans, thinking about precautions. Sometimes a stiff drink is the only thing that can turn the mind off. Small and large encounters with alcoholism aren't uncommon among Capricorns.

Insomnia is another result of this same tendency. The worst mental health hazard is, of course, an almost cosmic paranoia—the feeling that not only other people but fate itself is working against the Capricorn. There is an enormous fear that despite all efforts nothing is secure against the ravages of possible misfortune. At best this paranoia tends to add a little melancholy to the average Capricorn's life. At worst it causes chronic depression.

Capricorn rules the knees, and natives of the sign have more than their share of trouble in this area. Many Capricorns don't assimilate calcium easily and should make dietary compensations for this fact or risk a great deal of trouble with teeth and bones.

LOVE AND SEX

Even though they may not be the easiest people to live with, Capricorns were made for marriage. They're not likely to be overly demonstrative, romantic, or affectionate, but, like all earth signs, they can be among the most physically satisfying of lovers. Since they're not usually interested in wasting a lot of time playing around, marriage is the best framework for them to satisfy their powerful sexual needs.

Capricorns don't usually develop quick sexual rapport with people, so when they find that rare someone whose passions and habits are compatible, they like to secure that relationship with marriage. But one dilemma of the sign is that Capricorns don't often marry primarily for emotional, romantic, or sexual reasons. As in other areas their behavior usually reflects their goal-oriented intentions rather than their emotions. They like to look for someone who can do them some good, someone who can help them achieve their goals, or someone who is ambitious enough to appreciate the practical help that they offer. Giddy or foolish love is usually foreign to them. Even in romantic matters they tend to be quite practical and realistic. They know how to separate love and lust. Many of them will satisfy their passionate urges secretly, without ever losing the image of respectability.

Typical of this pattern is the eighteen-year-old woman who enrolled at Howard University for no other reason than to find a fourth-year medical student. She married one, moved to New Jersey, and helped him build one of the most lucrative practices in the state. He died at thirty-five and she married his bachelor friend, who was also a doctor, but during both marriages she has maintained an outside relationship with a man she has known for fifteen years. He has been her "satisfier," but she wouldn't think of marrying him because he's not a "good" prospect.

Love for Capricorns is based on respect, not passion, and they can be quite devoted to anyone who wins that respect. Theirs is an enduring vibration. Once the Capricorn has made up his mind to love, he will persist longer than most. Once he has gotten married, if at all possible, he means to stay married. Capricorns often believe divorce is a public admission of failure; and they like to avoid such an admission if there is any way they can remain married and still make something productive out of their lives.

Although the core of the marriage might move from the bedroom to the parlor, the Capricorn will likely resist the urge to go prowling the world looking for an ideal lover. Capricorns aren't idealists in romance; their love is seldom based on infatuation. It grows out of shared respect for accomplishment. In love Capricorns seek like-minded allies in the struggle with life.

The presence of rock star Little Richard among their ranks notwithstanding, Capricorns are usually conservative dressers with a serious, matter-of-fact manner. While this doesn't make them glamorous or style-setting trendsetters, their neatness and strength of character can be quite attractive. Muhammad Ali and Zora Neale Hurston are examples of very appealing but not particularly stylish Capricorns.

Capricorns sometimes dedicate so much of their attention to mundane affairs that it may take a lot of stimulation to free all of their powerful sexual nature. Though sometimes inhibited initially by a concern for social images, mature Capricorns are willing to do whatever is necessary to free that dammed-up sexual energy.

They are extremely pragmatic, believing ultimately in whatever works. They can be quite dutiful and compliant with a partner whom they find liberating. Though often jealous, nagging, and critical, if necessary they can learn to avoid these traits and become quite considerate and thoughtful.

Both male and female Capricorns are usually very aware of sexual difference. Most of the men conceal a secret lustfulness behind their serious exterior, and in most of the women there is an ease of manner that surfaces only in the presence of men. Other women may distrust her, but men find her pleasant because she knows exactly what to do with the male ego. They are born managers and they aren't content to let husbands make day-to-day decisions about their domestic lives or careers. Advice will be forthcoming even when not asked for, and pity the husband who doesn't heed her advice and then fails to get the promotion or the new job. On the other hand a Capricorn husband won't allow his wife to run the house without constant advice from him. He's the kind who's forever sticking his nose in the kitchen pot and commenting on the grocery list.

Capricorn's love life often grows in reverse—like the New Yorker who at twenty-two dated only women over thirty and now that he's thirty-seven dates no one much older than twenty-two. Capricorn is an "old soul" growing younger. The heroine in Zora Neale Hurston's novel *Their Eyes Were Watching God* is typical: When she was not yet twenty she fell in love with a man over thirty, and when she was forty-five, she fell for a twenty-five-year-old named, of all foolish things, Teacake.

LOVE AFFAIRS

(See other chapters for love affairs between
Capricorn men and women of other signs.)

CAPRICORN WOMAN, ARIES MAN

Aries men can be very domineering, but that's not a serious problem for a Capricorn woman. You easily cooperate and accept the decisions of a person you respect, as long as the person gives respect in return. If things are going well, all you ask is that he talk to you and give you a chance to participate. Your ambitions don't make you childishly rebellious as many other ambitious women might be. If Mr. Aries is successful, you can either help to contribute to his success or you can strike out and be successful on your own. There will be a lot of competition between you, but that's not always bad. You usually feel that success comes from careful planning and long, hard work; he likes to do it quickly by gambling. You like to save for a rainy day; he can act like the world's biggest spender. He's optimistic, while you tend to be pessimistic. You are big pills for each other to swallow, but swallowing these pills could be just what the love doctor ordered.

CAPRICORN WOMAN, TAURUS MAN

All your desires to build something solid could be satisfied by this man. He thinks like you do. He's practical and tends to be thrifty. He may not be as ambitious as you are, but you can whet his natural appetite for the finer things in life. You both see the world in pretty much the same terms. He's stubborn, and you know when not to push. You're moody and ill-tempered sometimes, but he's patient enough not to make any rash decisions because of that. The sexual vibrations are very good. You both have large physical sexual appetites. He may be a little more romantic than you, but you're more adaptable. You can make it what it has to be in order to get out of it what you need, and you can give him what he has to have to make him happy.

CAPRICORN WOMAN, GEMINI MAN

He's not much like you except that you're both very adaptable. Neither of you are likely to be carried away on a sea of emotion, and each might see that the other has a great deal to offer. The dryness of the emotional hookup can be moistened by the juices of your own ambitions. You're both schemers, and neither is blinded by idealism and romanticism. A relationship between you might be difficult, but you both know that life is never without its difficulties. Gemini men need a lot of freedom, and you may be able to accept that. You'll tend to be more practical and realistic, but he might be able to deal with that. The sexual vibrations aren't good, but the tension involved might make it all interesting. He needs a lot of mental stimulation and often you do, too, but your approach to sex is usually straightforward and mostly physical. You will both have to be very considerate, or you'll leave each other cold.

CAPRICORN WOMAN, CANCER MAN

Cancer is the celestial mother and Capricorn is the celestial father, so the roles are reversed. He's more romantic, sensitive, and easily hurt, more needing and more giving. He'll want you to be more emotional and more demonstrative. But Cancer men are very strong in their own way. If he's a successful man, the role reversal might work. If he's not, you'll never forgive him for being so fuzzy and indirect. If you hurt his feelings often enough, he'll crawl back into his famous shell, and you're neither sensitive nor needing enough to crawl inside looking for him. Criticize or needle him too much and he'll remain there, coming out only long enough to badger and meddle with you or to sidle off to someone else. Sexually you're likely to prefer a more domineering, forceful man. But Cancer men are often so sexually insecure that they work overtime to prove themselves, and there are few places where good hard work is more needed to yield the luscious fruit of the sexual bliss that is possible between you.

CAPRICORN WOMAN, LEO MAN

The two of you have very little in common except the determination of each to have his own way, and that could make you quicker enemies than friends. The initial attraction between you is likely to be based on the facades you both erect for the public. But it won't take you long to learn that he may not be as "together" as he seems to be, and he'll learn that you're not as jovial and outgoing as you often pretend to be. Your pessimism and practicality will bore him. His extravagance will seem like foolishness to you. But Capricorns like to work hard, and there could be some great rewards for the hard work involved with this relationship.

CAPRICORN WOMAN, VIRGO MAN

If you're honest with yourself, you'll see that in so many ways this man is made for you. A particular Virgo might not suit your fancy, but only among Taureans are you as likely to find such a good fit. Virgo men are intelligent, practical, and adaptable. He may not be as ambitious as you are, but he's willing to take the kind of advice that you're likely to give. He's home-loving, cautious, and generally very realistic, just like you. Both of you are likely to approve of the other's method of dealing with the world. In love neither is very sentimental, and both have very strong drives that may be covered by strong inhibitions. Like him you are likely to be inhibited in verbal expressions of love and tenderness, and both of you have considerable emotional reserve, so it's unlikely that either will ask more of the other than the other is willing to give.

CAPRICORN WOMAN, LIBRA MAN

When the ambitions inherent in this relationship are aligned, the connection can be very powerful. His world is made of ideals and human relationships. Yours is created of practicalities and realities. You are both good at building solid achievements. Capricorn Debbie Allen and Libra Norm Nixon have probably found this to be true. Even if he's effective, it's possible that you'll find him somewhat less goal driven than you like your life to be. Even if you are extremely effective, he will want you to slow down and smell the roses. Take each other's advice, even though it might go against your best instincts. He may be ever so handsome, witty, and entertaining, but you're usually drawn to a more rugged personality with more drive and personal ambition. Since he's open and optimistic, he may find you too closed and sober. Be mindful of the faults in yourself and you'll see the advantage in him. Ask him to do the same with himself and you. Everything that the other is, and everything that the other is not, is just what each other needs.

CAPRICORN WOMAN, SCORPIO MAN

There's bound to be a lot of mutual admiration between two reserved, ambitious, realistic, and hardworking people like you. The financial area will be one of your greatest areas of agreement. You are each likely to be quite sober in making money decisions. Capricorn women are usually attracted to Scorpio men because they are so solid. Scorpio men are usually attracted to Capricorn women because they know the value of ambition. If the two of you are working toward the same goals, there are few combinations that are more powerful. There will be a lot of jockeying for power, but this might do no more than satisfy the deep competitive urges in each of you, as long as neither of you subscribes to a win-at-all-cost strategy.

CAPRICORN WOMAN, SAGITTARIUS MAN

Crusader Rabbit might fall in love because he believes he can change you. He doesn't believe that sobriety and pessimism need to be permanent parts of anybody's nature. If he likes you, he'll want to give you some sunshine. You tend to prefer planning for your future, worrying about ill fortune, social standing, security, and the practical everyday realities of the material world. Hope he doesn't make changing you a quest, because when he fails, he might start to run a little, and that is tough for you to take. There are plenty of faults you can find with each other, but it is best not to start looking because you might not stop. Build on the interest that you are both bound to have in bringing something new and needed into the other's life.

CAPRICORN WOMAN, CAPRICORN MAN

The only difficulty here is finding something that you both want to work toward. With energy directed toward a common goal you two will celebrate your victories in the same way and suffer from defeat in the same manner. You'll understand each other's gloom and know what makes each other happy. You might play some, but mostly this will be a serious, sober relationship that thrives more on accomplishments than on personal gratification. You know how to be whatever you have to be in public, but you'll each have to learn to be more happy and congenial with each other. Otherwise arguments and harassment could take up a lot of your private moments. Since neither is much inclined to give up, there will be a long time for each to work out the means of comforting, helping, and loving the other, and admiring the reflections of yourself that you see in the other.

CAPRICORN WOMAN, AQUARIUS MAN

Aquarians are usually concerned about too many things that Capricorns could care less about, and vice versa. He's likely to be a gentle, progressive, perhaps eccentric, rebellious, humanitarian, generous, sympathetic man. But he's also quick-tempered and stubborn. Criticism brings out the worst in him, and you'll surely think he needs to be told about his helter-skelter way of organizing life. He may be ambitious, but most likely he's more concerned about lifestyle than about distant objectives. He may find you much too cautious and closed. He's generally optimistic, and you're usually cautious and pessimistic. His idealism will often seem foolish to you. Your realism will impress him as the crudest materialism. You're concerned about social standing in the community while he takes a certain delight in ignoring public opinion. There is much work to do, and you'll have to avoid feeling that you are doing most of it.

CAPRICORN WOMAN, PISCES MAN

Mr. Pisces will have to do a lot of changing, but there's no more adaptable personality in the zodiac. You won't let him be as vague and undisciplined as he is sometimes inclined to be. He'll recognize in you the strong support he needs to push him toward his goals. He'll probably have more imagination than you and a kind of emotional handle on situations that is effective for him. Underneath all his gentleness he's very tough and tenacious. Often his indirect approach will infuriate you, but you need something to be infuriated about anyway. You might start some arguments, but he can hold his own, and he's likely to have the sexual upper hand since it's he who can seduce and excite you as few men can. He'll complain that you're not emotional enough, or not sentimental enough, but the stabilizing emotions that you bring could produce an interesting pool of emotions for the fish to swim in happily.

CAPRICORN

(DECEMBER 21ST TO JANUARY 20TH)

FLORENCE GRIFFITH-JOYNER, Olympic sprinter	December 21, 1959
ARTHUR FLETCHER, labor leader	December 22, 1924
MADAME C. J. WALKER, entrepreneur, hair-care-industry pioneer	December 23, 1867
JAMES CLEVELAND, gospel singer	December 23, 1932
CAB CALLOWAY, singer, actor, entertainer	December 25, 1907
LITTLE RICHARD, singer, "Architect of Rock 'n' Roll"	December 25, 1935
RICKEY HENDERSON, baseball star	December 25, 1958
EARL HINES, innovative jazz/blues musician	December 28, 1903
DENZEL WASHINGTON, Academy Award–winning actor	December 28, 1954
ROBERT WEAVER, civil rights leader	December 29, 1907
TOM BRADLEY, first black mayor of Los Angeles	December 29, 1917
BO DIDDLEY, influential musician, singer, songwriter	December 30, 1928
BEN JOHNSON, Olympic track star	December 30, 1961
JOHN HOPE FRANKLIN, scholar and renowned historian	January 2, 1915
WILLY T. RIBBS, professional race-car driver	January 3, 1956
FLOYD PATTERSON, boxing champion	January 4, 1935
GRACE BUMBRY, classical singer	January 4, 1937
ALVIN AILEY, dance innovator	January 5, 1931
ZORA NEALE HURSTON, writer, anthropologist, folklorist	January 7, 1901
LITTLE ANTHONY, singer	January 8, 1940
BUTTERFLY MC QUEEN, actress	January 8, 1911

JOHN H. JOHNSON, publishing magnate, founder of *Ebony* and *Jet*	January 8, 1918
DEAN DIXON, classical musician	January 10, 1915
GEORGE FOREMAN, boxing champion	January 10, 1949
JAMES FARMER, civil rights pioneer and union organizer	January 12, 1920
MORDECAI JOHNSON, educator	January 12, 1890
MARGARET DANNER, poet	January 12, 1915
WALTER MOSELY, writer, creator of "Easy Rawlins" mysteries	January 12, 1952
JULIAN BOND, civil rights activist, politician	January 14, 1940
HARVEY GANTT, politician, architect	January 14, 1943
JOHN O. KILLENS, author, educator	January 14, 1916
MARTIN LUTHER KING, JR., religious and civil rights leader, martyr	January 15, 1929
MARIO VAN PEEBLES, actor, director	January 15, 1957
ERNEST GAINES, writer	January 15, 1933
DEBBIE ALLEN, actress, director, dancer, choreographer	January 16, 1950
SADE, singer	January 16, 1960
L. DOUGLAS WILDER, politician, first black elected U.S. governor	January 17, 1931
JOE FRAZIER, boxing champion	January 17, 1944
JAMES EARL JONES, stage, screen, and television actor	January 17, 1931
SHABBA RANKS, singer, rapper	January 17, 1966
MUHAMMAD ALI, boxing champion, "The Greatest"	January 18, 1942
DANIEL HALE WILLIAMS, first successful heart surgeon	January 18, 1856

**JANUARY 21ST TO
FEBRUARY 19TH**

AQUARIUS

THE WATER
BEARER

THE SIGN OF THE
REVOLUTIONARY

◆

BROAD-MINDED, FREEDOM-LOVING,
ORIGINAL

◆

Ruled by Uranus and Saturn

COLORS: Pastel Green and Blue

METAL: Uranium GEM: Garnet

LUCKY NUMBERS: 8 and 4

FORTUNATE DAY: Wednesday

THE AQUARIUS VIBRATION

AQUARIANS ARE VERY STUBBORN, ESPECIALLY when enraged. They are very rebellious, especially when there is an injustice, and most especially if the injustice is being done to them. They can be absolutely uncompromising when their humanitarian ideals have been violated. Take Rosa Parks, the Montgomery, Alabama, seamstress, who was tired on December 1, 1955. Her feet were hurting, but so also were her feelings. She had had enough of racial segregation on busses and public accommodations in Montgomery. She refused to give up her seat on a bus as blacks were required to do whenever whites were standing. Parks was arrested. Her courage inspired the boycott that brought Dr. Martin Luther King to fame.

Any list of Aquarians is bound to be full of courageous, defiant people. Under pressure Aquarius is the most rebellious sign of the zodiac. Cut from slightly different cloth than Parks is Aquarian Angela Davis, the California college professor who became a fierce fighter for racial justice in the 1960s.

A cofounder of the Black Panther party, the quick-tempered, fiery Huey Newton, was also born under the sign of Aquarius, the humanitarian. One of the things that drives many Aquarians is their love of justice and their need to help establish a more equitable social order for the benefit of mankind in general and the underdog in particular.

Ben Chavis might not have done well with the organizational politics of the NAACP, which he recently headed, but on the civil rights battlefield he was the most fiery member of the famous Wilmington Ten, who went to prison in the fight for African-American liberation.

Of course Aquarians are not simply lovers of freedom and haters of injustice. In personal relationships they can be very emotionally detached. They also read human character very well and are good at predicting what someone will do next. Aquarians are often touchy and hate to be criticized and, when criticized, tend to be unforgiving.

To a small extent the vibration is ruled by Saturn, which produces a restrictive, practical, extremely logical turn of mind; but Aquarius is ruled primarily by eccentric Uranus, the planet of change, creativity, humanitarianism, and nonconformity.

The seeming contradictory nature of many Aquarius personalities derives from these planetary influences as well as from the position of Aquarius in the zodiacal cycle. Aquarius, according to most astrologers, is the vibration in which humankind finally merges its consciousness completely into the Cosmic Whole. Sagittarians struggle to *understand* the Whole and Capricorns *work for* the Whole; but in Aquarius there is no separation, the individual becomes the Whole, the One. In its evolved stage Aquarius represents, quite simply, *individuality* perfected and united with the Cosmic Whole.

The well-known Aquarian tendency to demonstrate eccentric behavior is an offshoot of this implacable drive not just to seek the truth but also to live it. Traditional values, the counsel of friends, family, or lovers, even the dictates of the highest authority are not enough to convince the Aquarian of the virtue of an idea, a principle, or a course of action. No. All must be subjected to the Water Bearer's scrutinizing intellectual gaze or weighed against his or her internal sense of what is true for the collective Whole.

In fact, society's values are a threat to the Aquarian. She must resist the influence of society in order to remain unhampered in her quest to be true to her vision. In lofty Aquarians this relates to a vision of new ideas for the betterment of mankind. In some natives of the sign this can lead to eccentricity for the sake of being different. Even though they may be ridiculed by their peers or ostracized as being foolish or outrageous, most often they continue to follow their own counsel. What else from a vibration that combines probing intellectualism with such a deep inner sense of spiritual righteousness?

These and other factors combine to create a personality that can be quite breezy, outgoing, positive, optimistic, and friendly, but very emotionally detached. This casual, easygoing exterior, however, hides a willfulness that few see until an attempt is made to get Aquarians to do something they really don't want to do. Then they can be more pig-headed in their way than Taurus, Scorpio, or Leo can be in theirs. In the Aquarian this stubbornness is more surprising than for the other fixed signs since it's unexpected from someone whose style can seem so casual and at times unconcerned. Aquarians often seem so tolerant that you wouldn't expect them to have a temper, but they happen to have one of the quickest in the zodiac—quick to blow, slow to cool.

Still, in many ways Aquarians are living contradictions. They can live well without material things, yet they are often deeply concerned about owning many uniquely chosen things. They are prone to dress casually, even sloppily, but they also love clothes, and many will change their attire three or four times a day. Aquarians are supposed to be the most scientific people in the world, yet more Aquarians believe in the occult than do natives of any other sign. Aquarians reportedly hate snobbery and egotism, but many of the most pompous intellectual snobs are Aquarians. They have a reputation for being fun-loving and easygoing, yet they are often secret worriers.

Seventy-five percent of the people in the Hall of Fame of Great Inventors in New York City were born with Sun in Aquarius or with Aquarius rising. Aquarians are very inventive people. They like to do things in new ways. In fact they usually have a strong dislike for any established order or system. Yet there's no rut deeper than an Aquarian rut. Once they've found something they're interested in, they can be unswerving in their attention to it.

They have the remarkable ability to tune in what they want and to tune out anything they don't want to deal with; the brilliant Aquarius mathematician who doesn't know the zip code of the house in which he's lived all of his life is an example.

More than any other sign, Aquarians have the ability to focus their attention without being distracted. In addition to his outstanding athletic ability, basketball superstar Michael Jordan's biggest gift seems to be his ability to focus his attention on the basket. No matter that someone else is blocking his path or not, no matter that someone hits him, or he feels himself falling, or he is too far under the backboard, he keeps his focus. His knack of occasionally shooting foul shots with his eyes closed may just be a way of demonstrating that incredible concentration to himself.

One of Jackie Robinson's marks of success as the first black to play major league baseball was his ability to focus on the game despite the taunts and racial abuse that came from fans and other players. Under other circumstances an Aquarian would not have tolerated it for one minute.

One reason Aquarius is such a difficult vibration to define is that it's an air sign; air has no definite dimensions, and it imparts such an abstract otherworldly mentality that natives often use instead the characteristics of their rising sign in order to operate in the real world.

Aries rising makes Aquarians aggressive and determined. Taurus gives warmth, stability, and a great need for material security. Gemini makes them more witty and flexible. Cancer tones down the personality and makes it more sensitive and sympathetic. Leo rising makes Aquarians warmer but more ostentatious. Virgo provides a more practical focus in politics and career. Libra makes them more socially graceful. Scorpio gives hidden motives, makes them harder to get along with, and provides a deeper understanding of the nature of power. Sagittarius rising gives Aquarians more courage, but could make them conceited. Capricorn makes them more conventionally ambitious. Aquarius rising makes sun-sign Aquarians cool, detached, progressive, and perhaps rebellious; it also intensifies their ability to tune out almost anything that the native wishes to ignore or avoid. Pisces rising softens the Aquarian vibration and makes the native more affectionate and emotional; although it heightens their creative instincts, it could make them overly generous.

The rising sign or Ascendant is important in everyone's astrological chart, of course, and it can actually determine the face a person presents to the outside world. But in Aquarius this aspect of the chart is even more visible in the native's behavior.

Pressures that often force other vibrations to modify their behavior, such as pressures from peers, from the immediate environment, and from society at large, are often resisted by Aquarians. In no other sign are the unique ideas of the individual so persistently followed. It's not that they don't listen to others or value their opinions, it's simply that Aquarians are more attuned to another voice. The voices of society, family, and peers don't speak as persuasively to them as do the voices from within themselves. Aquarius is a sign that truly marches to the beat of a different drummer.

Aquarians often seem unconcerned about the mundane things or day-to-day annoyances that worry other people. Instead they seem to fret over things about which others are only vaguely aware. They are fun-loving, but not happy-go-lucky. Often their sleep is troubled. Virgos and Scorpios worry a lot, too, but they usually know what they're worried about. Aquarians often know only vaguely that something is wrong—what, exactly, they often can't define.

Aquarius is the Water Bearer. A mythological creature who holds a perpetually overflowing urn, its water constantly flows down for the good of mankind. The urn never empties, the uneasiness never ends—there's always something that Aquarius must do to make things right.

Because of changes in the earth's orbital relationship to the stars, mankind enters a new age about every two thousand years or so. Since the 1960s the public has been aware that we are leaving the age of Pisces and entering the age of Aquarius, which some astrologers believe will come in the year 2000. The Broadway musical *Hair* celebrated some of the most inspired themes of the new era. Love, peace, and freedom are the slogans for the generation that saw the dawning of the age of Aquarius. Inventions in electronics and telecommunications will play a profound role in the alteration of consciousness. High-tech advances in communications via radio, telephone, television, and computers, as well as in databanks, satellite communications, and space travel won't simply alter man's environment, they will change human consciousness.

These advances in electronics and telecommunications are ruled by Aquarius, and Aquarians are the first to accept the new changes in the society they herald. The previous Piscean age saw the rise of Islam, Christianity, and other religions with their brooding spirituality and the bloody wars that sometimes resulted from attempting to enforce religious faith. The Aquarian age will be more tolerant, more scientific, yet just as attuned to the mystical and spiritual aspects of life, but in Aquarians spirituality is free of emotional or institutional manipulations.

In her book *In the Spirit* Aquarian Susan Taylor, editor-in-chief of *Essence* magazine, expressed the nature of Aquarian spirituality. The book draws spiritual insights from all of the world's great religions and blends them into a free, personalized, new-age vision of human possibility.

Love to a Pisces can be a brooding, emotional affair; to Aquarians it's more free and easy. Their approach is more open; it is mental rather than emotional. According to most astrologers, the influence of this Aquarian objectivity and openness will launch the breakdown of gender, racial, and national barriers in the new age. Equality between the sexes and the races is a characteristic of this new age. Women's liberation, world revolution, free expression of alternate sexual lifestyles, the rise of unisexual fashions and hairstyles are all indications of the age.

It is not surprising that Oprah Winfrey has become the reigning personality of this transitional period. More than any other person she is using advances in electronic communications to affect human awareness of itself. She has said, "When I look at the future, it is so bright it burns my eyes."

Individual Aquarians may not believe in the new age, but no other sign is capable of understanding it better, tolerating it more freely, and fighting to defend it where it is threatened.

RELATIONSHIPS

Here you would definitely have to know what the native's rising sign is before you could say much about how he or she would relate to others. Generally it can be said that Aquarians are among the friendliest people in the zodiac. They're generally concerned about the welfare of others, especially the less fortunate, and they give sympathy and help more easily than most. They enjoy a full social life and love mixing with all kinds of people. Most of them love to entertain because they like to be responsible for making other people happy.

Aquarians aren't at all shy and they usually experience little difficulty meeting strangers. In fact, they are among the most socially adventurous of all types. They actively seek new friends, but unlike many other gregarious types, they don't neglect old friendships. Being an air sign, Aquarius is not nearly as loyal and dependable as the other fixed signs; as with Gemini and Libra there is a great deal of restlessness and detachment, which is in conflict with the stabilizing force of the fixed quality. Still, Aquarians do seem to keep their friends for a long time.

There is a soberness about the vibration that is often missing in the other two air signs, but like Gemini and Libra, Aquarians are witty conversationalists. All of the air signs are very concerned with the link between people and ideas in society. Gemini is concerned with gathering impressions, linking them together, and communicating them to society. Libra is concerned with promoting social balance and harmony by stressing the importance of accommodation between different points of view. Aquarians are more concerned with uniting larger groups of people around a common ideal; although they are sometimes quite hard to pin down on a personal level, they are usually firmly planted on the ideological level.

Aquarians tend to become involved with clubs, fraternities, sororities, or other loosely connected associations. They form many friendships or date many people rather than commit themselves to one person—this is one reason why large cities make the best locations for them professionally and socially. They form friendships rather than fall possessively in love, or create many attachments rather than confine themselves to one person. They gravitate naturally to the least restrictive relationships, which is why they mate so well with the other air signs. Their attachments to concepts or ideas are usually more apparent than their connection to an individual. It is ironic that the most humanitarian of all types often seems to be bound more closely to projects, causes, careers, dreams, and even flighty concepts of freedom than to any single human being.

PHYSICAL AND MENTAL HEALTH

Aquarius rules the ankles and bones of the lower legs. Active Aquarians are very prone to shin injuries, leg cramps, and charley horse. But more important, Aquarius rules the circulatory system, and natives of the sign show a greater need to purify the blood periodically. They're sometimes troubled by poor circulation and often complain of being cold in rooms where others are perfectly comfortable.

Physically, Aquarians are usually quite healthy and resistant to diseases. Most of them are gifted with handsome physiques, not overly muscular, but long and gracefully proportioned. Even when their faces are not particularly attractive, most Aquarians have supple bodies capable of loose, limber, and free-flowing movement. And, like Sagittarians, there is a tendency for the men of this vibration to display some feminine traits and the women to have some masculine physical qualities.

Mentally Aquarius is often a more serious sign than is at first apparent. No doubt the mixed influence of Uranus and Saturn is responsible. The Saturnine influence leads to suppression, suspicion, worry, isolationism, and pessimism. The Uranian influence produces rebelliousness, a great need for freedom, and a great deal of good humor. Aquarius produces genius far more often than any other sign, but under adverse circumstances it produces people who easily dissociate completely from reality and give in to personal fantasies.

LUCK, MONEY, AND WORK

Here again we have to speak of Saturn and Uranus, the two planets that rule the sign. The influence of Saturn makes Aquarians very money conscious and very concerned about material things. The native who falls under its influence is likely to be financially conservative. He will save for the future and seldom takes chances, although he may occasionally splurge in a conspicuous display of his wealth.

The Uranian Aquarius is something of a bohemian. She couldn't care less about money. Money is nothing more than a necessary distraction. It's simply a key that opens more doors to a fuller life; or, if the Aquarius is engaged in some all-consuming project, it's nothing more than a means for her to keep on doing what she's doing. It certainly doesn't represent power, as it would to a Capricorn, or security as it would to a Taurus. If she doesn't have money, she doesn't worry much about it. But even in tattered jeans she's likely to be stylish, for the artistic temperament is always very strong.

In these bohemian types the hoarding instinct is very weak. If they happen to make a great deal of money, they're likely to spend much of it on fun and travel. They like to experience new life in the manner described by Aquarian Langston Hughes in his aptly named autobiography, *I Wonder As I Wander*. During much of his life Hughes was a rootless, wandering poet whose curiosity led him not only to travel over many parts of the world but also to explore a wide variety of literary forms. He was a novelist, essayist, and dramatist as well as a poet, and he created the famous black cartoon character Jesse B. Semple.

Teachers of young children often comment that Aquarians have excellent writing talent at a very young age because they tend to see things differently. When this talent is cultivated in some way, Aquarians can grow up to be excellent writers. Alice Walker, the author of *The*

Color Purple, In Love and Trouble, and many other distinguished works, made her mark by successfully imposing her own personal view of life on her writing.

And of course Toni Morrison, Nobel Prize–winning author of *Beloved, Sula,* and many other works, has been heralded not simply for the unmatched lyricism of her prose but for her unique way of visualizing the world she writes about.

Aquarians tend to be somewhat lazy when working at tasks that they don't select; but when they're working at something they've chosen, they can be very persistent. They may be emotionally detached, but they're among the most mentally disciplined of all people. Their intellectual focus can be as narrow as their emotional focus is diffuse.

They make fine athletes partly because of this ability to focus their mental energies so well. Sports commentators often remarked that Bill Russell was a great basketball player not because of outstanding physical talents but because of the intense concentration he brought to the game.

Hank Aaron, baseball's all-time home-run king, and incidentally, Babe Ruth, the former "King of Swat," were born with Sun in Aquarius, and any batting coach knows that hitting home runs is not a matter of raw power but of focusing the mind on nothing else but that tiny white sphere sailing toward home plate close to one hundred miles per hour. This kind of focus can bring success to a wide variety of endeavors.

Aquarians also have good reflexes and good intuition. If intuition is defined as the power to know things without conscious reasoning, then it's no wonder that Aquarians have such a strong instinctive sense of the "rightness" of their decisions. They make good and stubborn scientists, maverick designers, excellent diagnosticians and doctors, psychics, and seers. They like to experiment and tinker. The key words of the sign are I KNOW; and although others may not know how they know, Aquarians do know.

Aquarians don't normally make good secretaries or businesspeople. Housework can drive them crazy. They like dealing with people, but they're often too temperamental to be good salespeople or personnel directors. They are likely to be occupational wanderers until they've found the right groove; then all the fixity of their nature comes out.

LOVE AND SEX

In love Aquarians aren't overly affectionate or demonstrative, but they're among the most sexually free of all types. Neither are they overly emotional; they make love with their mind's eye wide open. They are not selfish; in fact they love to give pleasure to others. But their game playing might be annoying to someone who is more intensely and blindly involved. Aquarians aren't usually jealous and in turn they hate for a partner to be clinging and jealous.

The sexual drive is occasionally very strong, but seldom steady. This is why they so often substitute playfulness for physical passion, technique or fantasy for ravaging sexual desire. When their mind isn't sufficiently stimulated, they can be among the most unimaginative of bed partners, but when their mind is titillated, they're extremely uninhibited. They're usually stimulated more by variety than by quantity. But because they're not sexually driven, they can be as faithful in marriage as they have to be, unless curiosity starts them thirsting for something new. Then they can be unfaithful without guilt. Sexual morality and sexual fidelity don't mean as much to them as to most others. Friendship means more.

Most weren't made for marriage, but because of their ability to tune things out, they often survive in marriage better than many types who are compulsively drawn to it. Men and women of the sign usually get along very well with their children. The relationship soon becomes one between friends rather than between parent and child.

Aquarians get angry and blow up very easily, but few people are more forgiving. Their love is sometimes difficult to define, but in their own distant way they can be very good lovers.

LOVE AFFAIRS

(See the other chapters for love affairs between
Aquarius men and women of other signs.)

AQUARIUS WOMAN, ARIES MAN

This one could work if he learns quickly that an easygoing, fun-loving woman like you can be just as serious and stubborn as he is. He's aggressive and likes to have his own way, but you're not the kind to play follow-the-leader. He is likely to be egotistical; you are not the kind to massage anyone's swollen ego. You two are likely to have many interests in common. Both of you like to explore life in all its variety, and you both like to travel and mingle with a lot of people. An active social life is forecast. In love he is open, direct, and passionate, and when you make up your mind to be, you are playful, imaginative, and skillful. Your uninhibited nature could open him up to new experiences. You'll like the fact that he is so ambitious. That means you don't have to be. But though he'll want plenty of freedom for himself, he's likely to be insecure if you insist on the same. You can both be possessive and jealous, but if you're traveling along together, there may not be that many occasions for jealousy.

AQUARIUS WOMAN, TAURUS MAN

There are many differences in the ways the two of you like to run your day-to-day lives. No matter how lighthearted he pretends to be, his life is tuned to a very heavy, deliberate vibration. Neither of you is very pushy, so it might take a long time before you realize that you're so stubbornly different. Instinct might tell you that he's jealous, somewhat private, possessive, steady, reliable, and sensual. And his caution might tell him that you're much too diffused and breezy. He may be so conservative and stodgy that you'd find him boring, and you may be so impractical that he'll find you foolish. If you can forget about your differences, the sexual hookup based on sexual appetites could keep this one together.

AQUARIUS WOMAN, GEMINI MAN

Here is a perfect meeting of minds. You both see the world in pretty much the same terms. For an Aquarian woman like you, no man is more mentally compatible, and no man is likely to object less to your cool, detached approach to love. The sexual vibrations are likely to be excellent. You're both free and uninhibited. You both need a lot of mental stimulation before you can do your sexual best. You both tend to like variety, but neither is very jealous. For both of you, companionship and friendship are the better parts of love. He's moody and you're just the one to leave him alone when he's in a bad mood, even though he's not inclined to do the same for you. His sarcasm might hurt you often, but you know that most of it is nothing more than the verbal games he has to play. You both enjoy an active social life. Your mingling with a lot of people on many occasions will provide relief from those stark private moments created by two minds that are often too logical, analytical, and similar.

AQUARIUS WOMAN, CANCER MAN

His love is like syrup or flypaper and could be much too sticky for a free-hearted butterfly like you. He's mellow, but once you get to know him, you're likely to discover that he's much too sensitive, emotional, easily hurt, serious-minded, possessive, and retiring for you. And he'll find you too light, superficial, and unfeelingly logical for him. His insecurities will lead him to worry a lot about money and the future. Your optimism leaves you rather careless about both of these. He prefers a more tender-hearted woman if he is to expose his own soft heart. You both like to wander, but in the end he's about the most home-loving of all men, and you are likely to be one of the least domestic of all women. This reversal of roles might be fun. He'll love your sense of freedom and you'll admire his intensely romantic nature—if he doesn't

let your freedom annoy him and you don't let his sentimental romanticism bog you down.

AQUARIUS WOMAN, LEO MAN

Attractions of opposites are always interesting. You two are 180
degrees apart on the astrological wheel. Some astrologers claim that this
makes for a successful match. True, you each have many of the qualities
that the other lacks. He's passionate; you're cool. He's very involved;
you're often detached. He likes to organize; you're often personally
disorganized. But he's also self-centered and can be domineering, and
you won't allow yourself to be dominated. He's egotistical and likes a
woman who responds to, and is somewhat dependent on, him. You're
not the kind to just join anyone's fan club. He is King Leo, who likes
to rule, but you can be most unruly. You'll both have to learn how and
when to give in.

AQUARIUS WOMAN, VIRGO MAN

He's likely to be very cautious, serious, and analytical underneath
whatever face he puts on. He can be charming but almost never carefree.
Even if he's one of those eccentric Virgos, his mentality is likely to be
too restrictive and realistic or pessimistic for you. If this one works at
all, you will have to tune out his unrelentingly critical view of life. If
he's an evolved Virgo, he won't mind since he probably wishes he himself could tune it out sometimes. He won't like your spending habits,
but he might accept them as the price he must pay for you. He's much
more realistic than you are, and often your idealism will seem like
foolishness to him. You are both more mental than emotional, but he
is mental, practical, and reserved, while you are mental, optimistic, and
friendly. In love he needs a lot of mental stimulation, but once he starts
loving, he is very physical and uncommunicative. He doesn't whisper
sweet nothings. In love you need a lot of mental stimulation, but your
sexual attention span is very short if your partner doesn't keep the
mental stimulation coming.

AQUARIUS WOMAN, LIBRA MAN

For the Aquarius woman, Libra is one of the best matches. His mind works like yours. He's logical and clever, and though he might complain that you're not as romantic as he is, you'll both know you are. All the things he likes to say and hear aren't things he deeply believes. They just sound nice to him. Love between you will often be a case of who's jiving whom. You both like it that way, since you both believe that life and love were made for fun and not for any deep, brooding passion. He'll share your love of style and finery. In fact, he's likely to love it more than you do. You are both likely to be good conversationalists with a fine sense of humor, knowing how to forgive and forget and certainly not holding grudges. Each needs freedom, so fortunately neither of you is jealous or possessive. Neither likes to argue, and both like a rich social life. The sexual vibrations should work out very well.

AQUARIUS WOMAN, SCORPIO MAN

Few people are as stubbornly different as the two of you. You need personal freedom, and he's suspicious of anyone who says they love him and yet remains so independent and emotionally detached. Many astrologers claim that he can truly love only that which he controls. You know that to be a problem right there. The idea of being controlled is more than you can usually handle. You're bound to bring out the most secretive part of his nature, and you'll then find it difficult to deal with someone who doesn't communicate his feelings and thoughts openly. He'll find it difficult to deal with someone whose mind is where he thinks a person's heart should be. You can each lead the other to a very different psychological space. The sex could be good in both spaces if each consents to go willingly with the other.

AQUARIUS WOMAN, SAGITTARIUS MAN

The dance begins when you meet each other. During first meetings you are both light on your feet and you enjoy playing lighthearted mental games. When love comes, it is likely to be just as lighthearted because you've normally both agreed on the terms. The most agreeable term is freedom. Since you both like it, you don't mind giving it. He's likely to be less jealous than you, and you bring out the player in him. He pulls you into a part of your personality that you like. You talk well together and are usually interested in the same things. Sometimes when Sagittarians get too much into the head game, they might lose some of their interest in the bed game. This is not an insurmountable problem, but he's the one who is likely to have to adjust.

AQUARIUS WOMAN, CAPRICORN MAN

There are parts of you that are just made for a man like him, and parts of him that fit perfectly with parts of you. This occurs mostly because Aquarians are ruled by both Saturn and Uranus. Capricorn is ruled by Saturn. There is a side of you that is determined, opinionated, practical, and businesslike and a lover of convention just like he is. But then there is the other side of you that is ruled by Uranus, the planet that makes you tend toward the humanitarian or the eccentric. Sometimes something might zing out of your mouth and he'll never know where it came from. The hope of this relationship lies in your getting him to accept that that's just the way you are.

AQUARIUS WOMAN, AQUARIUS MAN

Who can better understand the complex Aquarian personality than another Aquarius? You're both realized, easygoing lovers of adventure, excitement, and variety. You both enjoy having an active social life. If one is more reserved and Saturnine and the other is full of Uranian friskiness, then all this doesn't apply, but more than likely you're both high-spirited, idealistic, uninhibited, vibrant, and independent. Each will understand the other's emotional detachment. The sexual vibrations are bound to be compatible. Neither might be good at handling money, but neither is likely to worry much about it after each momentary financial crisis has passed. On the mental plane, where you both like to operate, this is a very good partnership. You two make good friends, and for both of you that can be the best part of life.

AQUARIUS WOMAN, PISCES MAN

Both of you have a great concern for other people, and both are likely to be sympathetic and generous at times and self-centered and selfish at others. You can talk to each other really well, so you can easily get this all in alignment. You each like to exert entirely different kinds of control in relationships. You dictate, but he controls the emotional undercurrents. You might seem to be on top, but he knows that can be the biggest of illusions. If this one is played with great savoir-faire, it could be very interesting.

AQUARIUS

(JANUARY 21st TO FEBRUARY 19th)

HAKEEM OLAJUWON, basketball star	**January 21, 1963**
BILLY OCEAN, pop singer	**January 21, 1950**
RICHIE HAVENS, musician, singer, songwriter	**January 21, 1941**
BENJAMIN CHAVIS, NAACP executive director, clergyman, activist	**January 22, 1948**
SUSAN L. TAYLOR, editor, television-show host	**January 23, 1946**
GLORIA NAYLOR, short-story writer and novelist	**January 25, 1950**
EARTHA KITT, singer, actress	**January 26, 1928**
ANGELA DAVIS, revolutionary writer, educator	**January 26, 1944**

OPRAH WINFREY, talk-show host, actress, producer	January 29, 1954
CHARLES DUTTON, actor	January 30, 1951
SHARON PRATT DIXON, first black female mayor of Washington, D.C.	January 30, 1944
JACKIE ROBINSON, legendary ballplayer, broke the color line in baseball	January 31, 1919
LANGSTON HUGHES, author, poet, columnist, founder of theaters	February 1, 1902
ROSA PARKS, civil rights activist	February 4, 1913
LAWRENCE TAYLOR, football star	February 4, 1959
HANK AARON, record-breaking home-run hitter, baseball executive	February 5, 1934
BOBBY BROWN, pop singer	February 5, 1969
ROBERT TOWNSEND, actor, director, filmmaker	February 6, 1957
BOB MARLEY, innovative reggae musician, singer, songwriter	February 6, 1945
EUBIE BLAKE, composer, producer	February 7, 1883
ALICE WALKER, award-winning novelist and poet	February 9, 1944
LEONTYNE PRICE, operatic singer	February 10, 1927
ROBERTA FLACK, Grammy-winning singer	February 10, 1940
JOSH WHITE, singer	February 11, 1908
REUBEN CANNON, film and TV producer	February 11, 1946
BILL RUSSELL, basketball star and coach	February 12, 1934
ARSENIO HALL, comedian, actor, talk-show host	February 12, 1958
GREGORY HINES, dancer, stage and screen actor	February 14, 1958
MICHAEL JORDAN, basketball star	February 16, 1963
LES BROWN, motivational speaker	February 17, 1945
JIM BROWN, football legend, actor, activist	February 17, 1936

MARIAN ANDERSON, internationally known opera star, civil rights activist	February 17, 1902
HUEY P. NEWTON, Black Panther party co-founder	February 17, 1942
TONI MORRISON, Nobel Prize–winning novelist, writer	February 18, 1931
AUDRE LORDE, poet, essayist, author	February 18, 1934
SMOKEY ROBINSON, soul-music poet	February 19, 1940

FEBRUARY 20TH TO MARCH 20TH

PISCES

THE FISH
THE SIGN OF THE DREAMER

◆

EMOTIONAL, SENSITIVE, POETIC

◆

Ruled by Neptune and Jupiter

COLOR: Lavender

METAL: Neptunium

GEM: Bloodstone

LUCKY NUMBERS: 5 and 8

FORTUNATE DAY: Friday

THE PISCES VIBRATION

DEEP INSIDE QUEEN LATIFAH, THE RAPPER, AC-tress, and businesswoman, and deep inside Shaquille O'Neal, whose power game is predicted to dominate basketball for the next decade, are two gentle souls that are compassionate, sympathetic, emotional, unworldly, impressionable, intuitive, supersensitive—dreamers whose feelings are relatively easy to hurt.

Ask their friends. You'll find that they agree with this assessment. Read between the lines of the stuff that has been written about both of them. The masters of the power rap and the power dunk have, like many other Pisceans, found suitable protection for their temperamental natures.

You can feel it in Queen Latifah's silence. When she's not laughing and throwing people off the trail to who she really is, she seems absorbed with her own secret matters. You can catch it in Shaquille O'Neal's eyes at the end of an interview. There is the sense that all along he has been conscious of something else. He was not totally there. Neither the basketball court nor what is being said in the interview was the main focus of his attention.

Sensitive souls born under African-American social circumstances have to find ways to keep from being constantly bombarded with the senselessness of the real world, which is full of racism and stupidity. One way is the rough exterior—Charles Barkley, novelist Ishmael Reed, Marsha Warfield, and Moms Mabley are in this hit-them-before-they-hit-you school of self-protecting Pisceans.

One of the most combative men I know is a Piscean. He is a small, belligerent, burly man who has a habit of referring to others with the most abusive obscenities and pretending that he will fight to back up what he says. Only those who know him well know that it's all pretense—a front. And in an *Ebony* magazine article Piscean actor and former football player Fred "The Hammer" Williamson was described as follows: "[He has] purposely cultivated a public image as an arrogant, egotistical tough guy but Williamson is, in private life, a quiet, gentle, studious man who spends much of his time with books." Pisceans can be very cold or sarcastic outwardly, but get beyond the surface and their essentially sensitive nature is readily apparent.

And then there are the camouflagers, who are really feeling something exactly opposite to what you think they are feeling. The best trickster slaves were undoubtedly Pisceans. In one story Master John asked a slave, "Pompey, how do I look?"

"O, Massa, mighty. You looks mighty."

"What do you mean, 'mighty,' Pompey?"

"Why, Massa, you looks noble."

"What do you mean by noble?"

"Why, suh, you looks just like a lion."

"Come, now, Pompey, where have you ever seen a lion?"

"I saw one down in yonder field the other day, Massa."

"Pompey, you foolish fellow, that was a jackass."

"Was it, Massa?"

To Pisceans the power ploy can be just as protective as the power play.

In Pisces, the twelfth sign of the zodiac, humankind achieves its ultimate spiritual maturity. Whereas Aquarius represented the final stage of *individual* maturity, Pisces symbolizes the point in the zodiac's evolutionary cycle where mankind is totally absorbed into the One, the Whole. Here the physical realm may be left behind entirely; in one sense the individual disappears. Pisces represents complete absorption into the Cosmic Whole, into pure consciousness. Natives of this sign have an instinctive awareness of the consciousness of our Oneness that is unequaled by other signs. Pisceans are capable of engaging all possible human viewpoints simultaneously.

For Pisceans the world is not so much an external reality as it is a state of consciousness. It all depends on how you look at it. The grandest intention of this vibration is to accept the mergence of self with consciousness and to recognize consciousness as the sole determinant of reality. There is tremendous power in this way of approaching the world, but there can also be tremendous confusion.

As a sensitive vibration, Pisces may try to protect its sensitivity by avoiding certain emotional situations. Pisceans will often attempt to keep some distance between themselves and family members or loved ones—anyone who they feel is in a position to hurt them emotionally. Emotional defense is usually more important than family ties.

Pisceans can also be very determined, industrious, and prestige conscious. But their method of attaining these ends is usually indirect and not outwardly aggressive. Charm, amicability, and a passive, nonthreatening demeanor are their tools, and for the determined Pisces this approach is very effective. They are mellow yet tough, forceful but seemingly nonaggressive.

The sensitive Piscean can reveal these different faces because—like Gemini, Virgo, and Sagittarius—Pisces is a dual sign. Gemini has the reputation for possessing a split personality, but Pisces may well be the most dual-natured sign of the zodiac. Upstream, downstream swim the fish—one toward encounter with reality, the other escaping from it. It is significant that in the symbol for Pisces the two fish are bound together by an unbreakable cord. It is possible to view them as if one were swimming outward toward the material world and the other plunging deeper into the subjective, emotional regions of the self.

If the plunging fish pulls hardest, the Piscean may become a depressed dreamer who has a hard time dealing with problems of the outside world. People of this type are often bored, fatigued, and unwilling to take part in everyday life. This reaction is often seen more among young Piscean men than among Piscean women because the traditional role for males in our society requires that they be outwardly dominant and aggressive. Consequently many afflicted Piscean men have earned a reputation for being weak-willed, confused, and indecisive.

When the personality is being pulled downstream into subjectivity,

Pisceans may also be completely unrealistic and impractical. They may be timid, lacking in self-confidence, and filled with feelings of inadequacy and inferiority. Finding it difficult to make up their minds, they are sometimes easily influenced by others. In order to protect themselves, they may become unreasonably suspicious. Feeling that they are vulnerable to everything, they refuse to open themselves up to anything until they must.

This extreme emotional sensitivity sometimes produces great works of poetry, art, and music, but it can just as well produce an aimless, muddled personality. It may produce a person with tremendous psychic insight into self and others or a self-pitying soul who is obsessively concerned with despair and melancholy.

When the upstream fish is pulling hardest, Pisceans will often display great perseverance and determination to reach whatever goal they have set for themselves. When Pisceans want something or someone, they don't give up easily. They have keen insight into how life is played and they are adaptable enough to play it as it lays. They are too mature to be idealistic and too mellow to be rigidly proud. Like willow trees, Pisceans survive and thrive by bending with the wind. They are not egocentric. They can sacrifice ego for objective; they move along with others knowing exactly what they want, and they can appear to be whatever they have to be in order to get to where they want to go.

They are usually connoisseurs of the best food, drink, clothing, and home furnishings. They are versatile and intelligent, with a quick grasp of how people and organizations operate, and they are flexible enough to use this knowledge to better their own position in the world. No sign is more adept at creating an illusory image for others in order to preserve a larger isolated area for their own spiritual freedom and personal indulgence.

Pisceans live with the tension created by these oppositely pulling fish: "Two thoughts, two unreconciled strivings; two warring ideals in one dark body whose dogged strength alone keeps it from being torn asunder," as Piscean W.E.B. Du Bois said in a different but not altogether unrelated context, as we shall see later. Pisceans never seem to get the two fish pulling in the same directions—and there is no need. Their goal should be to control them, training one to exert more influence during public life and the other during private moments.

A young Piscean woman who recently moved to Chicago illustrates the confusion that can result when these opposite forces are not balanced. She is a beautiful woman with an active professional and social life. She works as a receptionist for a large university—an undemanding job that pays well. But the moment you meet her, the muddled state of her private life becomes apparent.

She is generous when she should be selfish and selfish when she should be more giving. She often trusts the wrong people and is suspicious of people who would do her no harm. One instant she is too withdrawn, the next she is too involved. She is overly clinging on many occasions but far too independent at times when dependence might be more appropriate. What is obvious almost immediately, however, is that she enjoys this confusion.

On one occasion, after she complained about a headache, a friend asked her if she wanted an aspirin. "No," she pouted.

"Why?" the person asked.

"The headache might go away," she said laughingly.

Despite her laughter, everyone in the room knew that to some extent she was serious. Some Pisceans can be somewhat attached to their own pain. Their need for emotional and physical sensation can lead them to invite painful situations. They want to experience the entire range of human emotions—pity, sympathy, betrayal, devotion, and sadness. There are times when the fish loves nothing better than to swim in a sea of turmoil.

This is nothing more than a desire to come into the closest possible emotional contact with the world. In Aries, the first astrological sign, mankind is a child whose intent is to demonstrate its will and courage to the world. The key words for Aries are I AM. Ego is Aries' greatest strength and greatest weakness. By contrast, in Pisces, the last sign, the key words are I BELIEVE. Belief, or faith, is Pisces's greatest strength and greatest weakness.

An interesting bit of astrological lore holds that black America is ruled by Pisces. And there are some convincing arguments to support the view that the group vibration, the cultural soul of black America, is more Piscean than anything else.

The practice of placing an entire group of people under a sign is not unusual. Many astrologers contend, for instance, that both the United States and Africa are ruled by Cancer; southern Italy by Scorpio; Japan by Libra; Switzerland by Virgo; Jewish America by Capricorn. This is not always simply a matter of a nation's birth date, although that method is sometimes used. Signs are often ascribed on the basis of the spiritual essence of a place or how specific groups of people feel and behave. And just as the most appropriate ruling sign for Los Angeles is Leo, Pisces most adequately characterizes the style, direction, and group behavior of the Afro-American community.

The Piscean tendency to bend but not break under pressure, for instance, reasonably accounts for black America's ability to survive slavery without annihilation. A less flexible vibration, for example Leo or Aquarius, would most certainly have resisted enslavement and probably been destroyed. And the Piscean ability to absorb and merge with others is obviously reflected in Afro-America's spiritual and emotional impact on the hostile, foreign culture into which they were thrust. Then there is the Piscean instinct for pretense as a means of disarming an adversary while maintaining its own internal independence. Black folklore is filled with tales like the one about Pompey above.

On the other hand, Afro-America's tendency toward emotionalism and impressionability, its reliance on faith and religion rather than on practical, goal-directed behavior, and its attitude that it all depends on how you look at things may well account for the tendency to change the viewpoint, the consciousness, rather than try to change the external world.

Like supersensitive Pisceans, black Americans are often hesitant and indecisive as a people. They often seem to lack a sure sense of identity and a clear sense of direction. They are far less materialistic than most other groups; in fact, it often seems that money is of interest only to the extent that it will buy some of the finer things in life and provide for sensual indulgences. Like most Pisceans, African Americans seem not to have caught the modern temper, which regards money as an abstraction representing power or the illusion of control over other people or over natural and social forces.

Like the Piscean dreamer-poet, American blacks demonstrate an enduring belief that fate cannot be controlled; it can only be understood and appeased, suffered and enjoyed.

Pisces is associated with self-sacrifice and with the highest form of wisdom—the knowledge of the essential unity between human being and cosmos.

The lore holds that African-Americans, through their music, are the emotional guides who will lead humankind to love as the greatest and most enduring of the emotions. No matter how this message is distorted by the marketplace, it is the greatest lesson of African-American music, which is now the music of the modern world. The emotional guidance in the music attempts to lead the world toward what is important to love. When successful, it leads modern people to wider knowledge and a deeper consciousness and ultimately to a full and perfect union with the Whole.

Pisces is the most musical of the signs. Of all life in the modern world, African-American life is most vividly tied to music. As Piscean W.E.B. Du Bois wrote in 1903 in *The Souls of Black Folk:* "And so by fateful chance the Negro folk-song—the rhythmic cry of the slave— stands to-day not simply as the sole American music, but as the most beautiful expression of human experience born this side the seas."

These often anonymous slave artists had the ability to see the deeper strains of human character and to feel the more subtle truths of their times. It has been black music—spirituals, blues, jazz, rhythm and blues, and soul music—that has provided the world with its most useful rhythmical and lyrical metaphors for the sorrows and aspirations of modern man.

Pisces is associated with institutions of correction, hospitals, jails, secluded spots, private hells, and circumstances such as failure, loneliness, abandonment, rejection, betrayal, and self-betrayal that grows out of misplaced compassion.

Until they embrace the enduring qualities of God and end their emotional entanglement with the punitive, scolding gods of the major religions, which has blinded them to God as pure love (not sensuality) and as pure joy (not fun), Pisceans will remain lost, so the story goes.

RELATIONSHIPS

Pisceans are somewhat reserved at first. They aren't extroverted back slappers and hand shakers. They are more than a little cautious, and tend to keep their distance until they've checked a person out. They don't rush into friendships. Many of them are shy and can appear to be standoffish. They warm up slowly, but once they get to know you, they are among the friendliest people of the zodiac. If you have a Pisces friend, you've probably thought at one time or another, "When I first met her, I wasn't really sure, but now I think she's the nicest person I know."

Pisceans approach slowly, but, once involved, they remain close. They are often forced by circumstances to be independent, but their natural tendency is to join with others, to be involved in the lives of others, and to have others deeply involved in their own lives.

Still, Pisceans are not the most sociable people in the world. They usually don't get along well in crowds and seldom are they egotistical enough to hold the center of attention. They are at their best one-on-

one. They are introspective and self-absorbed, but they are not loners. They need to and do merge with other people.

For them friendship is not a small closed circle, as it often is with Capricorns and Scorpios. Although they're not fond of habit, routine, and social repetition, they are not like those Sagittarians or Ariens who neglect old friends in a happy-go-lucky search for new ones. In Pisces there is a balance between loyalty and adventurousness.

Pisceans make good business partners if they balance the tendency to be at one time too trusting and at another too suspicious and reluctant. Most natives are eager to enlist others in their projects. They dislike entering upon ambitious ventures without a cushion of moral support. Usually they are not self-confident enough to venture very far without someone to fall back on in case of trouble. They enjoy cooperation much more than confrontation but consequently can be secretly competitive. They like to surpass others, but they do not like to risk open rivalries.

They make excellent friends for people who are spiritually troubled. They are good listeners and have a great ability to perceive how others feel. People are always coming to them in times of emotional stress because they readily offer a shoulder to cry on.

Unevolved Pisceans like to prey on the emotional weaknesses of others. They are kind and generous until they have drawn the person in, won his trust, confidence, even love, and then they begin to lie and misuse.

LUCK, MONEY, AND WORK

At games of chance Pisceans are very lucky, but they don't make good gamblers. They are too emotional, they often lack self-control, and there is sometimes a self-destructive streak in them that keeps them going long after they should stop. Pisceans are susceptible to many varieties of addiction—gambling is one of them. Being partially ruled by Jupiter, however, they are usually very lucky in their day-to-day lives. They have good intuition and they often find themselves in the right place at the right time to achieve whatever it is they want to achieve, and they are often lucky at setting up a comfortable place for themselves.

They are not usually hardworking people, but they can be opportunistic, which means that they can work hard, long, and methodically when opportunity presents itself. Afterward they will usually return eagerly to the leisurely pace that they prefer. They are not overly ambitious or egotistical. They don't have to be on top to be happy. Comfort is more important than power; and money, for them, is useful primarily to increase their creature comforts. Only Libras and Taureans spend money with as much good taste as Pisceans.

In many astrology books too much is made of Piscean generosity. They are generous, but not foolishly big-hearted and open-handed as Sagittarians and Leos often are. Pisceans don't give unless there's a reasonable expectation that they will get something in return, and there is enough pessimism and insecurity in the sign to make them very anxious about their financial future.

Since Pisceans are talented, versatile, and adaptable, they are able to make money in a variety of fields, but they are not the kind of people who put everything into their jobs. Capricorns, by contrast, can dedicate their entire being to occupational ambition. What happens on the job can become the only important thing in their lives. To Pisceans what happens during personal time is more important. As we have said, not even Sagittarius likes to reserve as much free time for self-indulgence.

Pisceans make good doctors, teachers, and intellectuals, especially in philosophical and psychological fields. They are charming diplomats who are adept at all sorts of public relations work. If they are successful in politics or other leadership positions, it is because they inspire trust, and they often get to these positions because they have ingratiated themselves with the people in power. Actually most of the benefits that come to Pisceans come through the good offices of loyal friends in power.

Pisceans are convincing speakers, but they are far too sincere to make good salespeople. They are easily bored with routine office work, but they make good hosts, hostesses, waiters, and waitresses for restaurants, resorts, and clubs. They are definitely people oriented and not too proud to serve others. They are among the best social workers in the world.

The work that suits Pisceans is the kind that leaves them plenty of time to enjoy a full emotional life, a life with a variety of activities and involvements. So, of course, if they find a job that in itself provides variety and emotional involvement, they are doubly blessed. This is another reason why so many of them are fond of fields associated with the arts.

PHYSICAL AND MENTAL HEALTH

Physically Pisceans are not hardy, robust people. Most other signs produce huskier athletes. Pisceans succeed in sports usually because of style and grace. Julius Erving is the quintessential Piscean athlete. Shaquille O'Neal, the seven-foot-one, three-hundred-pound Orlando Magic center, grew up wanting to be a professional dancer, and was an excellent breakdancer as a teenager. Muscle-bound football star Herschel Walker is a ballet dancer in the off season.

Pisces rules the feet, an area of the body with which Pisceans should be extremely careful. Pisceans are especially susceptible to catching colds because of cold feet. In fact, Pisceans are not particularly resistant to most contagious diseases, such as influenza. But Pisceans are far stronger than most of them think they are. When they have to, they resist illnesses. It is primarily when they have little to occupy their minds that they become melancholic enough to bring on various illnesses that have an emotional origin.

After long periods of emotional stress Pisceans are apt to suffer from any number of fears and phobias. This is on the unconscious level, but on the conscious level Pisceans are also prone to use illness or helplessness as a means of gaining the sympathy they love. In addition, negative Pisceans like to feel sorry for themselves; what better reason for self-pity could there be than an illness? This negative pattern is reinforced by the Piscean tendency to overindulge in alcohol or drugs.

Pisces is the most impressionable of the signs. An unhealthy emotional environment during childhood will do more harm to them than to natives of any other sign. Even in adulthood it's necessary for Pisceans to have moments when they can rest their emotional antennae. The tense, unfulfilled, besieged Pisces can make an emotional wreck of himself. The others live longer, healthier lives than most.

LOVE AND SEX

Pisceans are sensualists, and love is one of the greatest sources of sensation. So is sex. Love allows a person to feel a wide range of emotions. It is not surprising, then, that Pisceans are love seekers. Many of them tend to be sexually promiscuous, but sex by itself is not what they're after. The desire is more emotional than physical. They seek to merge, to lose the sense of aloneness. Pisceans are not sexually aggressive. They are seducers rather than conquerors. They are romantic, sensitive, considerate, and giving, but they are also famous for carrying on more than one affair at a time. They can be quite deceptive, even fickle, in their affections; although appearing to be dependent and devoted, they have a secret love for intrigue and sexual variety. Their need for a secure, stable base of operation can keep them tied to one person for a long time, but all the while their sexual imagination is likely to be wandering. Like the natives of the other mutable signs, Pisceans have to fight to keep from being bored with repetitious sexual activity and situation.

In love there is that constant tug-of-war between the two fish. Pisceans can be extremely warm and affectionate one minute and very cold, aloof, and easily offended the next. They can be both dependent and manipulative in the space of a single act of love. They can use their honest feelings of need to gain power over others.

Pisces women deserve their reputation as good lovers. Of all women they are the most aware of their femininity. If the women's liberation movement had waited for them, it might never have begun, at least it would have taken an entirely different course. They know exactly what their "femaleness" will get them. They can throw men off guard by seeming weak, helpless, and in need of protection and direction. If a man's touch is firm and sensitive enough, they will let him dominate. Often they will enjoy the luxury of not having to deal with a lot of ugly realities. But if there isn't a man around, Pisces women can be surprisingly effective in their unaggressive, nonthreatening way. The strength is maternal.

For the Pisces man passivity is sometimes a problem. He is often not aggressive enough for women who like steel in a man. He may be too sentimental and dependent and too willing to avoid confrontation.

For the high-minded Pisces, male or female, love is like a religious experience. They keep making the leap of faith, jumping all the way in with little evidence that they should be there. Pisceans do not always love wisely, but they love deeply. And during the act of love there are no hard and husky egos, no overweening pride, no inhibitions, and no social taboos preventing Pisceans from doing whatever feels good to whomever is involved. Sensitive Pisces can be one of romantic love's best instruments.

LOVE AFFAIRS

*(See the other chapters for love affairs between
Pisces men and women of other signs.)*

PISCES WOMAN, ARIES MAN

There is bound to be a lot of attraction between rushing, masculine Aries and a Piscean sweetheart like you. He is romantic and idealistic and he'll enjoy all of that attention you shower on those you love. If you are not very sure of yourself, he'll certainly have the right medicine for your insecurity and indecision, but if you already know what you want, you might come to resent his domineering ways. Soon he might begin to wonder how anyone can be so ruled by watery emotions, and you might begin to wonder why anyone would want to be so ruled, as he is, by impatience and aggressiveness. He loves to argue; you avoid it. He can be egotistical and unbendingly proud. You know it is better to bend than to break. In moments of emotional stress you become very withdrawn, and he'll hate it when you don't react to his ranting and raving. When you came together, you knew you were very different. You'll have to work at learning to love the difference.

PISCES WOMAN, TAURUS MAN

There's likely to be no instant compatibility between the two of you, but there's much on which to build. You are both easygoing. He is romantic and sensual and, like you, he enjoys a life full of the finer things—good food, fine wine, and other pleasures of the flesh. Sexually the vibrations can be good since he supplies an earthy physical base for your boundless emotion. Of all types he has the greatest power to stabilize, and that is certainly what you need sometimes. He is possessive and jealous, though, and you sometimes get the roving eye. This could be a good match if he doesn't get too earthbound and unimaginative and you don't get too impractical.

PISCES WOMAN, GEMINI MAN

He could be an enjoyable playmate. There are four of you in the game—two fish and two dancing twins. Both of you can accommodate a high degree of commotion, and there is bound to be a lot of it. Both of you have a very happy mood and a very gloomy one. Luckily you both like to be alone when the gloomy one strikes. Pisceans do like social life, but sometimes they have to be led to it. A Gemini man can do that. This one works better if you keep it light.

PISCES WOMAN, CANCER MAN

This could make a lush love affair. You two could fill up a bedroom with sensitivity, gentleness, moodiness, sentimentality, affection, vulnerability, possessiveness, caution, suspicion, manipulation, and a host of other emotions. You'll both carry a lot of this out into the world, but both of you know that a person can be effective without being coldly practical, coldly logical, or impatiently aggressive. Using your own styles, the two of you can accomplish a great deal. There is enough of a difference between you to make the pairing interesting, but enough in common to bind it very tightly.

PISCES WOMAN, LEO MAN

In a lifetime you'll see a lot of Leo men who are attractive to you; most women do. Leo men are high-spirited and friendly. They like a lot of attention, and you give that. They are very dramatic and like to be on stage, and you enjoy watching things from a front-row seat. Sometimes you lack a sense of direction, and he has that even if it's the wrong direction. You're often unsure of yourself, and he's full of self-confidence. He's likely to be emotional, romantic, and imaginative in a way that will be charming for being so corny, sweet, and naive. Chivalry is not dead. It lives on among Leo men. He is gullible and you are clever and manipulative, often in a pleasant, useful way. You can make him feel good. He's generous, and you're eager to get. This is a wonderful combination if he doesn't get too domineering, foolishly proud, and ultimately self-centered; and if you don't get too sensitive, moody, and finally withdrawn.

PISCES WOMAN, VIRGO MAN

He can be charming, but he is not at all mellow and sentimental. He can be very thoughtful, but not really warm and free. He often has a hard time expressing his feelings just at the moments when they should be easiest to express. You'll swear he doesn't love you. Maybe he does, but he doesn't love anyone the way you need to be loved. He's loyal and dependable, but even if he's the artistic type of Virgo, he's likely to seem insensitive and emotionless at too many of the wrong times. He is emotional, but much of his emotional life is locked up inside instead of flowing out toward fusion with you. Getting the right formula for pulling him out will be your big challenge. Dealing with your impractical side is his big challenge.

PISCES WOMAN, LIBRA MAN

It's surprising that two incurable romantics like you don't get along better, but after a while it's apparent that he's light, playful, and a bit vain and detached, and you of course are deep and moody. Despite his romantic nature, he's very logical, positive, optimistic, and outgoing. Because of yours you are intuitive, alternately optimistic and pessimistic, and reserved. He loves freedom and an active social life. Often when you need him, he'll be off doing his social number. You can be clinging and very dependent, but when he looks around for you, you may well have withdrawn. The sexual vibrations aren't the best. He's fast, and you like a man with slow hands. There is some adjusting to do, but you are good at that when other things are right.

PISCES WOMAN, SCORPIO MAN

You're good for him because of the way you'll allow him to be. He doesn't like to show that deep emotional side of his nature unless he feels completely in control of the situation. He likes to make sure it's safe, and no one could be less threatening than you. He can't stand to be rejected, and you seldom reject deep emotions honestly given. Aggressive women might find him very physical and unaffectionate, but they can never get out of him what you'll get by being your nonthreatening self. He'll be extremely sensual and satisfying. He'll enjoy the way you like to flatter and take care of a man. Even his type of jealousy will make you feel more needed and loved. You're the one, the best one, to make him less sarcastic, domineering, argumentative, suspicious, and ungiving. After all this, what else could the sexual vibrations be but excellent?

PISCES WOMAN, SAGITTARIUS MAN

He'll turn you off often enough, but he's often very easy to forgive. He can't help being that way—blunt, independent, argumentative. You admire him because he seems very sure of himself and very sure he knows where he's going, even when he doesn't. He can be very affectionate and sensitive, periodically. He likes to live an adventurous life and he likes to share it with someone who's adventurous, artistic, appreciative, sensitive, and imaginative like you. He likes emotions, so he'll like you because you are a very emotional woman. But he hates to have someone clinging to him, and he will find it hard to understand how things that are so simple for him can be so confusing for you. He'll be a great friend, but the sexual vibrations between water and fire may not last. Over the long haul he's not as passionate, involved, or affectionate as he seems at first, but no one gets everything they want in a man.

PISCES WOMAN, CAPRICORN MAN

You'll have to give up a lot to get along with Mr. Capricorn, but it might be worth it since you each have a great deal of what the other lacks. He's one of the hardest of all men to please, but you're the most eager of all women to be pleasing. He likes to nag, interfere, and dominate. You're annoyed and hurt by nagging, but on the other hand, nagging can give you something good to sulk about. If you lack a sense of direction, he's about the most goal oriented of men. If you're somewhat artistic and unrealistic, no one deals more effectively with day-to-day reality than a Capricorn. If you're insecure, he's the man most concerned about giving at least financial security. The emotional vibrations will be poor at first, but he's likely to be very satisfying physically. He might also be smart enough to know he has to loosen up and be more affectionate toward you, especially if he's too proud and needy to want to let you go.

PISCES WOMAN, AQUARIUS MAN

It's odd that with so few things that could pull you apart, there are still fewer that would bind you together. Aquarians are the most independent and detached of men. They're affectionate, gentle, idealistic, and very much concerned about the feelings of others. But despite all this, they seldom seem to get deeply involved on a personal level. They're more logical than emotional. They hate to be smothered or hemmed in. Aquarians can be quite stubborn, quick-tempered, and argumentative. Nor are they stable enough to make anyone feel very secure. You are both going to have to work hard to keep finding joy in what is very different between you.

PISCES MAN, PISCES WOMAN

There are four fish in this affair and they may get along quite well together or they may swim around each other in confusion. Two people of the same sign can get along well together and understand each other, but they aren't always the best possible match. They often have the same strengths and weaknesses, leaving little possibility that one might have what the other one lacks. With Pisceans, however, this is not nearly as likely. There are lots of possibilities, negative and positive. If you're somewhat confused and not quite sure of your direction, you certainly don't want a man just like you, or if you've found your way, you may not be strong enough to carry a man who hasn't found his; he could feel the same ways about you. But then there's the best of all situations: If you're both pretty much in control of yourselves, if you both are playing the game and playing it well, you're excellent for each other. Nothing could be better than the give-and-take between two sensitive, artistic, determined, dreamy, creatively materialistic lovers like you.

PISCES

(FEBRUARY 20TH TO MARCH 20TH)

SIDNEY POITIER, groundbreaking screen and stage actor	February 20, 1927
NANCY WILSON, singer	February 20, 1937
CHARLES BARKLEY, basketball star	February 20, 1963
NINA SIMONE, singer, musician	February 21, 1935
BARBARA JORDAN, lawyer, politician, civil rights activist	February 21, 1936
JOHN LEWIS, civil rights trailblazer, politician	February 21, 1940
ISHMAEL REED, novelist	February 22, 1938
JULIUS ERVING, basketball legend	February 22, 1950
W.E.B. DU BOIS, scholar, spokesman, writer, intellectual	February 23, 1868
LOUIS STOKES, congressman from Ohio	February 25, 1925
GODFREY CAMBRIDGE, actor, activist	February 26, 1933
FATS DOMINO, musician, singer	February 26, 1928
BILL DUKE, acclaimed actor/director	February 26, 1943
CHARLAYNE HUNTER-GAULT, prize-winning broadcast journalist	February 27, 1942
RALPH ELLISON, influential novelist	March 1, 1914
HARRY BELAFONTE, singer, actor, activist	March 1, 1927
HERSCHEL WALKER, football star	March 3, 1962
JACKIE JOYNER-KERSEE, track and field star	March 3, 1962
MIRIAM MAKEBA, singer, "The Empress of African Song"	March 4, 1932
MARSHA WARFIELD, comedienne, actress	March 5, 1955
SHAQUILLE O'NEAL, basketball star	March 6, 1972
DICK ALLEN, baseball star	March 8, 1942
AL JARREAU, jazz singer	March 8, 1940
FLOYD MC KISSICK, attorney, social activist	March 9, 1922

RALPH ABERNATHY, civil rights activist	March 11, 1926
QUINCY JONES, musician, entertainment producer, businessman	March 14, 1933
LIGHTNIN' HOPKINS, blues musician	March 15, 1912
LEON DASH, Pulitzer Prize–winning journalist	March 16, 1944
SLY STONE, musician, singer, songwriter	March 17, 1944
NAT KING COLE, singer, actor, television star	March 17, 1919
BAYARD RUSTIN, political strategist and activist	March 17, 1910
WILSON PICKETT, singer	March 18, 1941
QUEEN LATIFAH, rap artist, actress, record producer	March 18, 1970
VANESSA WILLIAMS, actress, singer, first black Miss America	March 18, 1963
CHARLEY PRIDE, country-western singer, songwriter	March 18, 1938
ORNETTE COLEMAN, musician, singer	March 19, 1930
MOMS MABLEY, legendary comedienne, singer, actress	March 19, 1894
SPIKE LEE, filmmaker, actor, producer	March 20, 1957